A GREAT FEAST OF LIGHT

John Doyle attended University College, Dublin before
emigrating to Canada in 1980. He has been a critic for the
Globe and Mail in Toronto since 1997 and has written the
paper's daily television column since 2000.

'*A Great Feast of Light* is beautifully written, a significant
and different take on Ireland of the 1960s and 1970s. As
John Doyle illustrates, television changed Ireland and
thank God for television.' Danny Morrison

A
GREAT
FEAST

JOHN DOYLE

OF

LIGHT

Growing Up Irish in the Television Age

Aurum

First published in Great Britain
2006 by Aurum Press Ltd
7 Greenland Street, London NW1 0ND
www.aurumpress.co.uk

This paperback edition published 2007

ISBN-10: 1 84513 259 9
.ISBN-13: 978 1 84513 259 0

1 3 5 7 9 10 8 6 4 2
2007 2009 2011 2010 2008

Text design by C.S. Richardson
Printed in the UK by CPI Bookmarque, Croydon, CR0 4TD

For my parents, Sean and Mary Doyle

CONTENTS

A FLICKERING SIGNAL

ON A BLOSSOM-BRIGHT May morning in 1961, my father took me to school. It was my first day at school and although it was just an experiment to get me registered, sitting at a desk and familiar with the idea of school, it almost unhinged me. I remember tears and laughter. My father, who sold insurance policies and collected premiums, had an inspector working with him that day. The two of them took me into the schoolhouse and they followed as a teacher took me to a desk. Grasping the situation, I looked up at the rafters and howled. Hot tears flooded down my cheeks, but nobody stepped up to wipe them away and murmur something soothing to me. I looked over at my father and the inspector. Dad was frowning, as if he wanted to help me but couldn't. The inspector was laughing at my rage. After a pause, I stared up at the rafters of the schoolroom again, saw only pitch-black darkness high up in the criss-cross wooden beams, and howled once more.

Whatever else happened that morning is gone from my memory now. But this much I know—at lunchtime I legged it home. Out the schoolyard gate I raced, turned right and ran. Down Church Road, past the girl's convent school, the high-pitched roar of playing girls ringing in my ears, then with a faster sprint past the arched entrance to the old jailhouse where everybody knew the Cormack boys had been hanged in 1848 for a crime they didn't commit and their ghosts still haunted the old archway to mock the judges and lawyers who came and went, and turning right again but picking up a stick to clatter along the iron railings of the court house clang-bang-clang-bang to keep all ghosts away, running and panting for the sight of home. I raced across Wolfe Tone Terrace past the new houses with the doors newly painted in bright baby blue and yellow, catching the sun, with the scent of new-mown grass following me faintly from the court house grounds as I ran and ran and ran, heart pounding, looking for the gap in the stone wall that would lead me through long furrows of potato plants and beets to my own back yard.

I found the gap, climbed the big stones, stomped on small nettles growing there and raced in a straight line through the furrows to the gate of our yard. I wanted to call out, "Mam, Mam, I came home!" but I was breathless and stood there, panting. My mother was hanging out the washing on the clothesline and it took a minute before she noticed me.

"In the name of God, John Doyle, what are you doing here?"

"I came home."

"Jesus, Mary and Joseph, did you run across the whole town of Nenagh and tell no one where you were going?"

Mam sighed, took me inside, sat me in a sugawn chair—an ancient country thing made of battered old wood and hay ropes—and told me to keep an eye on my sister, Máire, who was sleeping in her cot. Mam went down the street to ask Mrs. Moylan, who was going over to the school to fetch her son Michael, to tell the teachers that I was safe and sound in my own kitchen.

Later, Mam stood me on a barrel in the back yard, and I helped her take down the washing. I was happy in the yard, a boy safe inside walls on a street inside an old walled town. From inside the walls of my back yard, and standing on the barrel, I could see the church spire asserting itself high into the sky while the tower of Nenagh Castle stood there beside it, solid as the past in which it had been built. Looking south toward Limerick, all anyone saw, always, were banks of grey clouds stacked on the horizon, usually obscuring parts of the soft-rolling hills of Slievnamon. It was a vista of greys, soft greens and subdued browns, a dull haze of colours from the clouds, the mist, the bracken and the brambles that seemed to cover the hills.

In the countryside around Nenagh, the people called the town "Nayna," not the proper pronunciation,

"Neena," which was used in town. They said "Nayna" with a shrug and a ghost of an exclamation point beside it. They were amused by Nenagh, its old, insular ways, and they thought it was a peculiar place compared with the countryside.

I'd heard Mrs. Moylan say "God made Nenagh." And I thought that was true then. I was getting on for nearly four years old and Nenagh was my world. First there was the walled-in world of our back yard and then the walled-in town of the winding streets, the castle, the church, and now the school. All of it was small, by any standard, but I was small too, and safe in its snug embrace. The streets and lanes were as familiar to me as my own knees and elbows. People would say "God is good" all the time, even if it was only because the weather changed and it stopped raining when mammies were going to hang out the washing on the line to dry. God made things nice and he'd made Nenagh nice.

All that afternoon, I played and hung around Mam in the kitchen. I practised lifting a ball with a small hurling stick and hitting it against one of the walls in the back yard. I raced up and down the furrows of potato plants, beets and cabbages, sometimes pretending I was being chased and diving down to hide. There was no fear of that. I could see my back yard from everywhere. If I wanted to see Sarsfield Street outside, I snuck down the alley and peered around the corner. Nenagh was all walls and alleys, a bound-in town and safe for a small boy who stayed inside his boundaries.

There would be nothing to surprise me on Sarsfield Street, anyway. If it was the first Monday of the month, it was Fair Day, when the farmers brought in their cattle and lined them along the street to buy and sell. If it was the last Friday of the month, it was the pig farmers' Fair Day, and the street would be full of pigs, the air smelling heavily of dung until the county council men came and swept and washed it all away. On any day, Monday to Saturday, Willie Heaney, the writer for the *Nenagh Guardian* newspaper, would be cycling endlessly around the town, talking to people, taking notes about their doings. Around five o'clock on any day except Sunday, the men who worked at Mrs. Burns's coal yard across the street would be walking home, their hands and faces blackened by the coal they'd hauled all day. Near six o'clock, the men who worked at the sugar beet factory would be cycling home in twos and threes, and if it was raining and they had no hat, they'd wear part of the heavy paper sugar bags on their head, cut like an army cap, to keep their heads dry.

That warm night, the air in the back yard and the surrounding gardens swarmed with midges. Masses of the tiny, silent insects moved around and muddied the light from the kitchen window. I sat on the back step, nursing a bruised knee, and watched the floating throngs of midges shift, it sometimes seemed to me, to the rhythm of the sound of flutes and fiddles on *Céilí House*, the program of traditional music on the radio in the kitchen.

Unknown to me, on that night there were other forces, unseen, in the air. The Irish Television Authority was already at work, silently sending out signals from a transmitter at Kippure in the Dublin Mountains. The signal was general all over Ireland. Throughout the country, pioneers and eccentrics were attaching aerials to their roofs and chimneys. In shops where televisions were ready for purchase, a set was occasionally, optimistically turned on to see if there was a signal yet.

Later that mild summer of 1961, an electrical engineer in Limerick, fifteen miles from my back yard, adjusted his aerial, descended from the roof and turned on his set. A test pattern card was crisply visible, but that wasn't all—a fly was buzzing around the test card, agitatedly zigzagging this way and that. The engineer sat transfixed. He was watching the first live-action broadcast on Irish television. It was reported in the *Limerick Leader* newspaper the next day.

On New Year's Eve of that year, television in Ireland was officially launched with the broadcast of a grand party from the Gresham Hotel in Dublin. Eamonn Andrews, in a tuxedo and Fred Astaire hair, talking in his semi-English accent, MC'd the party and introduced the acts. There were old Irish songs and smooth pop ballads. The Artane Boys Band, from the Dublin reformatory school for poverty-stricken and wayward boys, played too. Outside on the street a huge crowd gathered trying to catch a glimpse of the broadcast on a tiny TV set that had been placed on a pedestal.

Before the concert from the Gresham, President Eamon de Valera—a man who had fought and killed for Irish independence, been jailed and, according to legend, had first entered the Irish Parliament with a gun in his pocket—gave a speech to the nation. It was a warning. He sat in a book-lined study wearing a dark overcoat, and his weak old eyes peered at the camera. He said television could be a good influence and a bad influence. After the old man whom everyone called Dev came Cardinal D'Alton, the most important figure in the Catholic Church. He blessed the new broadcasting endeavour and warned too of its good and evil sides. The two old men talked solemnly, as if they knew that Ireland was to change utterly. When they stopped talking, the party started and the dancing began.

PART ONE

THE SPIRIT OF TIPPERARY

CHAPTER ONE

A LIGHT FROM OTHER PLACES

IT WAS AN AFTERNOON in May 1963 when Dad brought home a television set in the back of his car. He'd bought it at Jackie Whelan's electrical shop. Jackie, a great favourite of Dad's, was famous for his enterprise. He'd started off in the working world as a postman, delivering letters and parcels on a bicycle all around the Nenagh area.

He had soon noticed that he was continually delivering heavy parcels that contained batteries for the radios that most people used in their homes. There was a fierce demand, and the batteries never arrived quickly enough to satisfy the customers. Their radios were already dead and silent by the time Jackie carried the parcels to the door. He was constantly regaled with stories about the joy that would come to the house now that a new radio battery had arrived. There would be music, jokes and news from around the world.

Jackie was no fool, and in any case he was fed up with cycling to remote farmhouses in all weathers. He quit the post office and opened a shop selling batteries, radios and any other gadget for which there might be a market now that electricity had arrived in North Tipperary. He had television sets galore before there was a big demand for them and easily convinced Dad that television was the coming thing.

Dad took the car, a Volkswagen Beetle, into the lane at the side of the house so that he could bring the set in through the back yard. Mam carried Máire out, and I stood beside them looking at the big black set in the back seat of the car with its rabbit ears sticking up. It looked squat, dark and a bit preposterous sitting there, taking up most of the seat. Dad hauled it into the house and Mam cleared a space on a side table for it to sit.

We looked at it and waited for Jackie Whelan to turn up and attach it to the aerial he'd installed a few days before. Jackie arrived after he closed his shop and he immediately fussed about with wires. Then he advised us to stand back while he turned it on. The set flickered and slowly, glowingly came to light. There was snow falling on a grainy grey background. Jackie stared at it for a minute. Nobody said a thing. Then Jackie Whelan said, "That's not right at all. Sure, *Bat Masterson* is on now." Out he went and up on the roof with him. He called out to Mam, who kept an eye on the set until a distinct figure appeared, a man wearing a jaunty hat and a scarf around his neck. He was smiling a rueful smile. Mam beamed and scurried to the back door. "You have it, Jackie!" she called out.

Jackie came in and had a cup of tea. We all sat around the living-room table staring at the television. Jackie said that Mam would enjoy seeing Monica Sheridan's cooking program, although his own wife was disgusted that Monica Sheridan was always licking her fingers as she cooked. His own wife said that if you didn't allow it in your own kitchen, it shouldn't be allowed on the television. Jackie also praised Charles Mitchel, who read the news in a lovely voice and always ended his recitation of events with a little smile. Jackie said these things as an aside, because his eyes were on *Bat Masterson*. *Bat Masterson* was his favourite. "That's Gene Barry playing Bat," he said. "Oh, he's a rogue with the women, wait till you see! I think he must have Irish blood in him with a name like Barry." Jackie lifted his cup of tea in the air and hummed the cheerful theme song.

I watched Bat in his derby hat and ribbon tie. I saw the twinkle in his eye as he spoke to a lady in a long dress, her hands fluttering around her hair as Bat told her how purdy she was and how he'd seen all sorts of ladies from Cheyenne to Albuquerque but he'd never seen a pair of eyes so bright and hair so golden. He stroked his cane as he talked. I had been hoping for a gunfight but I was enthralled by Bat Masterson's style.

I was six and all I knew about action stories was what I'd read in comic books or seen at the picture house in Nenagh.

I galloped through books, especially if the story was about heroes and villains and finding treasure. Mam and Dad said I was a powerful reader and it would stand to me some day. I was shy and quiet, but Mam said it made no difference as long as I was reading. "John's a great reader," she'd say. "He'd rather be here with a book than any place. He'll stop being shy when he wants to." Once or twice I'd been to see the pictures on a Sunday afternoon at the Ormond cinema. It was crowded and noisy and frightening, with dozens of boys and girls who would suddenly start screaming and shouting because somebody slapped somebody or pulled their hair. And if you had a packet of sweets and dared to take them out of your pocket, somebody older and bigger than you would just reach over and steal them. It was very hard to concentrate on the story on the screen when somebody was stealing your sweets or you were sitting there rigid, waiting for somebody behind you to give your hair a pull, and some of them would pull so hard your eyes watered. I knew because it had happened to me.

Besides, the westerns I'd seen at the pictures were very old. You could tell because the film kept crackling and the voices went up and down like a fiddler playing an old tune. There was supposed to be a gunfight and Indians roaring and firing arrows, but half the time the cowboys were only acting the cod. One fella told another fella he'd eat his hat and then when he tried, a whole bit of the hat came away into his mouth. That was nonsensical because you couldn't eat a hat. You weren't supposed to be putting things like that in your mouth anyway and it was just stupid codology that hardly anybody laughed at. This man Bat Masterson was different. He was a rebel, you could tell by the cut of him, and he was in my own house where I could watch everything he was doing, without the bother of screaming children and the fear of somebody pulling my hair.

Transfixed and in a kind of reverie, I tried to imagine Bat Masterson in Nenagh. On a Fair Day he'd stroll along the street. His world of cowpokes, gamblers and rough cowboys wasn't a million miles from Nenagh, even though it was set donkey's years ago. People on *Bat Masterson* didn't have cars. They rode horses. But in Nenagh not that many people had cars and most of the men went to work on a bicycle. The farmers with their livestock and the grain merchants and the tradesmen who sold to the farmers were only a couple of steps removed from the saloon keepers, cowboys and gamblers in Bat's world.

I could see Bat intervening at the Fair, as two farmers haggled over the price of a heifer, one of them roaring that the other was a bowsie and a crooked dealer. Bat would stroll in and make a little joke. He'd name a reasonable price and make them shake hands on it. One of them would spit in his hand before shaking it firmly with the other farmer to seal the deal. That was the way deals were made on a Fair Day.

But that was where Bat's stroll in Nenagh ended. I could see him looking for a saloon and finding only the widow Ryan's pub on Kenyon Street. If he drifted farther, maybe he'd try Paddy Rohan's pub and find two silent old men holding pints of stout and waiting for Paddy Rohan to say something about the hurling match on Sunday. Or about the shocking price of coal at Mrs. Burns's yard. He wouldn't stay. He'd be looking for fellow gamblers, rogues and fine ladies. He wouldn't want to sit and listen and wait out the night until some old fella sang the song everybody in Nenagh seemed to know, called "The Old Bog Road."

My mother died last springtime,
When Erin's fields were green.
The neighbours said her waking
Was the finest ever seen.
There were snowdrops and primroses
Piled high above her bed,
And Ferns Church was crowded
When her funeral Mass was read.
And here was I on Broadway
A-building bricks per load
When they carried out her coffin
Down the Old Bog Road.

Bat wasn't a man for singing maudlin old laments and blubbering about his mother's funeral on the Old Bog Road. Bat was a dandy. They'd make fun of him in Nenagh, mocking his made-to-measure clothes and his sauntering, who-cares style. He'd stand out with his confident walk and who-cares attitude. Somebody would say that he never went to Mass, the same Bat Masterson, and what sort of a man never set foot inside the church for Mass? Was he a Protestant or what? He'd be doomed.

After *Bat Masterson* ended and Jackie Whelan went home, wishing us the best of luck with the television and telling us we'd enjoy it all, daily routine returned to our house. Dad considered the television set now sitting in a place of prominence in the little living room and told me that if I was talking to boys at school, I was not to be going on like we were special or rich because we had a television.

Getting a television set was all anybody was talking about. I'd heard visitors to our house say that people who only had the radio weren't keeping up with the times at all. "Times are changing, Sean," Jackie Whelan had said when he brought the television set to our house. "There's aerials all over the roofs of the town." Dad said it was true and that there were houses in Nenagh where, if you looked out the back window, you could hardly see the castle and the church for all the aerials that were poking up.

People who could hardly rub two pennies together could buy a television on the hire-purchase, and pay a little bit every week for it. They called it "the never-never." All they needed after that was a few pounds for the licence you got at the post office. There was the story of a widow out in the hills who had a bit of money put aside and decided to order a television set. A van arrived from the shop in Limerick one morning and the installation boys got busy climbing the roof and attaching the aerial, and then they carried the TV set inside. The widow decided she wanted to watch television in the kitchen, the room she rarely left. She'd bought a nice piece of fabric for the set to sit on and everything was in place for it.

One of the boys put the set where the widow wanted it and said, "Now, missus, if you'll show me where the electricity outlet is, I'll plug it in and get it running for you." The old woman looked at him with a puzzled expression and smiled. "God bless you, son," she said, "but it's only the oil lamps that I have and that's all I've ever had."

There was also the story of the poor family living in a county council house in Nenagh who had scraped together the money for the down payment on the set and committed to paying money every week for it. They loved it. Neighbours were invited in to gawk at it. Relatives from other towns and from all over the countryside were invited to come to stay and watch it.

The woman of the house, a mother of six children, was proud of it but a bit nervous about the new machine. It was covered in a newly bought tablecloth every night after it was turned off. About a week after it was installed, the mother turned it on at six o'clock for the news. But the screen just stayed dark. Panicking, the woman was unsure of what to do. She decided it was a case for the police, the Gardaí. She sent one of her children to the garda station and asked that a guard come to the house immediately.

A guard duly arrived and surveyed the scene. The mother, a visiting grandmother and a small army of children waited for him to take some action. He looked at the back of the television set and felt it. It was stone cold. He followed the cord to the electricity outlet and pronounced: "Sure you haven't the damn machine plugged in at all!"

The mother glared at the children and demanded to know who had interfered. It turned out that the visiting granny, fussy about safety and wasting electricity, had unplugged it the night before. The guard sighed, turned on his heel and left the house. Then he told everyone about the case of the granny and the malfunctioning television set and the eejits in the county council houses who didn't know what to do with their new contraptions.

I heard these stories and laughed too. We had a television set now and we weren't baffled at all. But everything in Nenagh was sifted through layers of fault-finding and snobbery. The town people said that country people were supposed to be a bit slow, but that they were devils for turning something to their advantage. You couldn't gauge their cunning. Still, when they came in to Nenagh town, well off though they might be with a fine-sized farm, they looked and acted a bit awkward. They were tight with money too. It was bloody difficult to figure out who among them had a bit of money. All that anybody in Nenagh wanted to know was who had the two pennies to rub together, and who didn't.

Dad said I should never judge a man by his job or by his house, by whether he wore a suit to work or a pair of overalls. Even if the seat of his trousers was covered in old patches and an old rope held them up, it was his manner that mattered. "Some workingmen have more savvy than a flock of doctors and solicitors. Workingmen are the backbone of Ireland. They fought for Ireland, when others wouldn't."

I was going to the little Primary School for boys out on Church Road. Some of us had dads who wore suits to work and others had dads who wore overalls and hob-nailed boots to work. There were two teachers, Mrs. McDonogh and Mr. Daly. They taught the whole crowd of us, dozens of boys, in a few rooms in the old building that had been manhandled from some other use into a school-house. Mrs. McDonogh and Mr. Daly taught us to read and write and be good Catholic children. Being a good Catholic child was the whole thing. Probably, the rich children would enter the stream meant for them, and the rest would be sent out on the worn path that lay in wait. We were tucked away in a country town that was comfortable, almost entirely Catholic and ignorant of the outside world, and we'd fit into our assigned places as easy as we sat in our assigned desks in the schoolroom.

Going to school was fine, once you got used to it. You walked the long walk past the court house, the old jail and the church, and you sat in school and often you just played with chalk or putty and you made things. At break time you ran around the schoolyard playing cowboys and Indians or kicking stones. It was amazing to me that some boys didn't want to go to school at all. Ciaran Sheridan was always trying to not go to school. Everybody knew that. He was always claiming to be sick and everybody said his mam coddled him. Sometimes, on the way to school, Ciaran decided he just didn't want to go. "I'm not going to school today," he'd shout and walk through the church gates. He'd hide under a bush in the churchyard and stay there all day. Even if it was raining, he'd stay under that same bush and get soaked. When we were going home from school, he'd come out and say he'd had a great time all day, not going to school. But you could tell from the state of him that he'd just sat there all day under the bush, in case one of the priests saw him and took him off to school by the scruff of the neck or somebody walking by on the road saw him hanging around and went and told his mam. My mam took me to school one morning when it was bucketing rain and she saw Ciaran Sheridan go off under the bush and she said he was a madhatter and he'd surely end up on the broad of his back in the county hospital with pneumonia. And his poor mother must be worn out from the worry already.

At school, if we weren't playing with chalk and putty, we were told stories all day long. Even the Catholic catechism, which we were taught every day, was a story, with lots of questions and answers. "Who made the world?" "God made the world." Then it was a list of sins you couldn't commit or you'd go straight to hell. There were mortal sins and venal sins. If you committed a mortal sin and it happened you were struck down stone dead in the road, you'd be roaring forever in the fires of hell. Nobody would help you then. You could say you were from Tipperary and name your father and mother and everybody who belonged to you, but nobody would give a tinker's curse where you were from. You were condemned for all eternity. There was a picture of the Sacred Heart in the school and that was Jesus showing us his heart to tell us he was full of love for every child in the world. Mr. Daly said we should look at that picture and see the compassion in the eyes of Jesus. Jesus wouldn't punish us if we were good boys. Even if it was frightening to think of hell, with the Sacred Heart picture and the compassion in Jesus' eyes, there was nothing to be afraid of.

The only thing to frighten anyone at school was the way some boys tried to make you feel like an eejit. Dad had told me not to boast about having a television because he knew Nenagh's ways. In the schoolyard, boys from wealthy families were always going on about what they saw on television. Other boys who went to somebody else's house to watch TV chimed in that they had seen the program too. But the retort was that they had to cadge a look at someone else's television. It was good to say you'd seen a program. It made you part of the crowd. But it was asking for trouble to say you had your own television set at home. If you did that, the wealthy boys would try to make you feel poor by talking on and on about what they had for their dinner before they watched the program. They'd start telling you they had steak and roast potatoes. Some of them made it sound like they had steak and roast potatoes every day.

Mrs. McDonogh was dead set against television. She told us that if we had a television at home we shouldn't be watching it all the time. It would distract us from reading books and only make us lazy. Reading books would make us good scholars at school and we'd go far in the world. If we didn't have a television, we shouldn't be going to other children's houses to watch it. Even if we were invited, we should stay away from the television. The television was ruining children's eyes and making people miserable, Mrs. McDonogh told us. She said it was habit forming. We didn't know what she meant by that, but Mrs. McDonogh said it was like eating too many sweets and getting fat because you couldn't stop and because you weren't leaving room in your belly for fresh meat and vegetables. We didn't think television was like eating sweets. You could eat sweets any time if you had a penny. You just went down to Acres' sweet shop or up to J.K.'s shop and bought the long sticks of sugar called Peggy's legs, or bulls eyes or Trigger bars—you could have what you could afford. Even if you only had half a penny you could buy broken biscuits with bits of chocolate in them.

Television programs were something you couldn't get just anywhere. They weren't like the short fizz of sweet taste you'd get from eating Peggy's legs and a Trigger bar. The feeling was different—you were excited, not just satisfied with what was in your belly. And the excitement was in your head. These were big stories that made you want to have adventures. And if you were little, and big people were always telling you that you were wrong and that you didn't know anything, television programs showed you a world you could understand. It wasn't complicated, not like trying to figure out what Mam and Dad were talking about when they said somebody in the county council had his hand in the till and that all the trouble was being hushed up because money was going under the table.

On television programs, it was clear what was good and what was bad. On *Gunsmoke*, Marshal Matt Dillon was in charge of Dodge City, a rough town in the Wild West where most people didn't want to obey the law. Every day he had to handle the problems of frontier life. There was cattle rustling, gunfights, brawls and fellas trying to steal other people's land. The man in charge had to be solid, sensible and brave, and Marshal Dillon was all of that. Even if you were small, you knew where you stood with a man like that. You wouldn't need to ask him a load of questions.

Mr. Daly used to read to us from a big book with gold trim on the side. The best stories were about Fionn McCool in ancient Ireland and his band of warriors called the Fianna. Fionn and his friends lived to hunt and fish, to fight and play hurling. They roamed Ireland, stopping to praise the beauty of the trees, the sky and the lakes, but mainly they were interested in fighting and showing off their fierce strength. They lived outside the law and couldn't be held back by anyone. They were hard men, the Fianna, but it wasn't clear why they were always fighting. On television, there was a point to all the fighting and the gunplay. Something was wrong and it needed to be put right.

One day at school, just after we came in from the lunchtime break, some of us were in the boys' bathroom. Mr. Daly and Mrs. McDonogh always told us to go to the toilet and then wash our hands after the break. The window in the bathroom was open to the air outside and a bird flew into the bathroom. Some of the boys screamed in terror as the bird flapped in a panic around the small room.

The screams could be heard all over the little schoolhouse. Mr. Daly came running, with Mrs. McDonogh following behind. Just before Mr. Daly threw open the door, the bird escaped out the window. Mr. Daly demanded to know why we were making a commotion. We all talked and shouted over each other about the bird that flew in and attacked us. Mr. Daly said he saw no bird. He said we were making it up and that he'd never known small boys who were so bold they could make up lies like that.

He took us back to the classroom and all of us got four short smacks on the hand with the cane that he kept inside his desk. The sharp sting of the cane stayed in my hand for hours. I tried to cool it by holding onto the cold metal legs of my desk. But Mr. Daly told me to stop, to let the sting of the cane heal itself, as a reminder that I'd been lying. The injustice stung like the red welt on my hand. Bat Masterson might laugh it off, but Marshal Matt Dillon wouldn't stand for it. He'd sort out the truth and make sure that innocent people weren't blamed for a crime they hadn't committed. You could rely on the truth coming out in Dodge City.

CHAPTER TWO

OUR HOUSE:
THE DOYLES, DECENT PEOPLE

WHEN DAD BROUGHT HOME the television set, the house we lived in was a small one, Bridie Toohey's house at 32 Sarsfield Street. Bridie Toohey was long dead and gone, but her belongings were everywhere. Dad said it looked like she'd left in an awful hurry, and you could hardly credit that the woman had so few friends and relatives that nobody had come to claim her possessions. Her name was in almost every book in the house, big damp-smelling books by Walter Scott, Samuel Lover, Charles Lever and Canon Sheehan. Once, my aunt Vera looked at the books, winked at me and said, "Lover and Lever, isn't that the way with the boys, John?" and she laughed her big sweet laugh.

Dad was furious with Bridie Toohey, dead though she was and God rest her. He had wanted to buy the house because he was getting married, and it was good house, a hundred years old. But there was a problem. Bridie Toohey had not been organized at all when it came to keeping records of anything, and the deed to the house could not be found, even though Dad and Michael Black the solicitor searched high and low. Dad went to Mass both morning and evening every Tuesday for nine weeks and took Communion every week, praying for the discovery of the missing documents. It was bloody awkward if you had any sort of job at all, but the Nine Tuesdays was supposed to be the cure for every tricky and tangled situation. Dad prayed to every saint he could think of, including Saint Jude, the patron saint of hopeless cases. He lit a candle to all of them. On the ninth Tuesday, the solicitor told him he had a solution to the problem: Miss Delaney next door could sign an affidavit to say that Bridie Toohey had owned the house all along. Dad was still annoyed, though. "Nine Tuesdays," he said. "God almighty, my heart was broke. And I lost count of the candles I lit."

Dad had worked for nearly ten years for Irish Life Assurance and was in fine form to buy a house for himself and Mam. He was sure of his ground. But there was another fella interested in the house, according to whispers on the street, anyway—a loner named Jim Spain.

Dad went to see him. Dad said to him, "Look, I want that house and I have Irish Life behind me. I'm warning you." Jim Spain smiled. So Dad gave him twenty-five pounds to back off. Still, Jim Spain smiled. The two of them went to see the auctioneer who was selling the house, to sort it out. The auctioneer witnessed them shaking hands and Jim Spain left, twenty-five pounds in his pocket and still smiling all the way. Dad said he'd never heard of Jim Spain until the bloody man turned up and tried to buy the house out from under him.

Dad's own connection with Nenagh only went back to his own father's time. Willie Doyle had been the porter at the Bank of Ireland for thirty-five years. He'd come to Nenagh from Dublin to work as a groom for one of the gentry who had horses, but he gave it up when the gentry fell on hard times. Willie Doyle was as famous for his kindnesses as for the spotless state of the bank building and the pleasant gardens around it. Often the old women in the town would say to Dad, "Sean, your father was a lovely man." Dad would agree politely and roll his eyes when they turned away. "My father was soft," he would say. "The women would admire the garden at the bank and ask him to help with their own gardens at home. He'd oblige everyone and never take a penny for it. My mother, God love her, despaired of him."

Willie Doyle's brother, Paddy, survived him, and Dad took great care of his uncle Paddy because Paddy reminded him of his dad. Uncle Paddy came to our house for his dinner every Sunday and watched television in the afternoon. Old Shirley Temple films were his favourite. A devout man, he attended every funeral he could, believing it was important to honour the dead. He went to the last Mass on a Sunday morning, and Mam would hope there wasn't a funeral procession afterwards because Uncle

Paddy would surely join it and be late for his meal at our house. His gentle nature and religious devotions hid a dry wit. When he had a drink, as he regularly did, he'd raise his glass of beer or whiskey and say, "A toast to temperance!"

Dad's brothers and one sister were spread out across Nenagh. Everyone knew them. Joe Doyle had taken over Willie's job in the bank and lived a few streets away from us. Peter lived up in Summerhill, where the Doyles had lived for years. He worked for a while at the little aluminum factory in the town and then left to work as a labourer. Eventually he worked in a quarry and became an overseer. A quiet man of solid opinions, he doted on his wife, Mary, a delicate, sweet-natured woman. Peter, like Dad, also doted on Breda, their only sister. Breda was a woman wearied early by life and she rarely smiled. She had worked at the aluminum factory for a couple of years and there she met Danny Mullen, a dapper man who was looking for a wife.

They were married in a year and it was soon obvious exactly what Danny Mullen wanted in a wife. Danny came home from work, ate his dinner and went to the pub. He drank pints and talked sports until closing time. He did this five days a week and on Saturdays and Sundays he broke the routine to go to the bookies on Saturday and to Mass on Sunday. A man of great discipline, he was renowned for his punctuality and work attendance. Danny Mullen was wary of the Doyles. All those brothers fussing over Breda annoyed him. If he happened to be at home when one of the Doyle brothers dropped in, he'd make an announcement about an urgent meeting with a man in a pub and disappear.

Dad's brother Tony was in America, in the Bronx, and married to a girl named Tess. Tony wrote lugubrious letters home about how much he missed everything in Nenagh. Many Irish in America kept the home fires burning by sending over money and gifts. In Tony's case, it worked in the reverse way. The Doyles had a small industry going sending packages to the Bronx. The *Nenagh Guardian* was posted regularly, and shirts, ties and sweaters were sent off quarterly. When it was coming on Christmas there was a rush to send over food. Packing rashers and sausages so that they wouldn't spoil on the trip was a constant source of anxiety and debate. Shopkeepers were consulted. The countryside around Nenagh was scoured for anyone who might be travelling to New York City and might take a package of Roscrea sausages to Tony.

Tony's reports on the state of the rashers and sausages sent to him were highly anticipated. Sometimes he hedged, saying they'd arrived and he was grateful. The best bet for food items that stayed fresh were the blood puddings. Sometimes he commented favourably on the black pudding that had sizzled in the pan in the Bronx and made him think of Nenagh. Dad fretted about Tony, far away in America as he was. After school, Tony had started working at the aluminum factory, like everybody else. Then he joined the army but left after a year. Then he joined the merchant navy but left after a year. He'd poked around Nenagh for ages, looking for work, and then he'd scraped together the money to go to America. According to Dad, Tony was always restless and innocent. "He'd see his chance, but he was too innocent to take it," Dad said.

Nenagh was small but it was big enough to keep all the Doyles separated. Mam was from the country, not from the town, so the Doyles took a very polite attitude with her, but acted as though she was from the back of beyond, and it would be years and years before anyone got to know her. When there was work to be done on the house, it was Mam's people who came into Nenagh and laboured at it, not the Doyle brothers. I knew if one of the Doyles came, they wouldn't stay long, but Mam's people would arrive and make themselves at home. They were always helping out, and it was needed.

When Dad bought the house, a year before I was born, it had no running water. There was an outside toilet and a single tap in the yard. When I was a year old, Mam's brother Peter came in and built a new extension into the yard, putting in a kitchen, a bathroom and plumbing all over the house. Mam was delighted with the new kitchen but Dad missed the old kitchen inside. It had an ancient Stanley 8 range, fuelled by coal and wood. I thought Dad missed it because he often talked about the time a cat had wandered into the old kitchen and, surprised by finding people, had jumped up on top of the Stanley 8, which was heating up. Cornered and panicky, the cat danced a jig on the hot range until Mam chased it away, with Dad laughing till tears came down his cheeks.

Bridie Toohey's husband had been a cooper. He'd made barrels in a shed in the back yard. There was an L-shaped laneway leading to the back yard and a contraption at the crook of the L for hoisting materials into the yard and loading finished barrels onto a horse and cart. Old bits of rusted pig iron and warped wood stood in an enormous pile outside the back gate. Saving the shed and the yard from dilapidation was a long and thankless battle. Dad had started to clear the yard loads of times. Mam's brothers had helped him but they'd given up when the pile of rubbish from the cooper's trade reached the top of the wall. Wallflowers sprang from the pile in summer and stayed upright for months, swaying purple and green, attracting wasps and bees until someone took a swipe at the stalks with a stick. Dad was too busy to do that kind of thing. It was usually a job for one of the policemen who lived on our side of Sarsfield Street and leased huge plots of land at the back for growing vegetables.

Sarsfield Street was a street of tradesmen and policemen. Everybody called the police "the guards," except a few people who called them "police officers," and Dad said people who used that English term were eejits. They were called the guards because their official name in Gaelic was An Garda Síochána, the Guardians of the Peace. There were four guards on our street; some were high-ranking men and others ordinary uniformed officers. Paddy Cross, the detective guard, lived up the street. Dad called him the Defective Guard because his wife was always in trouble for stealing from the shops. He had his hands full, Dad said, with the crime in the town and the crime in his own home.

Jackie Murphy, a uniformed guard, also lived up the street. Jackie was a nice, quiet man and doted on his only child, Jenny, who danced the Irish dancing like an angel, according to Dad. Sergeant Cardiff was a few doors up from us, a gruff man, most at home in his garden. The guards had the pick of the adjacent empty lands for their gardens. Cardiff, Murphy and Cross grew potatoes, cabbage, carrots, beetroot, onions and scallions. The only non-guard with a plot was a quiet eccentric named Johnny English, who grew flowers. He came and went like a ghost, while his tulips and daffodils bloomed and soared in the spring and summer sun. Nobody paid a bit of attention to him.

Having all those guards on Sarsfield Street made some people feel safe. Mam liked them, because they never got drunk or made a show of themselves on the street. Dad was of two minds about it. The guards were good prospects for insurance policies because they had steady work and expected promotion. But sometimes the sheer number of them on the street irritated him. When Dad was out late and drove back to find Sarsfield Street quiet as the grave, he'd park the car at the top of the street, get out and close the door gently, take off his shoes and walk home in his stocking feet. Even in the rain. "You never know when some nosy guard is wondering who's walking down the street after midnight. Some of them would take note of it, the same nosy boys."

Dad said that before the guards came to Sarsfield Street and started following each other there, the way guards always do, it was legendary for its tradesmen. Some were still there. Dad said a man that works with his hands is set for life, if he has some enterprise and gumption in him. It was the training that was the hard part, getting your hands good at what they do, and that could take years. And that was the way I saw the world. There were men who worked with their hands, making things in their own shops or out in the aluminum factory, and then there were men who sold things in a big shop, and after that there were men who wore suits and went around writing things down and doing sums, like my dad.

Mansy Ryan the shoemaker was down the street. Farmers traipsed to his door on Fair Days to get their boots mended and new shoes made for weddings and wakes. Morgan Murray the stonemason was nearby. A small, quiet, solemn man with a tall, buxom wife and a plethora of daughters, Morgan was happiest in the company of stone and marble. Everybody knew it and talked very softly to him, whether passing the time of day or bargaining for a headstone. Morgan's many daughters were Máire's friends, and I liked being in their house, full of girls playing and Mrs. Murray smiling at me and telling the girls they should get used to having a man around because soon enough there would be young fellas courting them. Morgan Murray would come into the house from his stone yard and drink tea out of a delicate china cup, never saying anything to anybody, but happy to look on, in silent contemplation. Tad Sullivan the harness maker lived up the street, but he was getting old and there was no call for harnesses, except from the gentry, the horsey set. He stood wistfully at his door on Fair Days and watched the farmers parade the cows, sheep and pigs into town for selling. There was hardly a horse to be seen. Mick Bunfield, who lived below us on Sarsfield Street, was a tradesman of a different sort. The way Dad put it was, "He got you what you wanted when you couldn't get it elsewhere." He sold cigarettes during the war when they were few and far between. Dad said he was a good businessman: "He capitalized when nobody else could. Fair play to him."

When you're small and in a small town, people think you're blank, hardly there at all, but you're picking up hints and attitudes all over the place. When I was walking down the street with Dad and we'd pass two guards on their patrol, Dad would just say "Men!" to them as he passed and they'd nod back. If it was a doctor or a solicitor, Dad would say polite words and get some back. "Isn't the weather awful changeable for the time of the year, Sean? But please God, we'll get a good summer." Dad would say, "Sure aren't we bound to have rain, with all the farmers praying for it? The ground is awful dry out near Toomevara and Kilruane." It was easy chatter. Dad had worked as a clerk in a solicitor's office when he first left school, and he wasn't impressed by solicitors. Doctors he didn't mind, if they weren't full of airs and didn't act like everyone else was a specimen to be examined. In Nenagh, it was a businessman who expected respect and got it.

In an ancient market town of five thousand people surrounded by prosperous farming land, the aristocracy was the merchant class. Those who bought and sold ruled. The three broad main streets were filled with shops—draperies, bakeries, butchers, sweet shops and vegetable shops. Their owners lived in tall houses on the Dublin Road, and the workers lived in the labyrinthine lanes that snaked behind and linked the main streets. In the lanes too were coal merchants, cattle-feed merchants, barbershops and lumberyards. They sold to the locals and to the old gentry, the landed Anglo-Irish toffs who lived just outside Nenagh and owned vast stretches of land. The Bernells, the Riggs, the Polls, the Gasons, the Cartwights, the Baileys and the Webbs were the landed gentry.

Unless you knew who the old gentry were, they weren't all that visible, but they were there. The few remaining gentry, who were sometimes just called the horsey set, insisted on having the North Tipperary Hunt every Saint Stephen's Day, the day after Christmas. They'd gather together on their horses, in their red coats and little caps, just outside the town, near the top of Sarsfield Street. They were off to hunt a fox. But first they had to stand around, having a drink and making a show of themselves. Some people from the town would gather to watch them, as they sat grandly on their horses and in their red jackets. There was occasional jeering but it was more a low murmur than a protest. Old men would just stare at them in stony, hostile silence and old women would smile at the ostentatious activities of a class that was doing what it had always done. The first time I saw the hunt, Dad held me in his arms to see over the crowd. "You might as well see that specimen now," he said. "There's few of them left."

After the North Tipperary Hunt moved off on its Saint Stephen's Day jaunt, everybody else would drift over to a nearby field for the other traditional local event of the day. That was hare coursing. Live hares were released into the long field, and a minute later, dogs were set free to chase and kill them. Some people loved the hare coursing, and at the back of the field bets were placed on the dogs. When I saw it the first time, I was too small to see the dog catch the hare and tear it apart. I only saw the dogs bound out of their traps and race after the tiny little hare. My attention was on the activity at the back of the field, where men were arguing furiously and waving wads of money in their hands. When the first dog caught the hare you could hear the roar of delight from the back of the field. Somebody had won a bet.

Some people thought that the coursing was cruel. Mam wouldn't go to see it and she kept Máire away from it too. But it was the town's amusement while the gentry rode around the fields like eejits in their red jackets, looking for a fox.

When Dad collected insurance premiums from the girls who worked as skivvies at the Bernells' big house, he was told in a whisper by a nervous maid to always be on alert for the arrival of Mrs. Bernell. The servant girl told him, "If Mrs. Bernell comes into the room, you have to bow to her and say, 'Good morning, Mrs. Bernell.'" But

Dad wasn't going to bend and bow down to that old bag of bones. Instead, he went to the back door and collected his money there.

Some of the Nenagh merchants were worse than the gentry, adopting their ways and attitudes. Dad once went to Donie Cantwell's warehouse, hoping to sell an insurance policy. Donie Cantwell sold dry goods to the local shops and lived in a large new house out by the hurling field. Dad made his pitch, which included mention of the fact that he was a local man trying to establish himself. He mentioned where he was living and all his brothers and his sister who were born in the town. Donie Cantwell looked at him and said, "I care as much about you and all the Doyles as I do about the dirt under my feet."

Dad never forgot that insult, and no one blamed him. When Donie Cantwell died suddenly, his business in ruins because his own sons had mismanaged it, Dad didn't gloat. But in later years, if he mentioned the insult as an example of Nenagh's ugly, calcified ways, he'd say, "The same Donie died roaring. And then he went to his grave, buried in the dirt under his feet. Dirt to dirt. But God be good to him, wherever he is."

Many of the rich and important in the town were golfers and Dad was a golfer too. In this, as a man from a working-class background, he was unusual, and he knew it. When he was ten years old, Dad and his brothers started earning money by working as caddies at the Nenagh Golf Club. A group of boys would traipse out to the golf club on Saturdays and Sundays, and every evening in the summer, to see if they could earn money carrying the golf bags for the players. According to Dad, sometimes three of them would travel out on one bicycle. They'd earn a shilling for carrying the bags over a whole eighteen holes.

On the golf course, Dad saw up close the gentry, the bank managers, the solicitors and shopkeepers who ran the town. He knew who was willing to pay the boys a decent fee and who would try to get away with giving them a few pence for the afternoon's slog. What irritated him was being treated like dirt. There was a tradition that after playing eighteen holes, the players would go to the club house for drinks and a meal and order some sandwiches to be sent out for the caddies. Some of the players, especially the old gentry, would never bother to arrange to feed the boys who had been carrying their bags. There were times, Dad said, when he and his brothers would leave the golf club starving. They'd travel a couple of miles on the way home and find a field where turnips were growing. All the better if they knew the field was owned by one of the toffs from the golf club. They'd check that nobody was watching, climb the ditch and pull a few sweet turnips from the ground, cut them open with a penknife and eat them, just to keep themselves going until they got home.

Through the summers, Dad got to study the golfers and assess their skills, and he decided he'd like to play himself. After years of observing, he was good at it. When he got his job with Irish Life, he applied to join the club. There was token resistance from the oldtimers, but most of the club officials knew he was a good player and let him in. By the time he was married, he wasn't awed by the gentry, the rich and the important men in Nenagh town. He played their game, but he could and did speak a different language.

Dad spoke Gaelic fluently and often in the house. Gaelic was also the first thing you heard when you turned on the television. Radio Telefis Éireann came on the air at 5:35 in the afternoons, by which time we had settled in to watch the television most evenings. Mam said the television was great company. And it was, a boon on fall and winter afternoons, warming the house with talk and music as darkness settled on Sarsfield Street. There was only one channel, RTÉ. It was said that up in Dublin some people could also receive the BBC with their aerials, the signal flitting across the Irish Sea without any attention to the border and customs regulations, but in Nenagh we knew nothing of that. Sometimes Mam turned it on a few minutes before the programs started and we'd hear soft Irish music playing while the St. Brigid's cross just sat there, a pattern from ancient Ireland.

There were twenty-five minutes of children's programs on RTÉ when it came on the air each evening. On some, puppets talked and wobbled around a little stage. The show that all we children watched was *Daithi Lacha*. Even the teachers at school told us to watch it. Daithi Lacha was the Irish for David Duck. It was a crudely drawn cartoon with Daithi the duck going around a lake having little adventures. When he talked to anyone, Daithi spoke Gaelic, and that reminded us that Gaelic was the other official language of Ireland.

Some children and many adults watched *Daithi Lacha* in utter mystification. They didn't speak a word of Irish and it was only the glamour and novelty of the television and the charm of the cartoon that kept them glued. I easily understood *Daithi Lacha* because Dad talked Gaelic around the house all the time. It wasn't strange to me at all.

Being familiar with Gaelic and connected to the ancient language set you apart in Nenagh. It was a snub and a scoff at the gentry and the other remnants of the old order that had commandeered Ireland under English rule. When the like of the Bernells weren't out on their horses hunting foxes, they were in their big sprawling houses and estates outside the town, being as English as they could. When they had been in charge, speaking the Irish language had been an act of secret rebellion, and the idea of Ireland being an Irish-speaking country again was something they'd never have tolerated. Some of the old gentry were still known by their British army rank from the First World War or the Boer War. There was Colonel Webb and the moustache-twirling la-di-da gent known as Colonel Lancelot Bailey. Dad despised them all. There used to be a club for "gentlemen" in Nenagh, the North Tipperary Club. Dad could recite its motto with a fine, theatrical sneer: "Strictly gentlemen by profession and gender." They were chancers, every one of them, he said. Dad liked to dwell on the death of the North Tipperary Club, because he'd had a part in erasing it from the town. The club's building was taken over by the Gaelic League in 1952. Dad was one of the league's four founding trustees in Nenagh.

I knew the story was important to Dad because he'd tell it in a way that showed he was enjoying all the detail of it. "We gave 'em a push, the ould gentry," he'd say and then he'd smile and act like he did on a Saturday at lunchtime when he was sitting down to a meal of bacon and cabbage and Tadgh Connors was coming to the house to discuss important matters about plays and the language movement. It was a delicious story for Dad.

The purpose of the Gaelic League was not just to revive the Irish language but to make it the main language of Ireland. The league had already been going for fifty years and, although there was no sign of the country suddenly talking Irish in everyday life, it was a powerful, tenacious organization. In structure it was based on a pattern as old as the hills. It met every week, and *timirí*, or messengers, came from other branches with news of the league's doings. Often there was a travelling teacher who gave classes on Irish-language poetry and politics. Dad wore a *fainne*, a gold ring, in his lapel to let everyone know that he was an Irish speaker. Sometimes people came up to him in a pub or a shop and started talking Gaelic, fluently or hesitantly. He greeted them all with a warm smile, and the big issues of politics, or small issues of the weather, were discussed in the old tongue.

Inside Nenagh town there wasn't what anyone would call an intense interest in the Gaelic League, but there was great respect for it. Acquiring a bit of fluency in the Irish language was considered a shrewd move for anyone with an eye on a civil service job, but, as most people saw the situation, it was only if you were a cunning striver and determined to get a good, pensionable job with the government that the added flair for Irish was any use at all. We children were taught Irish in school every day, and if you couldn't pick up a smidgen of it from the Christian Brothers or the masters in school, you'd have to be an awful eejit.

Dad's technique for keeping the Irish language alive in our house was to use it in everyday conversation, dropping in enough bits of it to make some of it stick. If we were having our dinner, Dad would say, in Irish, "Pass the salt and pepper, John." Or he'd repeat in Irish something I'd said in English. If I announced I was going out to play, Dad would say, *"Tá mé ag dul amach anois,"* which meant "I'm going out now," and hope it stuck with me. And he always said any of those endless expressions that came with being Catholic in Ireland—"God rest his soul," "God willing," "God protect you"—in Gaelic. It worked with me. Dad was delighted that I wasn't watching *Daithi Lacha* only for the pictures.

Both Dad and Mam liked me to read too. The most important book in our house was *The Spirit of Tipperary*. It was a little book we had to study at school too, and Dad loved it because his friend Padraig O'Meara, a crony from the Gaelic League, had compiled it and got it into the schools. It was all rebel songs and poems about Tipperary and the fight for Irish freedom over the dark centuries of English rule. Mam liked it because it was about things that happened in other parts of Tipperary and, she said, it was good for people to know that Nenagh wasn't the be-all and end-all of Tipperary. Because the way some Nenagh people talked, you'd think there wasn't another town or townland in the whole county. At the front, all the songs and poems were in English, and at the back, they were all in Irish. I knew whole parts of it by heart.

> *Were you ever in Tipperary, where the fields are*
> *so sunny and green,*
> *And the heath-brown Slieve-bloom and the Galtees*
> *look down with so proud a mien?*
> *Oh 'tis there you would see more beauty than is on*
> *all Irish ground—*
> *God bless you, my sweet Tipperary, for where could*
> *your match be found?*

In *The Spirit of Tipperary*, the Tipperary men were big, strong fellas who lived to fight the English and walk around Tipperary admiring the scenery and being hard but quiet. They were called the matchless men of Tipperary.

> *Let Britain boast her British boasts,*
> *About them all right little care we,*
> *Not British seas nor British coasts*
> *Can match the men of Tipperary.*
> *Lead him to fight for his native land,*
> *His is no courage cold and wary,*
> *The troops live not on the earth would stand,*
> *The headlong march of Tipperary.*

All the men of Tipperary roared with delight at the sight of English blood, and the only people they hated as much as the English were the informers who spoiled their plans to attack the English. If a Tipperary man was captured fighting the English, he climbed the scaffold singing a rebel song, to let the cowards and the traitors know that some men were prepared to die for Ireland. Sometimes I wished that there were more programs on television about the men of Tipperary so that I could see them having their adventures fighting the English, in places that were only down the road from me, not a million miles away like America. But the more poems and songs I read, the better I understood why.

Can the depths of the ocean afford you not graves,
That you come this to perish afar o'er the waves
To redden and swell the wild torrents that flow
Through the valley of vengeance, the dark Aherlow.

Sometimes on RTÉ there was an announcement that the program or the film would contain scenes that might make some people nervous, and that was usually about some killing or blood in the film, and there was an awful lot of blood and killing in the stories of the men of Tipperary, even if it was only the English invader they were killing so that they could live freely and be proud of Tipperary and Ireland.

There was a small, hard core of Republican sentiment in Nenagh, well outside the Gaelic League. But it had become diluted into party politics, factions and old feuds about who did what in the Irish War of Independence back in 1919 to 1922, and then in the savage Civil War that followed for a year. There was a man who lived over in a lane behind Pearse Street who, as far as the town was concerned, was the fella who shot Michael Collins dead in 1922. That meant he pulled the trigger in the assassination that killed a glorious Irish leader. Collins had wanted to stop fighting and build a country. The other side in the Civil War wanted to keep fighting until there was an all-Ireland republic that included Northern Ireland. They felt betrayed. The man over in the lane behind Pearse Street had pulled the trigger because he didn't agree with the treaty that Collins had signed with the English. Mam said it was hard to believe that yer man had shot Michael Collins and if the truth were known, there was probably a fella in every town in Ireland who was supposed to have shot Michael Collins. They were ten-a-penny, Mam said, the heroes and villains of the old war.

The anti-treaty forces had started the Civil War to save Ireland from being a partitioned country. They didn't want to finish the fight with a clatter of people still in charge in Northern Ireland who wanted to remain loyal to England. It was all about betrayal and the dishonour of compromise. Accusations about giving up the fight for Irish freedom had seeped into the bloodstream in every town and village, including Nenagh. The inheritors of the anti-treaty crowd were the Fianna Fáil party.

Fianna Fáil dominated Nenagh politics, but Mam and Dad were Labour Party people. They believed in better wages and more rights for working people. They disliked Fianna Fáil because being a Fianna Fáiler was all about whom you knew and who might do you a favour. Dad said Fianna Fáil was all about the wink and the nod and money under the table. He'd rather deal with straight, decent labouring people.

Dad didn't say much about politics when he did his Irish Life job or he talked to a man in a pub. He didn't want to argue with or insult people he'd have to do business with. But in our house he raged against the ridiculous pomposity of Fianna Fáilers. He didn't need to prove that he was an Irishman. Dad was a quiet Republican. Many of his Irish-speaking cronies were active in what was called the Movement. The last time the Movement had done anything was in the late 1950s, when the remnants of the old Irish Republican Army had carried out a desultory campaign against the existence of the border between the Republic and Northern Ireland. Dad knew many of the men involved, and some had been arrested and interned at a camp in county Kildare. Because Dad owned a car, he often obliged the families of men who were still interned by driving them to the Kildare camp on a Sunday to visit the men inside. Police detectives sometimes followed his car back to Nenagh. Occasionally, he collected men who had been released. He'd offer them a stay in our house before they continued on to their old home out in the country. But they never stayed. "There were too many guards living on the street," Dad explained later. "You'd be watched all the time."

Many of these men had taken Irish language classes while they were jailed. Dad enjoyed talking Irish to them and helping them improve their Irish skills. Dad's wallet, which I liked to hold and study when he let me, was made of leather and it had been handtooled by a man in the camp. It had intricate Celtic engravings, like the patterns on the long spine of the big book that Mr. Daly had at school. Dad believed in the language movement, not the military movement. He stood apart because he was a Labour Party man, not an old-fashioned Republican. But he had nothing to prove to anyone.

CHAPTER THREE

JESUS, MARY AND JOSEPH.
HOLY MOTHER OF GOD!

AFTER *Daithi Lacha* AND THE other children's programs, everything stopped on TV for the angelus at six o'clock. This one-minute break featured bell ringing, accompanied by a religious image on the screen. As far I knew, it was all about the Virgin Mary. We were all supposed to stop and pray to the Virgin Mary for a minute when the angelus came on. If you were out on the street when the angelus bells rang from the church, you'd see people pause, bless themselves and say a prayer. You were supposed to do exactly the same thing if you were watching television in your kitchen or living room.

Nobody thought it was peculiar to have a religious intrusion and an invocation to prayer in the middle of television viewing. Weren't we all Catholics? Weren't we supposed to pray to and honour Our Lady, the Virgin Mary, at every opportunity? That's what the teachers told us at school, and if a priest came to the school to quiz us about our religious knowledge, he said it again. Every night when RTÉ closed down, at about eleven, the broadcast would end with a priest saying a prayer. You couldn't have television interfering with people's religious practices. Wasn't the fight for Irish freedom all about being free to be Catholic and not having the English trying to shove Protestantism down our throats? It was in all the ballads and songs.

At Easter, television almost disappeared completely. The only thing you'd get on Good Friday was the Stations of the Cross being broadcast for hours in the afternoon. Then RTÉ would just close down until Easter Sunday morning. It was to remind us that the anniversary of the resurrection of Our Lord was more important than anything going on in the world. We had to go to Mass or benediction over and over between Thursday and Easter Sunday. Everything stopped in Nenagh from Thursday to Saturday. Even Willie Heaney stopped cycling around the town on his bicycle and talking to people for his stories in the *Nenagh Guardian*. Before we had the television, at Easter it was just waiting all the time and then getting ready to go to church. I would be trying to keep my clothes clean if the weather was fine and I was outside playing. If it was cold or bucketing rain it meant staying in the house and being very quiet. After we had television and I had to stay in the house because the weather was atrocious, it was hard to look at the television set sitting there like a dead thing and it was hard to believe that they couldn't put something on, just something for small children who had nothing to do except wait for the next time we had to get ready and go to the church.

Nenagh was full of religion. The town seemed to have an army of priests, Christian Brothers and other organizations devoted to the Church. The most powerful was the Legion of Mary. The legion was for men and women. Some people laughed at the Legion of Mary, but they were afraid of it. You could tell because they whispered about it and would just snigger and change the subject. At school the teachers told us to think about joining the Legion of Mary when we were older, but at home I heard people talking about it and I knew they were laughing.

The Legion of Mary was devoted to Our Lady, the Virgin Mary, Mother of God. It was about Mary's perfect obedience, her angelic sweetness and spotless purity. Mam and Dad went to Mass and confession, but they weren't in the legion. I could tell from the way they talked about it that the legion was for a particular type of person. You could make a smart remark about the legion in your own house, but you didn't say much about it outside your house. The members of the legion met every week and said prayers. Then, according to some people, they sat around and gossiped about the town, trying to figure out what matter they could interfere in. They were great men and women for visiting the elderly and the sick at home, or people in hospital. But they didn't bring some

51

fresh fruit, flowers and good cheer like everybody else did. They brought religious pamphlets and made the sick person say prayers with them. They were also liable to descend on families who, as far as Nenagh gossip was concerned, were going to hell altogether. Maybe they weren't going to Mass or maybe some daughter was reputed to have been seen talking to a married man on the street. Some people said the Legion of Mary could stop a film from being shown at the cinema in Nenagh if they didn't like the sound of it.

In our house, Mam paused and crossed herself quickly when the angelus came on the television. Dad did the same and muttered a prayer to himself in Irish. I knew they took it seriously, as everybody was supposed to do, but they weren't fanatics. Dad didn't believe in being a fanatic for anything. If he met a man who jawed on and on about some issue that was dear to his heart, Dad would later call him "a fanatic" and sigh. Soon enough I learned that "fanatic" meant someone who'd keep you talking for hours when you wanted to do something else.

We all went to Mass on Sundays, and sometimes Mam or Dad went to Mass during the week if they wanted to say special prayers because somebody was ill in hospital, or somebody in the family was hoping for a bit of good luck with a job or a promotion, or one of the children needed help. We didn't eat meat on Fridays. We had our Sunday breakfast hours before going to Mass so that we could take Communion. I went to confession, and Máire did when she was old enough, and I told my venal sins, living in dread of when a grumpy priest would take issue with the small matter of disobeying Mam and Dad and give me a long lecture, ordering me to say an enormous number of Hail Marys in penance. I'd have to kneel in the church after coming out of confession and by the length of time I was there, other people would know I was a bold, brazen child and maybe if they were in the legion they'd start coming to our house and make me get down on my knees right there on the spot to say my prayers and renounce the devil.

You were supposed to say a polite hello to priests you met on the street. But if you were small, you'd say "Hello, Father" and most of them would just ignore you. The worst was when they'd look at you, deliberately, and still ignore you, like you were dirt on the ground. They'd march along the street, the black suit and coat flapping like they didn't need to look where they were going because everybody got out of the way. Dad had no time for priests who sat on their comfortable behinds in the parish house, drinking wine, eating cake and going out with a cross look on their face when they were called to give the last rites to somebody who was dying. There were enough of those boys around, according to Dad. They were nothing but arrogant fellas who'd been getting it soft ever since their mammy decided they were going to be a priest. When they became priests they devoted themselves to sitting in the parish house and expanding their backsides. They never did a tap of work; they were only bags of wind.

Sometimes Dad would use the old Gaelic expression *"Ná bí mór ná beag le sagart"*—don't be too close or too distant with a priest. Dad respected the priests who actually did something in the town, who organized committees, raised funds for new buildings or took part in running a hurling or Gaelic football team and were definitely not fanatics about religion. He liked the man in charge in Nenagh, Monsignor Horan. In the 1950s, when there was the IRA campaign against the border with Northern Ireland, one of the old IRA men in the Nenagh area, Sean South of Garryowen, had been killed in the campaign. Monsignor Horan had accompanied his coffin on the long funeral march. Dad said it showed great respect for the old rebel traditions of Tipperary and he was sure the bishop had given Horan an earful about his action.

One priest, Father Molloy, was active in the Gaelic League for a while and occasionally came to the house to see Dad. He was a bit standoffish and Mam didn't care for his presumptuous ways. He expected to be fed, always, and Mam never failed to provide him with a meal. He'd always say, when he finished, "That hit the spot!" But he would never say an outright thank you. Mam took to calling him Father Hit-the-Spot, and she'd mutter a few choice insults when he was out the door, noting that his prominent, well-fed belly preceded him by several inches. I listened to it all and watched the way the priest expected to be treated like an important man, but he really hadn't the manners that I was supposed to have, saying please and thank you all time, and as soon as he was gone from our house, there were plenty of hints to tell me that some priests were only a pain in the arse and no good to anyone but themselves.

Having the angelus on television, and on the radio at noon, was nothing to think about at all. It was the way it was. Being a good Catholic was as obvious a part of living in Nenagh as eating potatoes with your lunch and dinner every day. It was a business too. Dad's twin brother, Paddy, had the angle on the business side. His wife Lizzie's family, the O'Morans, were long established in the merchandising of religious wares. Paddy expanded the business to the point where he sold religious goods in towns and villages across the whole southern half of Ireland.

The bedrock of the business was the missions. The missions were a fact of life in every parish. A town would be invaded by the Redemptorist, Dominican or Franciscan priests. They were there for two weeks: a week for the women and a week for the men. That meant early-morning Mass every day and a big sermon every night. The purpose of the mission was to provide an annual spiritual stimulant for the local congregation. One time only, I went to a mission for small boys and I thought it was mad. It was exciting, like going to see one of the amateur plays Dad was involved with, but it still seemed very peculiar. It was hard to know what the big priest was talking about, as he stood at the pulpit and shouted at us. We had the gift of faith, he said, and we should live in fear of losing the gift of faith. Mam said there was no fear of that in Nenagh, with the number of priests in the town, the Christian Brothers and the Legion of Mary prying in everyone's pocket. Mam and Dad were skeptical about it by then. The country was 95 per cent Roman Catholic, and instances of people switching religion were few and far between, but as far as the mission priests were concerned, Ireland was going to be destroyed by modernity and their goal was to halt it. Dad said they were headcases, every one of them.

When the mission priests came, it was an event, and the towns and parishes were galvanized by it. There was something to do every day during a mission. It was an entertainment to some, and it was a chance for many wives and mothers to get out of the house. A mission was a week of terrifying, bellicose warnings. It was an ideal opportunity for contemplating the delectable dangers to traditional purity. Nightly, the mission priests would rail against every single dilution of holy, Catholic Ireland.

They complained about the cinema and the television and the radio, about dancing and newspapers and magazines. They saw lewd behaviour everywhere. They railed against small families and said the fashion to have two children in an Irish Catholic family was an abomination and the result of vile English influence. Four children should be no bother to decent, God-fearing Irish Catholic mothers and fathers. No bother at all. God provided for everybody.

They glowered from the pulpit and shouted. Anyone who wasn't actually in the church for the mission was up to no good. Men and boys who stood on corners smoking cigarettes and eyeing women were striking examples of moral decline. Women who courted men in doorways and alleys or dark lanes should be reported to the parish priest and their movements noted until their behaviour improved.

They were hard men, the mission priests. Spittle and foam flew from their mouths as they promised hell to people who listened to foreign music and danced to it. Television was to be used for the news only, and for important announcements by bishops and cardinals. Everything else on television was rubbish and filth to be avoided. Some mission priests swayed and almost fell exhausted to the church floor when they'd finished roaring about hell and lascivious behaviour. Dad said he was always surprised that there wasn't a round of applause. According to Dad—in the safety of his own home, mind you—many of the men who were mission priests had mistaken their vocations. They had a calling for the stage but instead they went into the Church. Jimmy Cagney had nothing on some of those lads waving their arms and roaring from the pulpit.

According to the mission priests, people needed to be reminded of their Roman Catholic faith and of Our Lord and the Virgin Mary both at home and at work. There shouldn't be a wall without a holy-water fount or a shelf without holy statues, and a picture of the Sacred Heart should be visible everywhere in the house.

This is where Paddy came in. Paddy had the goods. He'd get a list in advance from the Redemptorists or Dominicans of the towns they would visit on a mission. Paddy would be outside the church at four in the morning, setting up his stall in the best spot, nearest the church gate, and he'd unload his crates of mission goods. At the early Mass, a mission priest—usually the older, gentler men took the morning duty—might remind the congregation of the value of having a statue of the Blessed Virgin that was highly visible inside the home. The congregation would leave the church and there in front of them would be Paddy's stall with an array of statues for sale. At the evening Mass, a mission priest might shout in a frenzy of passion, "Every person in this townland should have a miraculous medal!" Outside, Paddy sold them by the dozen.

A miraculous medal was a small aluminum commodity, with a saint's likeness embossed on it, and the image was endorsed by the Church. It was supposed to save you from harm or bad luck. Everybody had them. People wore them inside their clothes to ward off illness or put them in the little saddle bag on their bicycles as a preventative against accidents. They were put in children's schoolbags. I had one in my schoolbag and one pinned to the heavy woollen gansey I wore going out to play in the winter. The farmers put them everywhere. They were attached to cows and pigs and were nailed over outhouses. Sometimes they were attached to fences or hung from the brambles near where sheep, chickens and pigs gathered.

Dad respected the mission business. He'd seen it all himself. He used to go with Paddy to remote places, where Paddy would need help transporting the boxes of statues and medals and setting up his stall, and where a few words of fluent Gaelic might go some way with the locals.

In 1960 he went with him to the Aran Islands, the three forlorn, rocky islands at the mouth of Galway Bay. They did a roaring trade on Inis Mór, the big island. Then they followed the mission priests to Inis Meáin, the smaller island. The sea was rough and Dad and Paddy clung to the crates of statues, Sacred Heart pictures, holy-water founts and miraculous medals as the Atlantic pounded the trawler. It went on for hours, as sight of Inis Meáin came and went in the wind and sleet. Eventually they were told the sea was too rough for the boat to dock.

They waited, swaying in the trawler as the waves rose higher, and Dad expected the boat to just turn tail and make for the port at Inis Mór that they had left earlier. But the trawler just idled, with the sea slashing into it. Then, in the sea around them, there appeared several local fishermen, out in their little boats to bring the passengers in to the island. But they couldn't carry the crates of mission goods. Dad watched as Paddy talked to the trawler captain about the tides. There was much nodding and pointing. Paddy made a decision. Dad was dubious, but Paddy said he knew what he was doing.

They threw all the crates overboard and watched them float off, bobbing up and down in the high waves. Then they climbed gingerly into the little fishing boats made of canvas and balsa wood, boats that seemed to glide on top of the rolling waves, and they were taken safely to the island in minutes. They went to their lodgings, changed out of their wet clothes, enjoyed a good meal and slept soundly. At dawn, Paddy woke up Dad and they set off for the shore. There, on the small, rough beach, were all the crates of mission goods waiting for them. They hauled the wet crates to a track where a man with a donkey cart would carry them to the church gates and they could start selling the statues and miraculous medals that now smelled heavily of the salt sea.

Dad told me the story over and over. He was in his own world when he told it, remembering the treacherous sea and the sight of the crates floating away from the boat. He loved the Aran Islands because the people there spoke only Gaelic, and Paddy would have been lost without him. It was old Ireland, he said, and the mission was great entertainment for the islanders. Dad said that the mission priests, roaring away at the people in their schoolbook Gaelic, tormenting people with their cracked pronunciation, were wasting their time. The mission priests went to the Aran Islands to warn against the evils of modernity and they preached to the last truly isolated peasantry in western Europe. They preached to people who knew only Gaelic and who in almost every aspect of their lives were back in what Dad called "old God's time." The people on Inis Meáin had no quarrel with modernity because they knew nothing of it.

By the mid 1960s, when I had my only experience with the mission priests, the missions were in decline. There were too many distractions keeping people away from morning Mass and nightly sermons about the horrors of hell that awaited those who indulged in non-Irish, non-Catholic behaviour. Even on those forlorn, rocky Aran Islands, whipped by the wild Atlantic though they were, the light from other places would fall. Television arrived, and with it the hints of glamour, modernity and sophistication. The angelus bells still rang on Irish television to remind everyone of the faith of their mothers, fathers and forefathers, but in my house and in my mind, the angelus was only an interruption between entertaining programs and stories.

CHAPTER FOUR

KNOWN FOR THEIR LAWLESSNESS

AFTER THE ANGELUS ON RTÉ, there was the news, usually read in a solemn voice by Charles Mitchel. All the news was about Ireland. Occasionally there was a report from America, and it always involved one of the Kennedy family. Poor John F. Kennedy had been assassinated, for reasons that nobody understood. I heard people say that maybe he'd been shot because he was a Catholic, or because he was too good a man to deal with all the wickedness in America. His picture was everywhere. Almost every house in Nenagh had a photo of him on the wall. He was in framed pictures sold by Paddy in his mission stall. In those it was John F. Kennedy beside the Pope's photo, and the writing at the bottom of the photo said, "Men of Peace." On the news, there might be a mention of the Soviet Union's latest launch of a rocket into space, but the Soviet Union wasn't of much interest unless it was threatening war on America or making a display of persecuting Catholics. Nothing seemed to happen in England that was newsworthy. Sometimes there was news about the British government putting unfair duties on goods, food and livestock imported from Ireland. They were always out to get us.

The news was mainly an account of the government's doings. The prime minister, Sean Lemass, was lamenting what the British government was doing to the Irish economy while he opened a new sugar beet factory or a creamery for pasteurizing milk somewhere in the country. At the same time, a bishop was opening a school or blessing yet another commemorative statue of a sainted figure from Ireland's past. The government or the Church was the gist of it on *RTÉ News*. RTÉ had a correspondent who covered the Vatican and Church affairs, and news from Rome was more plentiful than news from Belfast or London.

After the news came the farming report. That's when everybody in Nenagh stopped watching and ate their supper—though some people might keep an ear cocked for some mention of an agricultural crisis that might affect business in the town. The farming report was entirely concerned with livestock and grain prices and the activity at various cattle marts across Ireland. The commercials were aimed at farmers and at selling them cures for diseases that apparently plagued farm animals. It was a matter of stamping out mastitis, liver fluke, roundworm, tapeworm and scour. Even people who never set foot on a farm were familiar with the mastitis problem.

After the farming report, there was often a western. Apart from *Bat Masterson*, there was *Have Gun Will Travel*, *Gunsmoke*, *Bonanza* and *The Adventures of Kit Carson*. The town people tuned out the farming news, and they didn't pay much attention to the westerns. The westerns were for children, or for people who lived outside the town, on the farms. Nenagh people thought the westerns appealed to people in the rural areas because they were all living in the old style out there. They weren't modern at all.

It was true that westerns were especially savoured in the countryside. Farmers and farmers' sons saw themselves as cowpokes, making a living on the land and raising a few cattle. Even the shops they visited were not so different. The general store on a western show sold feed and grain, like many shops in Nenagh. The saloons were similar to the traditional Irish country bars, with their sawdust on the floor. Many men drank measures of whiskey just like the cowboys and gunslingers in the westerns.

I noticed the similarity, and knew that the frontier towns seen on *Bat Masterson* or *Have Gun Will Travel* had the same class structure as a town like Nenagh. There were always the rich, the poor and a few in-betweens. The doctor and the schoolteacher were respected. The things you saw on the shows about modern America—the world of big cars, telephones and people travelling on airplanes—were almost as far away from the old American frontier towns as they were from Nenagh.

In the hills outside Nenagh, they'd been living the frontier life for hundreds of years. They were just a bit beyond the mannered ways of the town, and they knew it and liked it that way. Mam's people, the Aherns, lived in Castlecranna, seven miles outside Nenagh. The Aherns were decent, honest country people, known down the generations as skilled carpenters, cabinetmakers and small-hold farmers. Mam was the only daughter of Martin and Mary Ahern. They were true country people, but Martin Ahern was not a farming man. He was a skilled labourer who worked for the county council and rose, through the years, to become a supervisor to the road crews that laid tar macadam on the roads, fixed potholes and kept the ditches and hedgerows trimmed. Tall, upright, with piercing blue eyes and the manner of a man who was proud to supervise and keep order, he could be distant in public and standoffish in pubs but displayed his wit and warmth at home. He and his wife lived in a small bungalow at the top of a gentle hill. The house had no running water—every day my grandmother carried two big metal buckets of water from the well at the bottom of the hill—and electricity had only recently arrived. When I was two years old, Martin Ahern lifted me up in his arms and had me reach up to turn on the first electric light in the house. Mam told me that story and said my arrival in Cranna that day was a sure sign that the townland was going places.

Cranna, as it was always called, was rebel territory. Back in 1842, an English magistrate had declared, as he was sending a few locals off to Australia for their petty crimes, "Throughout history, the peasants of Tipperary have been known for their lawlessness." He surely had Cranna in mind.

Cranna people had their own ways and nurtured long and bitter memories. What had happened during Cromwell's invasion of Ireland or during the potato famine might as well have happened yesterday. The Aherns loathed the Herrick family. Martin Ahern would spit, with a great cough of disgust, if the Herrick name was mentioned. Sometime during the famine, relatives of the Aherns had been starving and unable to pay the rent to their English landlord. They were evicted from the land, and they lived in ditches until one of them was strong enough to work and earn money to rent a tiny plot of ground. Meanwhile, the Herrick family had moved in and taken the Ahern land.

They were still there, a reminder that some old wounds can never heal. The Herricks had acquired more land over the years and grown wealthy. Knowing they were disliked, they developed a superior attitude. The Aherns simply avoided them on the street, on the roads or in a pub. Mam's younger brother, Martin Junior, was the only one who enjoyed meeting one of the Herrick family. If he ever came across one of them, he'd say, "Fuck off, you!" and keep walking. He was famous for it in Cranna and Nenagh.

The famine meant little to me when I was small. It was occasionally mentioned in Cranna and sometimes called "the great hunger," but hardly anyone talked in detail about it. Whenever the famine was mentioned in the

Ahern house, my Gran said the English were to blame. The Irish starved and died or emigrated and that was good for the English rulers, according to Gran. All I knew was that it had happened in Cranna, and it was the reason for the Aherns hating the Herricks so much.

Cranna and the surrounding townlands of Shallee, Newport and Burgess were hilly, with narrow, winding roads leading to small rivers and lakes. Cranna had always been impossible to govern, and some of the Cranna people still believed they were beyond the law. It was a hotbed for the making of poitín, the moonshine whiskey. Almost every house had some poitín, and a large number of the local men had a sideline making it. Great hoards of bottles were in the ditches and under sods of soil by the roadside.

Sometimes the pubs stayed open late and the local guards made only token efforts to clamp down. Besides, the pubs up in the hills had the advantage of being able to see the guards coming in the squad cars or on bicycles, so the guards might arrive to find a locked, dark pub, and they'd get frustrated when they'd hear giggling inside and smell the pipe smoke and cigarettes but there would be no response to their pounding on the doors.

On one of Dad's first visits to Cranna, Mam's brothers Jerry and Tom took him to the pub for a drink. On the walk home afterwards, saying nothing, they took Dad on a detour to Mooncranna River. There, Jerry disappeared into the trees and began breaking down branches and sharpening their points with a penknife. Dad asked Tom what Jerry was doing, but Tom told Dad to be quiet. They stood around, studied the moon and peered into the water.

Then Tom disappeared for a few minutes and returned with a sack full of sods of peat turf. He handed the sods to Dad, took out some matches and set an end of the turf alight. He whispered to Dad to move closer to the water and hold the blazing turf over it. When Dad stood by the water he looked down and saw dozens of salmon swimming there. Jerry moved silently up and down the bank, spearing them, and Tom slid them into the sack. They did this for half an hour. Dad thought everybody was living on fresh salmon in Cranna, but they weren't. Jerry took the salmon into Nenagh the next morning and sold them to the hotels. The Aherns had fished the Mooncranna River for centuries and if they felt like fishing by night, they did. Cranna people were wild.

Mam had four brothers. Peter, a gifted carpenter, had moved away to Portroe, in the hills nearer the Shannon, and he'd married young. He'd wanted a little distance between himself and Cranna, and he got it. As a carpenter he was able to get work building the new housing estates that were starting to dot the land around Limerick city. He lived with his wife, Mary, in an ancient farmhouse at the top of a steep hill, with a spectacular view of the Shannon estuary. To get there from Nenagh or from Cranna you had to follow a tortuous route of small back roads and lanes. When Dad and Mam visited Peter in Portoe (he was always referred to as "Peter in Portoe," to distinguish him from Peter Doyle in Nenagh and to mark the fact that he'd up and left Cranna), Dad liked to return before darkness fell. Once or twice he'd gotten lost in the hills.

Jerry Ahern was a brilliant man with a glorious brain. According to some people he was as odd as two left feet, but he paid no attention. He lived a few minutes' walk from his parents, with his wife, Winnie. Jerry was a miner, working in the ancient mines in the village of Silvermines, where the silver had long run out but there was lead and zinc to be gouged from the ground. Jerry hated it. He had an active, restless mind that came alive when he was away from the mines. He loathed authority and received wisdom. He was full of opinions and could turn the most mundane remark into an occasion for lively debate. He liked to engage people with very large questions. He might ask, "Why is there all that music in the films?" As silence greeted his question, he'd begin asking more. He could mesmerize a crowd in a pub with his questions.

Once, he decided that the English language was a complete fraud. It was all a cod. He pointed to a sign in a pub advertising Smithwicks Ale and pointed out that if the English language made any sense at all, the *w* would not be there in the word because it wasn't used in pronouncing the word *Smithwicks*. It was sticking out like a sore thumb, completely useless. He got nods of agreement. Emboldened, he began an assault on the ridiculous uses of the letters *c* and *k*, an assault that involved a lengthy rhetorical questioning of why the words *Cassidy* and *Kildare* were pronounced with the same sound for the first letter when they were different letters. The madness of

English and the harum-scarum system of pronunciation was his theme for months.

Jerry lived to argue, but not to win the argument. A genius with words, he wanted a good fight about something and he got annoyed when people only shrugged at his "Why?" questions. When Mam or Dad mentioned Jerry's name, the words "highly annoyed" often came with the story. He was notorious for being highly annoyed about something. But he wasn't really annoyed at all. He was only perplexed by other people's acceptance of the ordinary. Sometimes, in the pub, he'd get disappointed with the disinterest of every man and woman in the place, and he'd be so testy he'd practically spit. He'd go to drink his pint standing in the doorway. That way he could study the cars coming and going. Cars interested him, but he declined to own one. He went everywhere on a bicycle. For a time, he considered filling the little living room in his house with seats and sofas made from car seats. It stood to reason they'd be more comfortable because they were designed for people to sit in them all day. They were bound to be more comfortable than most of the sugawn chairs and stuffed couches that were in the houses around Castlecranna.

Jerry loved television and watched it avidly. He enjoyed everything, from *Green Acres* to the old Hollywood movies that RTÉ would air on Sunday afternoons. He was like a bored man who had suddenly found something to spark his interest. It was *Have Gun Will Travel* that Jerry loved in particular. The main character was Paladin, a loner who lived a mysterious double life and was obsequious to no man. He lived in a fancy hotel in San Francisco and left only when somebody hired him to visit a remote place and sort things out with his gun. He was an older fella, and craggy faced, but dapper, smart and, apart from being a loner, a great one for questions.

Dressed in black, he would arrive in the little town where someone had hired him and ask questions about why the problem arose or why people weren't getting along in the town. Then he'd sort it all out with sharp common sense. Maybe in the end he'd have to use his gun, but he wouldn't want to. Often Paladin would be highly annoyed about the problems he was asked to sort out.

Once, Jerry was in Nenagh on greyhound racing business. He'd started raising and training greyhounds as a sideline. He was always starting up a sideline, because he was bored. He was in our house and decided he'd watch *Have Gun Will Travel* before he met a man about the greyhounds. He told me I should watch with him, because your man, Paladin, was the best of the cowboys. Paladin wasn't my favourite cowboy, because he wasn't a cowboy at all. Or even a gunslinger like Bat Masterson. He was old and he didn't seem to be having a lot of fun on his adventures. There were hardly any fist fights or attacks by the Indians. Still, I watched with Jerry because Jerry was always good for commentary. In this episode, Paladin was asked to go to New Orleans to sort out an argument between two fellas who were going to have a duel. One of them had insulted the other and they were all set to sort out the matter "with honour," according to somebody who was telling the details to Paladin.

Paladin was annoyed about the carry-on. "My time is too valuable to waste on matters of such stupidity," he declared, and Jerry was beaming at him. Paladin called the two fellas who wanted a duel "nincompoops," and Jerry laughed when he heard it. He looked at me like I should be taking note of what was going on. Near the end Paladin said to another fella, "We have fallen among idiots." "Good man yourself!" Jerry said at the television.

When I told Jerry that I liked *Bat Masterson*, he told me I was an eejit. He said *Bat Masterson* was all a cod. None of the stories made any sense. I liked Jerry, even when he said I was an eejit and *Bat Masterson* was all a cod. Jerry had what Dad called gumption, but he wasn't interested in using his gumption to make loads of money in a shop or a business. I liked that he'd talk to me all the time. He wasn't choosy about the people he would argue with. If it was a small child, well and good, you could talk about television or something he'd seen in a film. Mam saw me talking to Jerry, when there were few grown-ups I'd talk with. She told me other people considered Jerry awkward and peculiar and I wasn't to take him too seriously. But she also said he had great brains.

Tom Ahern lived another few minutes' walk from Jerry. A sweet-natured, always active man, Tom was passionate about politics, his wife and his children. His wife, Vera, was the favourite of everyone, especially Máire and me. Exotically beautiful, Vera looked like she had Spanish blood. When she laughed, as she often did, her head tilted back and her raven-dark hair cascaded everywhere. Vera had merry eyes and loved to hug and hold children. Her lilting voice always had a touch of gentle mockery in it, as if she was amused by everything. She was the happiest woman in the world. Martin Ahern Junior was the most mysterious to me. Young and wild, he was always on the move. He'd smile at me and wink, letting me know he had mischief on his mind. He was a quicksilver presence and it would be years before I knew him well.

Mam's full name was Mary Jane Ahern, but only her mother and Vera called her Mary Jane or Jane. When we visited the Ahern house in Cranna, Máire and I often heard our grandmother calling, "Jane, Jane!" and we knew it meant that Granny had another errand for Mam. She did everything in the house when we were there—cook, clean, garden. She was used to it, and did it with great efficiency. As the only girl in the Ahern family, she'd been cooking and cleaning for her brothers all her life.

Mam had gone to a one-room school in Shallee, in the hills near Cranna. With every other child, she'd carried a sod of turf each day to school, for the fire that heated the tiny building. At the age of twelve she'd left Shallee and attended the Vocational School in Nenagh, cycling the seven miles there and back in all weathers. At home, under oil lamps, she had cooked and cleaned. Her one indulgence was doing the crossword puzzles in the only reading material that came into the Ahern house, *The Sacred Heart Messenger*, the *Irish Catholic* or *Ireland's Own* magazine. She read and did the puzzles at night after the entire family had knelt on the floor to say the rosary together. She achieved small fame in Cranna for her expertise in the crosswords. Twice she'd entered the Christmas competition in the *Irish Catholic* magazine, and twice she had won a fancy wool sweater. People deferred to her for her knowledge of words.

But Mam, in her way, often dismissed her schooling as almost non-existent. When I'd ask her to explain something to me, she'd say, "John, I never went to school. I only stood on the road and met the scholars on their way home from school. It was little enough I picked up from them."

At the Vocational School in Nenagh, she'd learned English, commerce and home economics. That meant she was trained to write letters for job applications, balance a household budget and cook. When she graduated from the Vocational School, she went to work at Bridgie Gleason's bakery, an institution in Nenagh. Bridgie Gleason's was a teashop and sold bread and flour, mostly to country people who were in Nenagh to shop for supplies. That's where Mam met Dad.

She was serving the customers and Dad came in for tea and buns. He chatted her up and they started courting. Mam was pleased to be working and courting, but she knew that Bridgie Gleason was underpaying her. She was shrewd and bided her time. After two years, Mam went down the street to work at Sheehan's, another bakery, where she was paid a shilling more a week. She married Dad when she was nineteen years old and he was thirty-two. She had me, her first child, when she was twenty, and Máire was born eighteen months later.

Although Mam had gone to school in Nenagh and worked in Nenagh, she wasn't a Nenagh woman at all. She was a country girl in Nenagh and was treated as such by some of the Doyles and by Nenagh people who knew no better. But Mary Jane Ahern merely gave the impression of being an innocent, naive country girl whose world was only as wide as the distance between Nenagh and Castlecranna. Mam was quiet-spoken and polite to the Nenagh people. She held her tongue and kept her opinions to herself. In truth, I knew that at home and away from the in-laws and the insular Nenagh people, she savoured words, phrases and the insults she could, if she wanted, fling back at the whole shower of them. She had a countrywoman's quiet contempt for the false niceties of town life. She was beautiful, smart and witty. She had enough energy and humour to light up the town of Nenagh.

The devil featured prominently in her remarks. "May the devil choke him," she'd say of someone who'd said something critical. A particularly evil person—usually someone who was uncharitable or just plain mean spirited —had a soul "as black as the riding boots of the devil himself." If there was a married couple and the wife was as mean spirited as the husband, she'd say, "Put the devil on horseback and he'll ride straight to hell." A blowhard who didn't have much in the way of size was "no bigger than two halfpennies on a bar stool."

It was Mam's quiet opinions that influenced me in thinking about Nenagh and the way people carried on there. One time she said, "Nenagh was never funny. It was other people from Cranna and television coming into the house that brought a bit of life into it."

CHAPTER FIVE

BAGSY, SCROOPE AND FERRET

DAD THOUGHT NENAGH WAS very funny. He'd grown up in it and knew all the characters in the town and all the stories of famous incidents that had happened in it. Witty or sarcastic answers that somebody in Nenagh had made years ago came easily into his mind when he watched television with me. He loved stories and drama.

It was westerns and gangster dramas that really appealed to him. He'd grown up on them, going to the pictures every week, watching Tom Mix, Gene Autry and John Wayne fighting off howling Indians. He'd also seen dozens of American gangster films with James Cagney, Edward G. Robinson, Humphrey Bogart and the Irish-American Pat O'Brien as the priest. The likes of *Bat Masterson* were a bit too sly and slow moving for him.

There wasn't enough action, like you'd get at the pictures.

When Dad was growing up in Nenagh, going to the cinema was an event. Only courting couples went to the cinema during the week, but everybody went on Sundays. Still, if you wanted to go see the films, or "the pictures," as they were usually called, you had to plan for it and work for the entrance money. But then you'd enjoy it all the more, Dad said. I heard about it until I knew every detail of how it used to be.

Dad said that when he was small he always went to see the double bill on Sunday afternoons. It cost two pennies, and he and his brothers had to use cunning and enterprise to earn the money. For a start, there was the pig that Dad's own Mam and Dad kept in the back yard. They'd buy a piglet on a Fair Day, fatten it up and sell it. The pig had to be fed constantly, and Dad and his brothers would collect buckets of offal for it. If they brought enough buckets during the week, their Mam would give them a penny each. That was half the money needed for the pictures on a Sunday.

The other way to get money, the one that made my eyes go wide in amazement when Dad first told me, was by skinning rabbits. There was a fella who'd go out on a Saturday and trap a brace of rabbits. He'd go around the houses on a Sunday morning selling the rabbits for Sunday dinner. He'd skin the rabbit for an extra penny, but Dad would offer to do it himself, and after he'd used a sharp knife to get the skin off the rabbit, his mam would give him a penny. On Monday the rabbit skin could be taken to a shop where the owner would buy anything at all you had to sell, and you'd get a penny for a rabbit skin. Providing he could hold on to the money for the week, that was the start of the money for the next weekend's pictures.

If there was no pig to be fed or rabbits to be skinned, Dad would collect jam jars and get a halfpenny each for them. With that much work, Dad said, when you went to the pictures you enjoyed yourself. Dad would describe vividly the scene in the cinema to me, with the young boys and girls in the cheap seats, called the pits, shouting back at the screen, the girls calling Jimmy Cagney a bowsie but the boys imitating his Yankee sneer, and the women sitting in the rows behind the pits, many of them doing their knitting as the action progressed on the screen. It was great fun for every man, woman and child because nearly the whole town of Nenagh would be there.

Except, of course, for people who didn't want to enjoy themselves. They didn't want to spend the two pennies at the pictures. That was Nenagh. Dad always mentioned with a sigh that, of course, there was somebody who saw the cloud, not the silver lining, or they were just out to spite you. They'd begrudge enjoyment for other people. Dad hated that type of person. He'd be outraged just talking about it. "There was a young fella named Geurin who used to knock around with us. He'd collect the jam jars or take out a bucket to collect the offal and he'd get the money, the same as us. But he wouldn't go to the pictures. He'd hold on to his money. When we'd come out of the cinema he'd be standing outside with a grin on his face. He'd hold out his hand with the money in it. There, he'd say to us. I have two pence now, and ye have nothing. God, he was an awful pain in the neck."

The pictures had a lingering effect on Dad. Big drama and funny stories were what he wanted. Dad watched television sometimes, but he was often gone. He was always on the move. Apart from his job, which had varying hours, and the Gaelic League on top of that, he was the co-founder of the Kilruane Players, an amateur acting company based in Kilruane, just outside Nenagh. He started it up with Tadgh Connors. Tadgh was a farmer, a dreamer and a born actor. I knew him well because he was often in the house, and his big, broad body and dramatic gestures fascinated me.

He'd come for a meal at lunchtime on Saturdays and discuss all kinds of literary and theatrical matters with Dad. Once, there was only Tadgh and me left at the table. He had become distracted by an argument with Dad about a poem published in the *Nenagh Guardian*. Instead of tucking a napkin into his trousers, he'd tucked in the table-cloth. He went to leave the table and everything went crashing to the floor—plates, cups, knives, forks and a full jug of milk. Mam came running. "Jesus, Mary and Joseph, what happened?" Mortified and unsure of what the hell had happened, Tadgh looked over at me and said, "Look what you're after doing now!" I stared at him in disbelief. I was about to start crying when Mam sized up the situation and told Tadgh to get moving before the noise woke up every child on Sarsfield Street and had them all bawling.

Dad and Tadgh travelled Tipperary and beyond with

the Kilruane Players. Their headquarters was a pub called The Lucky Bags, out in Kilruane, a place that was more a crossroads than a village. The O'Meara family, who owned The Lucky Bags, loved the theatre and were anxious to be assigned roles in every production. Thus, The Lucky Bags was used for rehearsals. But a lot of travel was involved. There was always a drama competition going on somewhere. The Kilruane Players did one-act plays, and when they started winning prizes, they got ambitious. In preparation for a new production, they hired professional directors from the Abbey Theatre in Dublin. The directors, many of them important figures in Dublin cultural life, would stay in Nenagh or Kilruane for a week, rehearsing the amateur actors and advising Dad and Tadgh. Dad had no formal training in theatre, but he had an intuitive understanding of drama and storytelling. It made watching television with him a madcap, helter-skelter kind of entertainment. Stories criss-crossed this way and that.

Dad had little patience for complicated serial dramas on television, but he studied the acting techniques and the pacing. Watching *The Fugitive*, when the Fugitive fella was explaining his situation in detail to somebody, Dad would say, "Look at that now. Your man is talking away but it's not dramatically correct to have him just jawing on and on, when there's no movement. People lose interest. So that little scene is broken up there by having him lift that cup of coffee and taste it—that adds a dramatic pause to it."

If Dad was watching TV with me, the programs had to compete with his own stories of life in Nenagh. He'd see a

81

bald man on *Gunsmoke* and say, "By God, your baldy man there reminds me of Nick Scroope, and the time that Bagsy Gregan told him where to get off."

Then came the story of how Bagsy Gregan, a Nenagh man who sold newspapers at the bus stop down on Pearse Street, got on Nick Scroope's nerves. Scroope hadn't a wisp of hair on his head, which was as smooth and polished as a billiard ball. He ran a butcher shop and he was particularly busy on Saturdays. On a certain Saturday he didn't have his son John to help him and he was in a bad mood all day. Dad said John was missing because he'd been on the beer in the widow Ryan's pub the night before and he was in bed with a sore head. Nick Scroope was a very orderly man and he hated any change in routine or in behaviour. Anyway, the women came into Scroope's butcher shop all day, looking for a good bit of bacon or a lump of mutton for the Sunday dinner. When they pawed the meat, Scroope was always testy with them, worse than a schoolteacher, and he used a fly swatter to smack their wrists and keep their hands off.

It was a warm day and the sweat was pouring off his bald head. He moaned and moaned about John's absence. But it was Bagsy who was really getting on his nerves. Bagsy was on the street outside, and Bagsy was a demon whistler. He had a terrible stutter, God bless the mark, but he could whistle like a bird all day. He was devoted to whistling. Inside, Scroope was passing remarks that it sounded like a bloody canary was outside. The women encouraged him, enjoying the tension between the cheerful whistler outside and the agitated man with the fly swatter inside. One of the women suggested that Scroope have a word with Bagsy if he was so annoyed by the whistling.

Eventually he couldn't stand it and he put his bald head out the shop door. "Hey, sonny," he said, "where do you buy your canary seed?" Bagsy had a fair tongue on him, stutter and all. His face red with rage, he looked round at Scroope and, just about controlling his stutter, said, "The same place that you buy your fu-fucking hair oil!"

Inside the shop, the women roared with laughter. "Good man, Bagsy," one of them shouted, to acknowledge he'd won the duel. As Nick Scroope flayed away with the fly swatter, the women scattered from the shop and many made a point of stopping to buy a newspaper from Bagsy. They all told the story later to family and friends and the incident entered Nenagh history.

One night, while I was watching Bat Masterson, all suave and smooth in a saloon where some purdy lady was serving him liquor, Dad said, "That woman reminds me of Ferret Gleason." Ferret, who had a real name that most people had forgotten, was an old school pal of Dad's. "We were doing that play at school, years ago, the one about Robert Emmet the rebel leader, and it was only boys were in the play so Ferret had to play Sarah Curran and he was every bit the glamour girl playing her. She was Robert Emmet's lover. The scene called for a party of officers to have drinks at Emmet's house, and Sarah was doing the serving. We only had fizzy lemonade on the stage but we were supposed to be having whiskey. We hardly saw lemonade in those days so we were all guzzling it as fast as Ferret could pour.

"He came to me to serve me at the table and when I got some of it, I drank it off and I raised my glass for more. Ferret looked at the decanter, and it was almost empty. He looked down at me, smoothing the folds of the dress he was wearing, and says, 'Jaysus, Sean Doyle, will you not save me a drop?' We all started breaking our sides laughing. Of course, we were supposed to be having a drunken party in the scene so the audience thought it was great acting. Poor old Ferret was furious with the whole crowd of us."

Ferret, though I never met him, was real to me. What was on television was something to dream of, to wish for, like Bat Masterson's easy way of talking with people. Everything on television was something to dream about. In between the TV programs, RTÉ aired commercials, and they were as good a fantasy as any drama or comedy. There were ads for toothpaste or things for sale at department stores in Dublin and Cork, like fabulous new gadgets that could wash clothes or clean carpets. Mam washed our clothes in a large metal pail and used a washboard to scrub them. The people in the ads weren't real to me at all. Besides, in Nenagh all we knew of advertising was a few inches of space in the *Nenagh Guardian* or a sign stuck in a shop window. The most popular form of advertising in Nenagh was as old as the town itself. As Mam washed the clothes, or as I settled in to watch TV, Tom Tierney, famous for his loquacious oratory, walked through

Nenagh carrying a sign and ringing his bell in rhythm with his slow-paced walk, and he'd call out, "Gents' suits reduced at Slattery's drapery shop this week! Come one, come all!" Everybody knew him and he knew everybody. If Dad passed him on the street he'd say, "God bless the work, Tom!" And Tom would nod, without even looking to see who it was, and say, "Howya, Sean!"

In Nenagh, people loved knowing everything that was going on in the town, and if there was a little bit of drama attached to it, all the better. But their stories were always the same, going around and around until everybody knew the punch line. They were always about farmers and shopkeepers and how the world was fixed with everybody in their allotted place. On television, events changed things. The truth came out and justice was done. I knew that teachers and adults weren't as instantly entranced by television as small children were. And I knew why, without anyone explaining it to me. Grown-up people were stuck in their ways and their old stories. They knew everybody they were ever going to meet.

But that would change too. Television would break through all the layers of habit and conformity. The smallness of their old world would become clear as day.

CHAPTER SIX

PILLARS OF THE HOUSE

On the RTÉ schedule, if it wasn't an early-evening western, it was a light and breezy American show. The westerns gripped the country people, but in Nenagh it was the comedies about American families that had people talking, especially the women. Women and mothers were the stars of these shows, and it was strange for me, at first, looking at mams who weren't like my mam or Mrs. Moylan down the street. All the mams in Nenagh were basically the same, except the rich ladies who were married to a shopkeeper or a doctor or solicitor. I could see that all the mams did the shopping at the same shops, cleaned the house in their aprons that all looked the same because they all bought their aprons in the same shops, and sometimes they walked the children to school. It wasn't like that on

The Donna Reed Show, which was on RTÉ all the time. Donna Reed was Donna Stone, the mam of the Stone family, who lived in the suburb of Hilldale with her husband, Alex, and her children, Mary and Jeff.

Our house was different from many in Nenagh because there was only Máire and me, with Mam and Dad. Loads of families had lots of children and everybody except me seemed to have many brothers and sisters. Some families had as many as ten children, but most had five or six. On *The Donna Reed Show* it was only the two kids, and every other family on the program seemed to be small, too. Everything was neat and tidy in Donna Reed's house. The show always started with Donna coming down the stairs as the phone rang, and her husband, who was always wearing a suit, answered the phone and Donna kissed Mary and Jeff as she gave them their lunch bags to take to school. Then a neighbour came to the door with a cup and the story really started from there.

In Hilldale there were gadgets like vacuum cleaners and things for drying your hair. Everybody had a car. There were times when Donna and the whole Stone family played together, throwing an American football around and having barbecues with their neighbours in the sunshine. Donna and her daughter, Mary, sometimes wore narrow trousers, like the men, when they were doing that. You never saw any mam in Nenagh wearing trousers. It was always dresses or skirts. The way that the mams coped with their husbands and the children was the gist of many episodes of *The Donna Reed Show*, and even that was different. The mams were the smart ones. They needed to be smart and cunning to take care of things and make the husband feel like he was in charge when he really wasn't in charge at all. So much about the ordinary family life was different. Nobody on the show got down on their knees at night to say the rosary. Nobody mentioned the Legion of Mary and how the legion was hopping mad because of some film that was going to be shown in the local cinema. Nobody had bacon and cabbage for dinner on a Saturday. The men never went out for a pint, leaving the women at home minding the children. When Donna Reed did the house-cleaning, she looked like she was ready to go out for cock-tails if anybody happened to ask her. I liked watching *The Donna Reed Show* with Mam because I knew she enjoyed it so much. "You can't believe the half of it," she'd say, but she didn't stop watching and neither did I. It was a mad, care-free way of life those people were living in America. They were afraid of nothing.

It wasn't only *The Donna Reed Show*. *I Love Lucy* and *The Jack Benny Program* were also popular in Nenagh. All the women loved Lucille Ball, with her mad antics and count-less ways of getting into trouble with her husband and then laughing it off. After my mam and my aunt Vera, Lucille Ball was the funniest, happiest woman that I'd ever seen. Sometimes it was just the look on her face that made you laugh. Some people in Nenagh said it was all codology, the way Lucy carried on. But Lucy wasn't afraid to dress in ridiculous costumes, like a child, or to try out harebrained schemes. Even though the result was always the same—a husband calling out, "Luuucy, you got some explaaaaining to do!"—I could tell that Lucy's life was about the joy of skittering away from what she was expected to do. It was clear to me that Ricky and Lucy loved each other, like many mams and dads in Nenagh, but they had mad humour in their lives. There was nothing they wouldn't do for a laugh. The verbal snap and gentle jokes of their home were vastly different from the savoured meanness of insults thrown around by grown-ups in Nenagh. It was about joking, not mocking people. Sometimes Mam said I was too quiet and I had a cross look on my face all the time, like I was trying too hard to figure everything out. But she said there was a smile on my face when I was watching *Lucy*. And it wasn't only me. When I went out shopping with Mam and we were waiting in the butcher's shop, I'd hear the mams talking. "Isn't she great?" they would say to each other and giggle as they discussed last night's antics from *Lucy*.

Jack Benny was a favourite of Mam's. Oh, she liked Lucy, but Jack Benny was a caution. I could picture him fitting right in in Nenagh. Tight with his money and never admitting to being a day over thirty-nine when he was obviously a very old fella, probably drawing the old-age pension, he was annoying but very droll. I liked the way both Jack Benny and Lucille Ball had no notion of conforming to what a schoolteacher said or what the parish priest ordered or of bowing to the people who owned shops. They hadn't a care. The mission priests never came to town to rant and rave about moral behaviour. Nobody turned up to tell them to quit laughing and get back to school or get back to work. Nobody told them that they were putting on airs. In Nenagh somebody was always accusing somebody else of putting on airs. If somebody got something new, even if it was a toilet inside the house instead of a toilet at the back of the yard, somebody else was ready to be sarcastic. Words hurt more than anything, I knew. It was in the little schoolyard that I heard a boy shout to another boy that he was always going to the toilet at school because at home he went to the toilet in a bucket, and he probably had the mark of the bucket in his arse from sitting there. "Show us your arse and the mark of the bucket in it. Go on, show us your arse. It was far from flush toilets you were reared, and everyone belonging to you."

Even in our house, where Mam was kind and Dad was always busy, the television was a comfort from the hardness outside. Sarsfield Street was narrow and steep and it seemed more so in the winter, as if it was squeezed together by the cold and the rain. On television, the sun shone all the while. Sarsfield Street never changed. It was gloomy and wet in winter and in shadow all summer long. If Mam sent me up the street to Paddy Rohan's pub to tell Dad his dinner would be ready soon and he should be home in ten minutes, I always knew what I'd find. After six o'clock the doors of the shops would be closed and the lights would be off, making the darkness darker than ever. A man on a bicycle, cycling fast downhill to his dinner somewhere in Nenagh, would pass like a ghost.

At Paddy Rohan's it was always the same. The pub was small, the wood panels were nearly black and the mood was quiet even if there were half a dozen men there. If a farmer came in on a Fair Day, Paddy would ask his name and how the family was keeping. If there was any connection to be made at all, Paddy would go down to the cellar and return to produce ancient ledgers showing that the farmer's mother, father, uncle or aunt had been a customer and, maybe, there had been a wake for a family member in the pub. He could tell the customer how much whiskey and porter had been consumed at the wake and how much it had cost. Dad was taken with Paddy Rohan's meticulousness and said it was the sort of thing I should keep in mind if I ever went into business myself, God willing, when I was grown up.

On television, nobody said "God willing," "Please God" or "Jesus, Mary and Joseph" all the time. You didn't even know if the people were Catholics or not. There was no angelus bell and nobody talked about the saint they were devoted to for small miracles and a bit of help. When Donna Reed told Mary and Jeff to smarten up she didn't tell them to say their prayers. In Donna Reed's house there were pictures on the wall of sailboats and family members, not pictures of the Sacred Heart and the Pope. It wasn't like Sarsfield Street, and even when I was glad to walk home from Paddy Rohan's with Dad, I kept the picture of Donna Reed's house and the sunny yard in my head. When it rained and the street was dark, it was like keeping sunshine in your head.

By 1964, almost every household in Nenagh had a TV set. Dropping in on neighbours or relatives was turning into an awkward endeavour. The TV set was always on and some people expected visitors to sit and watch with them, instead of talking and gossiping. If the TV set was switched off, an air of resentment from the hosts filled living rooms and parlours. So people took to talking about television. Gay Byrne was a hot topic.

Gay Byrne landed in every living room in Ireland in the summer of 1962. He was the host of a Saturday-night program called *The Late Late Show*. It was meant to be a kind of town hall meeting with musical acts and comedy. It turned out to be the most extraordinary television program of its time, but nobody knew it then. There were other shows on RTÉ that involved interviewing politicians, writers or the clergy. But Gay Byrne had an audience of several hundred people in the studio, and he wasn't content to have them sit there and be entertained, smiling at the camera when it panned them. Instead, he'd listen to his guest politely and then turn to the audience for a reaction.

It was asking for trouble, glorious, scandalizing trouble. According to a lot of people in Nenagh, your man, Byrne, was causing ructions. It had turned out that Irish people could and would speak their hearts in the heat of passionate argument on live television. People poured out anger, vitriol, sarcasm and ridicule. Their frustrations were magically unleashed on television. Adding to the drama, you never knew when the program would end. Sometimes *The Late Late Show* was an hour long and sometimes it was much longer. If a topic was being argued and people in the audience were clamouring to say their piece, the host would negotiate more airtime and the show would just keep going. In the middle of it all was Byrne, a dapper Dubliner in his early thirties, who was smooth, ingratiating and mischievous. Women adored him.

Gay Byrne was dangerous. Everybody knew that. Yet nobody could nail down what made him dangerous. It wasn't what he said; it was what he didn't say. On *The Late Late*, as everybody called it, he simply allowed his guests and the audience to speak their minds. If they criticized the Catholic Church, he didn't dismiss them or admonish them. He turned to the audience and called for another opinion. Gay Byrne didn't agree with them or disagree with anyone. Often he didn't say anything at all. He was so smooth and unruffled, and with that fair-play-to-everyone attitude, he made people who were pompous and snobbish look absurd and stupid. In kitchens, parlours and pubs across rural Ireland, Gay Byrne put people on edge. He wasn't an American, like the characters on the cowboy shows and the family comedies. He was Irish and yet unknowable.

I had only seen *The Late Late* once or twice because it aired on Saturday nights long after I was supposed to be in bed. But one Saturday night I woke up and heard the sounds of shouting and arguments from the television, and I went downstairs. Mam was watching *The Late Late*, in the company of Mrs. Griffin, who sometimes came to babysit Máire and me. Mrs. Griffin was in her fifties, and almost blind. She sat near the television set, a glass of whiskey in one hand and a cigarette in the other. She stared intently at the screen, her mouth firmly set and the ash on her cigarette growing long. Mam was watching too, and an occasional "hmmm" escaped from her.

I stood and watched them watching the TV set until Mrs. Griffin noticed me. Mam told me to come and sit beside her. I expected to be fussed over, and anticipated a dozen questions about whether I was sick or having nightmares. Mrs. Griffin was a great one for telling me not to listen to stories about ghosts and banshees. She told me that there was no such thing as a banshee. There were no women ghosts wandering around outside in the night, crying because they were dead. Only an eejit would believe in a banshee and I shouldn't be worried about things like that. It was probably only a sick cat that people heard. This night, Mrs. Griffin and Mam didn't care. They were oblivious to me.

A priest was on the panel and he was under attack. That much I understood instantly. He had a self-conscious, uneasy smile on his face, the kind of smile that children adopt when they know they are being watched by adults and are trying to control their natural urge to run, scream and play. In the host's chair, Gay Byrne swivelled constantly, back and forth from the priest to the audience. A man in the audience was criticizing the priest for something that had happened to his wife and involved the Church. The priest said that women who didn't go out to work but stayed at home to raise children were the "pillars of the house." Mrs. Griffin snorted. The man in the audience was still upset and pointing his finger. There were mutters from people around him. Another man shouted at Gay Byrne for allowing the priest to be embarrassed and attacked on Irish television. What Byrne said, calmly but with great force, stuck in my mind forever: "We have a program, and we are proud of it as a program on which you are allowed to say what you want."

In my child's muddled mind, when Gay Byrne said "proud" he was being Irish and Republican. The word *proud* was in all the rebel songs I knew. To be proud was the opposite of being a traitor or a sleeveen, someone who was a slave to English rule. It was the opposite of being a go-by-the-wall, the sort of fella who crept along by the wall instead of walking proudly as an Irish person. I was supposed to be proud of being Irish and being from Tipperary. To be proud was the be-all and end-all of being Irish. Gay Byrne sounded to me like he was being very Irish, being proud of his program and letting people have their say.

There was no stopping the talk about Gay Byrne and *The Late Late*. When Gran out in Cranna finally got a television, it was the one thing she wanted to see. If I was allowed to stay up late in Gran's house while Mam and Dad were out taking Granddad for a pint, I'd watch Gay Byrne with Gran, sitting beside the ancient black range in a sugawn chair. "Give him his answer, the dirty scut," Gran would say to some fella who was arguing with somebody she didn't like. She'd sit there, sucking a hard sweet, never taking her eyes off the television, even when she asked me to give the fire inside the range a stir. I'd lift the lid off the range with the tongs and stick a poker inside to move the turf and coal around. When I did that during the day, there was always somebody watching me in case I burned myself. During *The Late Late*, Gran kept her attention on the television all the while.

One Saturday night, *The Late Late Show* was going great guns, even though there were no serious discussions or arguments. Gay Byrne was having a mister-and-missus quiz show. A husband and his wife were asked questions about each other. The idea was to gently embarrass them with their mistakes. The audience in the studio loved the banter. Then, while answering a question about what she had worn on her wedding day and later on her wedding night, the wife declared that she hadn't worn anything at all in bed on her wedding night. The audience roared with laughter.

Watching at home, the bishop of Galway was incensed. He picked up the phone, called RTÉ in Dublin and complained about the filth that was being allowed on the air. Then he called a newspaper. The next day, the country awoke to what became known as "the Bishop and the Nightie Incident."

Politicians in the Parliament in Dublin, especially those from rural areas, saw an opening to attack the Dublin-based power and popularity of Irish television and to support the powerful bishops and parish priests in the country towns and villages. In the midst of the furor, the rural member of Parliament and famous conservative Oliver J.

Flanagan got himself into a lather of complaint about promiscuity in Ireland and the influence of television. He declared, "There was no sex in Ireland before television."

The phrase was quoted for years in Ireland, a long-standing joke about how old fellas like Oliver J., so sincere in their devotion to the Church, hadn't a clue about anything, really. Even when I was small and everybody was going tut-tut about *The Late Late*, I knew it was peculiar that a television program could make people react like that, all furious about Gay Byrne or full of mischief if they liked him, week after week. When I was older I understood it a different way. Television brought stories into the living rooms and kitchens of the most isolated homes, like my Gran's house in Cranna. When people saw *The Donna Reed Show*, *I Love Lucy* or *Jack Benny*, they saw people comfortable in their skins, untrammelled by Church expectations and traditional pressures. When they heard arguments about sex, sexuality and religion on *The Late Late Show*, the arguments didn't seem so fantastical. Eyes had been opened, not only by a light but by a lightness of feeling that came from far away, and it was there in the corner, every evening, after darkness fell on the complacent town of Nenagh, and a thousand others like it.

CHAPTER SEVEN

COWBOYS, SPIES AND REBELS:
I AM IRELAND

I was a quiet child. I took great delight in my own company. Shy and sarcastic, I stared and listened. My sister, Máire, said once that she had little memory of me before I reached the age of about fourteen. No wonder. I was small, was slight of frame and slipped away into my own world. Adults forgot I was there, reading a book in the corner, or sitting silently on the backyard step. I could have been mistaken for a houseplant. If I was noticed, my silence sometimes annoyed the adults. They felt I was sizing them up, maybe disapproving of them. I often had a sour puss on me, according to my aunt Breda.

Cowboys, spies and rebels interested me. I loved some of the poems I learned at school. In my head I savoured the force of the dramatic short verse "Mise Éire"—"I Am

Ireland"—written by Patrick Pearse, the leader of the rebel rising of 1916. It was a few lines long and I knew it in both Gaelic and English.

> I am Ireland,
> Older I am than the hag of Beare.
> Great my pride,
> I it was who bore the god-like warrior Cuchulainn.
> I am Ireland,
> Great my grief,
> My own sons betray their mother.
> I am Ireland
> More lonely I am than the hag of Beare.

It was coming up on the fiftieth anniversary of the Easter Rebellion of 1916 and Ireland was going mad with the rebel spirit again. The ballads on the radio were always stories of bold Fenians who had defied the English and fought and died for Ireland. Everyone knew the words to a few of them:

> Glory O! Glory O! to her brave sons who died
> For the cause of long down-trodden man!
> Glory O! to Mount Leinster's own darling and pride:
> Dauntless Kelly, the boy from Killane!

Some were sentimental and others were attacks on traitors and informers. All were stirring. It made you want to go out and fight the English, with a song in your heart. Even the laments for the fallen could arouse anger against the English. Brave Kevin Barry was hanged for his rebel deeds, but he held his head high as he went to the gallows. It was better to be proud than meek.

I didn't want to be Kevin Barry or Kelly the boy from Killane, but I liked thinking about rebellion. I'd picked up Mam's unease with Nenagh town and all its petty prejudices and jibes. Somebody was always complaining or criticizing. And I'd picked up Dad's ideals, that faraway feeling that there was more to life than the mundane routine of work, the pub and church. I immersed my little self in rebel songs from the radio, stitching together narratives from the lyrics and imagining them enacted. On the television I saw stories of wildness and devil-may-care disrespect for old laws. Cowboys were rebels, and secret agents were rebels. It was all that was in my head.

In 1965, when the long, slow commemoration of the 1916 Rising was being stoked, I was now with the Christian Brothers after leaving what was called baby's school, and the marking of the anniversary of the Rising was something that came up every day. The heady proclamation made by the leaders of the Rising, those poets, dreamers and socialists, was on every classroom wall. We had to learn it by heart: "Irishmen and Irishwomen: In the name of God and of the dead generations from which she receives her old tradition of nationhood, Ireland, through us, summons her children to her flag and strikes for her freedom."

That was only the start of it. The proclamation continued on, about blood and sacrifice, and we were questioned daily about its meaning. Weekly, we practised marching for our part in the Nenagh celebration that would happen at Easter 1966. We learned about each leader of the Rising and how they had died. The person impressed on us daily was Pearse, the most intense and mercurial figure of the Rising. A teacher, poet, playwright and fanatic, Pearse's words from a graveside oration were drummed into us: "Life springs from death, and from the graves of patriot men and women spring living nations." It was a lot of talk about death and sacrifice for small boys to absorb.

While the Christian Brothers talked on and on about the sacrifice for nationhood, in 1965 we were all mad for *The Man from U.N.C.L.E.* Autumn nights in Nenagh were cold, and a damp, sullen mist always hung over the town. We were transported from Nenagh's glum streets by *The Man from U.N.C.L.E.*—the dashing heroes, the sunshine, the smoothness of the talk and the wit.

The thing was, there were *two* men from U.N.C.L.E. There was Napoleon Solo, who was tall and gangly and wore tight-fitting suits. He talked out of the side of his mouth, and was always smoothing the bit of hair on his head and smiling at women. He carried an exquisite gun, a long, thin thing with a silencer, and he was good and fast with it. The other man from U.N.C.L.E. was Illya Kuryakin, a blond with a Beatles haircut, turtleneck sweaters and a sort of Englishy-Russian accent. His gun was more squat and fat, with a thick silencer on the end of it. Illya was the action fella. Solo was always more interested in staying inside to have cocktails with women in short dresses. Illya was the fella for racing through the woods, in the night, undercover and gun ready. The pair of them talked in endless sarcasms and communicated with head office by muttering into pens they kept in their pockets.

In the schoolyard we argued endlessly over who was the best and the toughest. Most of the lads went for Solo, because he was the ladies' man and a silver-tongued devil. I liked Illya because he was more quiet and less flamboyant, a knowledgeable fella who could spout yards of information about music, geography and technology. Brooding and mysterious, he spoke in staccato rhythms and always gave the impression that he had better things to do than wave ridiculous guns around. It seemed that unless somebody implored him, he couldn't be bothered with the nefarious agents of THRUSH who arrived disguised as a dozen go-go dancers. He wasn't in it for the girls. He was a dreamer and an idealist.

We all carried U.N.C.L.E. agent badges. They were triangular bits of plastic, but were important to us. They came in packets of crisps, so everybody could afford them. One day, word spread that Goff's shop was selling *Man from U.N.C.L.E.* guns. After school we raced down to look at Goff's window, and sure enough, there was a long cardboard box with a picture of a rifle with a shiny telescope lens. "The Man from UNCLE" was written in big letters on the box and there was a picture of Napoleon Solo. Illya Kuryakin got a much smaller picture in the corner.

We stared at the box for ages. None of us knew what it cost but we all knew that few of us could afford it. We argued about who should go into Goff's to ask how much it was. Along came Donie Meaher on his bike. Meaher was a couple of years older than us and much taller. His father owned Meaher's drapery shop, a few doors away from Goff's, and he loved to remind us of it.

He cycled right into the middle of us, the front wheel of his bike making us jump back. "And what are you eejits looking at?" he said with a sneer. He looked into Goff's window and saw the big *Man from U.N.C.L.E.* gun. He smirked at us. "There's not one of youse eejits has the money for that. I'm the only one who has the money for that. If I ask me mother or father, they'd buy that for me in a minute. Go home, you little bastards. Go home to your cabbage."

We looked at him in stunned, embarrassed silence. Many of us were in fact going home to have cabbage for our dinner. Still, we resented Meaher lording it over us. He was Nenagh through and through, a shopkeeper's son who acted like the little lord of the manor.

Ger Hacket was the tallest among us and he was strong. Sometimes he'd lift one of us on his shoulders, and not a bother on him. He knew he was the only one who could take on Donie Meaher, and he did. "You go home to your mammy and tell her what to buy you," he said. "Maybe if you cry she'll buy you something nice." Donie Meaher started to get off the bicycle and he was aiming for Ger Hacket. But he wasn't fast enough. Ger Hacket raised his arm and in one swift movement he smacked Donie Meaher across the face. Meaher's big, white face went red as a beetroot and he was too shocked, for a second, to say or do anything. Then he swung his arm out wildly and we all scattered, racing up the street as fast as we could. Behind us we heard Donie Meaher wailing after us, "I'm telling my da, I'm telling my da."

For days I crept around the streets, terrified of Donie Meaher and his da. Every time I saw a schoolboy on a bicycle, I stopped and edged backwards, hoping for a lane to escape into if he came after me. He was a mean, belligerent bowsie and we all knew it. I knew that Donie Meaher would remember every boy who was in the little group he had encountered outside Goff's window. He'd try to get us all. He'd probably tell his da, too. Maybe I'd be in Meaher's shop with Mam and Donie Meaher's father would be there. He'd see me and then he'd start telling Mam that I was one of a group of corner boys who were bothering his son, a quiet boy.

The thing to wonder was what Illya Kuryakin would do. He wouldn't put up with that nonsense. He'd stay quiet and use stealth to hit back at his enemy. I fingered my little *Man from U.N.C.L.E.* badge in my pocket, but it gave me no power. I didn't have a gun with a silencer to frighten Donie Meaher.

The only other notion available to me was what an Irish rebel might do. I thought of Patrick Sarsfield, whose name was given to the street I lived on. Sarsfield was a brave and devil-may-care officer who led the Irish Catholic forces for

James II against the invasion by the Protestant William of Orange. The exact details of that war were faint to me, but I knew of Sarsfield's one glorious deed. He had been in charge of the fortified city of Limerick as the English forces tried to take Ireland. The enemy had camped, with ammunition and cannon, at Ballyneety, a few miles from Nenagh and not far from Cranna. In the night, Sarsfield led his troops from Limerick on a dangerous mission to destroy the English camp. Sarsfield persuaded a famous highwayman, the gallant Galloping O'Hogan, to show his men the path to Ballyneety. They moved under moonlight, stealthily surrounding the English camp. First they captured a man on lookout and made him give them the password for entering. The password was "Sarsfield."

Sarsfield insisted on leading the charge into the camp himself. He appeared, suddenly, as if by magic and by moonlight, in front of an armed guard, who asked, "What is the password?" Sarsfield answered, "Sarsfield is the word. And Sarsfield is the man!" With a great roar he led his men into the camp and destroyed the English position.

I longed for Sarsfield's bravado and Illya Kuryakin's cunning. There was no use in dreaming about a moonlit attack on Donie Meaher's position. It was better to take on Illya's attitude of apparent uncaring quiet, and wait. He was unlikely to be impressed that Donie Meaher's father owned a shop in Nenagh.

All the Doyles thought I was coddled and strange. Instead of asking questions about cars and motorbikes, I asked questions about Galloping O'Hogan the highwayman, and I watched too much television. One day, Peter Doyle came to the house to see Dad, but Dad was out. I was in the corner watching *Get Smart*, a show I didn't really like because there was too much tomfoolery in it. But I loved the little jokes about Agent Maxwell Smart getting things all muddled up. It seemed to be all about spoofing the fancy guns and gadgets that were thrilling on other shows, the sleek machines to help spies and other heroes do their work: radar devices; pens that acted as transmitters and microphones; telephones in shoes, pocket watches and eyeglasses; laser-beam pens and a TV set inside a briefcase. We didn't even have a telephone in the house. Hardly anybody in Nenagh did, except maybe the doctors and solicitors.

I was watching Maxwell Smart get things wrong while Uncle Peter looked at me and sighed. He was an impressive figure looming over me. Tall and bulky, dressed in the traditional workingman's outfit of battered old tweed suit and cloth cap, with a dusting of quarry sand on him, he brought the rough working world with him into our little house.

He spoke to Mam. "That boy will never turn out to be much. He's always in the house with you. What is he doing? Reading newspapers, reading books and watching the television. He should be out there with a stick on Fair Day, getting a few shillings from the farmers for helping with the cows. He should be out there with a stick, ready to earn money."

Mam told Peter that I was doing well in school. Not one of the teachers had a bad word to say about me. There was nothing wrong with reading. Reading would get me a better job than swinging a stick for farmers and herding a few cows on a Fair Day. And if I was at home reading and watching television, didn't she know where I was? She knew I wasn't running around the streets of Nenagh stealing sweets from shops, like certain boys were supposed to have done last week. Mam said this softly, without seeming to take offence at Peter's interfering notions. But she seethed.

Mam had plans for Máire and me. She took us to elocution lessons, so that we wouldn't always sound like children from Sarsfield Street in Nenagh. At the elocution lessons I said little. I spoke slowly and resentfully. When asked to say "Good morning" and "How do you do?" in plummy tones, I kept it flat, unsure of why I was being asked to sound that way. I lasted two lessons. Máire kept going for months. Mam's plans for us were in line with the middle-class aspirations of many families in Nenagh. But Mam wasn't stuck up. She loathed the petty snobberies of Nenagh. In particular, the nuns drove Mam mad. They were the very worst offenders because they instilled snobbery in small children. They were tyrants and cruel, according to Mam.

What happened in the playground of the girls' school was a disgrace. At play time, when dozens of small girls tore around the schoolyard playing games, the nuns didn't only look on. They ordered the children around, telling them whom they should play with. A doctor's daughter couldn't play with a labourer's daughter. The nuns forbade it and intervened if they saw the wrong girls getting too friendly. They tore asunder the friendships formed by children who didn't know whose dad did what job in Nenagh.

There was one big, ignorant nun, about six feet tall, with hands like a boxer. And she loved to use them. One time, she hit Máire a blast across the shoulder blades, for allegedly putting the girls' choir out of tune. Máire fell to the floor and hurt her knee, and she was still in shock and sobbing when she came home.

Mam got the story out of her. Immediately, Mam went hot-footed to the convent and found the big, ignorant nun. She asked her why she hit Máire. The nun said Máire had put the choir out of tune. Mam told her where to get off and suggested the nun use her hands to do something more useful for God than hitting small girls. The nun was speechless. When Mam came home, she told the story to Dad, with Máire and me listening. Over and over she used the words *big, ignorant nun*. When she'd finished she said, "Sisters of Mercy, my arse!" I liked Mam being angry at the nuns, because the nuns were bullies. It made Mam a rebel, somebody standing up for their rights and the rights of their children. But I couldn't understand why we had to take elocution lessons and try to sound different.

My own school, the Christian Brothers, was just across Sarsfield Street and down John's Lane. The building was old and crowded. After a few weeks inside the old building my class was put into one of the portable classrooms that had just been built in the yard. It was much brighter and sunnier than the old building but it had only a tiny heater, and when winter came we all shivered inside it. Some of us left on our coats until the room warmed up. The head brother came in one day and saw some of us sitting in our coats at our desks. He told us to take them off. "If ye can't stand a bit of cold, ye'll never be Tipperary men."

Most of the brothers were young and bored. They were also thick, and some were as ignorant and violent as the nuns. In my class we had Brother Spellacy and Brother Riordan. Spellacy was definitely thick, and testy and vicious on top of it. He carried his leather strap under his long black cassock and liked to wield it. He didn't use it often, but he liked to whip it out like a gunslinger on a western show. Even then, he preferred using his fists and hands to punish and frighten us. Brother Riordan was bored and smarmy. Both were in their twenties, not long out of the Christian Brothers College.

One day, Spellacy told us we had to compose a poem for English class. He sneered when he told us this. Pinch-faced, choleric and already middle-aged in his twenties, he adored giving orders and savoured the moment when he could raise his long, thin nose in the air and assess the reaction of small boys to his orders. Instead of ordering shop assistants around, he enjoyed the power of screaming at children and hitting them. We children knew it.

For the poem, most of us struggled to create a rhyming sequence that would satisfy Spellacy. Some boys went for a sporting motif and wrote lines that were no more than limericks about the stick, the ball and the fierce men of the hurling field. I wrote a piece of rhyming doggerel about going to the sea and sailing away. Spellacy collected our assignments from us and made us read a Wordsworth poem in our textbook, to start learning it by heart. While we read Wordsworth, he read our verses to himself. Finally, he pronounced. He told us that most of the boys were poltroons and bowsies who would end up pushing a wheelbarrow for the county council while other boys might sit in nice offices in a wool suit having conversations with county councillors and solicitors. But there was one boy who would go very far. Just one boy. If he minded his manners and applied himself he might even find himself at university in Galway or Dublin.

Then Spellacy asked Fergus O'Brien to step forward and entertain the class with his outstanding composition. O'Brien, a tall, slope-shouldered, slow-moving farmer's son whom none of us knew very well because he was always missing school to work on the farm, was scarlet faced and stunned. He got up from his desk and walked slowly toward Spellacy at the front of the room, eyeing him warily, as if waiting for a smack across the face. Spellacy handed him his composition book and said, "Read it out, boy. Do it justice. Read it out now in a fine, strong voice!" O'Brien looked down miserably at his own handwriting and began reading aloud.

> When children are playing alone on the green,
> In comes the playmate that never was seen.
> When children are happy and lonely and good,
> The Friend of the Children comes out of the wood.

Nobody heard him, and nobody saw,
His is a picture you never could draw,
But he's sure to be present, abroad or at home,
When children are happy and playing alone.

The rest of us looked on amazed. One or two of us recognized the lines, glanced at each other and smiled. The same poem was in a book we'd all had to study in our last year at the junior school. Dan Finnegan started giggling. Somebody nudged him in the ribs and he went on giggling, worse than ever. Spellacy called a halt to Fergus O'Brien's whining rendition of Robert Louis Stevenson's poem and lunged at Dan Finnegan. He hit him a whack on the shoulder and then grabbed Finnegan by the ear, hauling him out of his desk. "You miserable little gurrier," he roared. "You atrocious little sniggering poltroon. Do you want to end up a corner boy? Do you want to end up standing on corners with your hands in your pockets without a job and asking your poor father to oblige you with the price of a pint? Is that what you want, Finnegan?"

The class looked on, half of us laughing. Spellacy shoved Dan Finnegan back into the desk and glared at us. "Every one of ye is bound for the wheelbarrow and the shovel," he shouted. "It won't be a pen that one of ye is using for work, but a shovel." Then he called on Fergus O'Brien to continue reading. O'Brien stared down on us with the look of a man facing the firing squad. He began reading, quickly gathering a head of steam, and finished the poem at a gallop. There were a few stifled giggles, but Spellacy kept us under control.

At lunchtime I ran across Sarsfield Street and home. Mam was in the kitchen, putting away groceries. "Mam, Mam, that O'Brien fella read out a poem from the book we had in Mr. Daly's class in school. He said he wrote it himself. Brother Spellacy didn't even know!" Mam looked at me, taking a minute to grasp the story. She smiled a long, satisfying smile. "It wouldn't be the first time I heard of a Christian Brother teaching school who never saw the inside of a school himself when he was a child. That's a Nenagh education for you. If a child can fool a Brother, it's harum-scarum schooling you're getting over there."

Brother Riordan was a smiler and touchy-feely. A boy himself, smooth faced and with a lonely look about him, he gazed out at us in the classroom and saw his own youth, just passed and missed. He tried to ingratiate himself with little boys by watching television and talking about the shows with us. He was taken with *Get Smart*.

Every week he asked us if we'd seen the show. If he asked a boy a question in math class and the boy didn't know the answer or gave the wrong one, he'd say, "Sorry about that, Chief!" hoping we'd all join in his little joke. One day, he even took off his shoe and tried to imitate Maxwell Smart using his shoe phone. We all saw Riordan as a softy, but some of the boys—the ones who would be corner boys or poltroons, according to Spellacy—despised him.

Once, Micky O'Brien, who came from the working-class enclave of St. Joseph's Park and knew a fool when he saw one, asked Brother Riordan about his favourite parts of *Get Smart*. As Riordan began to talk about Maxwell Smart's many bunglings as a spy, Micky O'Brien said, "But what about Agent 99, sir? Do you like her?"

An expectant hush fell on the class. Micky O'Brien had hit the nail on the head that day. Agent 99, played by Barbara Feldon, was, especially to nine-year-old boys in Nenagh, an exotically sexy creature. A lanky brunette with her hair cut in thick bangs hanging heavily above her large and knowing eyes, she talked in a husky drawl, and every little boy sensed the meaning of the languorous way she moved. She slowly batted her long, long eyelashes at Maxwell Smart and drawled a cooing joke that straight-out advertised carnal desire. Any eejit could see it.

We all waited for Brother Riordan to pronounce on Agent 99. Either that or he was going to grab Micky O'Brien and drag him by the ear to the front of the room and unleash a leather strap on his hands and arse. "Well . . ." was all Brother Riordan said, with small flashes of blush appearing on his soft white cheeks.

Then Micky O'Brien upped the ante, like the rebel he was. My dad would have called him a cute hoor for the manner of his manipulations. "She was dressed like a man the other night, Brother. She was acting the driver for yer man, Maxwell. Trousers, cap and all, Brother. Did you see that one?"

Riordan's eyes flashed. Intuitively, he knew he was being led into hell. Of course he'd seen Agent 99 dressed as a chauffeur, in men's boots and pants and her cap at a jaunty angle. He was being mocked. A small boy with an innocent look and an anarchist's mind was talking to him about lust.

Riordan composed himself and sighed deeply. He went toward Micky O'Brien and sat on the side of O'Brien's desk. He settled a hand on O'Brien's face, tracing his finger on the prominent cheekbones and along his chin. "Now, Micky," he said, "there are many women we must admire. But Agent 99 is not one of them. We must admire Our Lady, Virgin Mother of God. And Saint Brigid, whose cross appears on the television every night. Will you pray to Our Lady, Micky? Will you say five Hail Marys when you go home today?" Micky O'Brien said he would, a terror having struck him deep inside with Brother Riordan's tender touch.

But Micky knew, as the rest of us knew, that Agent 99 was more a model to his many sisters and all the young women in St. Joseph's Park than the Virgin Mary would ever be. I was nearly ten and I'd started to have the feeling it was good to be young. The teachers and all the other adults never had television when they were young. We had different stories from theirs. We had stories coming to us from America every day. We could catch the teachers out and sometimes it looked like they didn't have a clue and they couldn't see what was going on under their noses. It was the teachers who needed to get smart, not us.

CHAPTER EIGHT

A TERRIBLE BEAUTY

ONE DAY IN THE SPRING of 1966, the head brother at school addressed us. All the boys gathered in the school-yard for his speech. He had two things to say. He wanted to remind us that there would be more drills in the school-yard in preparation for our march in the great parade to mark the fiftieth anniversary of the 1916 Rising. The other thing was a warning about standing on the roads hoping for photographs from a showband's tour bus passing through. He said the guards had asked him to warn the pupils about this dangerous occupation. He seemed bewildered by what he was asked to say. Brother Riordan stood beside him, grim faced and composed, but young and shrewd enough to know that his boss was trying in vain to quell a strange and base desire among children who were supposed to be besotted with dead rebels, not pop singers.

In 1966 Nenagh's young were flirting, in a flitting, hesitant way, with the modern world of pop music. This was a movement driven more by rumour and hints from television than by radio. The showbands were coming into their prime. Showbands were cover bands that performed imitations of songs from the hit parade. They played in the dance halls once ruled by traditional Irish ceilidh bands and mini-orchestras that played waltzes for middle-aged customers. Almost ten years after Elvis arrived and in the midst of Beatlemania, the showbands aped the outside world of dizzying pop, and brought it, diluted, to small-town Ireland. *Pickin' the Pops* aired on RTÉ every Saturday night, and a handful of the cover bands, usually dressed in suits, would perform a cover of a song that was already a hit in England or America. There was a thriving ballroom circuit, with the ballrooms often being built on the cheapest land, miles from any town. A dance hall near Nenagh, almost surrounded by bog water, was known as the Floating Ballroom. In summer the showbands would play in tents erected out in the fields. Buses would take the dance-goers to the ballrooms on weekend nights. During Lent, the showbands would disappear from Ireland to play to the emigrants in London or Manchester. At home in Ireland during Lent, people automatically followed the Church's advice to deprive themselves of fun and frolics. In England, apparently, this didn't apply.

Many of the showbands had lead singers who swivelled their hips and danced like Elvis. There was Brendan

Bowyer of the Royal Showband, the most famous of them all. Bowyer never stood still onstage. He wiggled his hips and pouted his pulpy lips, and in every show he'd leapfrog over the bass player. He made people giddy. The Royal sometimes passed through Nenagh on weekends, heading to dance halls in Limerick, and without anyone having to tell anybody what to do, groups of girls and boys gathered on the Dublin road, waiting for the bus to pass by. Signed photographs were thrown from the windows of the speeding bus. Teenagers were starting to hoard them. Occasionally, a showband played in the ballroom of one of the hotels in Nenagh, and when that happened, the showband's bus was surrounded all night by boys and girls too young to get inside the ballroom but wanting to be close to the glamour.

On Saturday nights, groups of local girls, dressed to the nines in clothes they'd seen on the American TV shows and had made themselves at home, walked to Pearse Street to get a bus to the dance halls where the showbands played. I'd seen them myself, especially Mrs. Griffin's many daughters, with their faces heavily made up and their eyelashes as long and false as those of Agent 99.

When the head brother made his speech about the Easter 1916 commemorations and the dangers of hanging around waiting for a showband's bus, he had to shout at us to get our attention. He didn't have the clanging bell he usually employed to call the boys to order—my dad had borrowed it as a prop in a play the Kilruane Players were doing. I told Dad about the head brother's speech concerning the boys and girls standing on the road waiting for the showband's bus. He smiled. "You can't blame the youngsters," he said. "And I must give that brother back his bell. It doesn't work very well anyway. It hardly makes a sound. You wouldn't scatter birds with it."

I was too young for dances and pop music, but Ireland was given to me through television, and it was through TV that I could see the change. Everything on television had an allure, especially when it was Irish people suddenly made glamorous by appearing on it. Between the shows on RTÉ, an announcer reminded us about the menu for the evening. My favourite announcer, and Mam's, was Thelma Mansfield. Thelma looked and sounded like she came from Dublin. She talked in a soft voice and smiled coyly, and even when she tilted her head, her blond hair never moved.

Thelma Mansfield was instantly a cult figure. Naturally, people wondered what she got up to when she wasn't sitting in front of the camera telling viewers what time the news came on. Everybody knew what time the news came on anyway. Most people had the RTÉ schedule memorized. People wondered what else Thelma Mansfield did, and it was assumed she got up to no good. A woman like that was dangerously sensual, smiling at the whole country several evenings a week. Aunt Breda disliked her but watched her intently. All the women did. They knew that smile. It was a smile that made women uneasy and made men silly. From the Nenagh perspective, people such as Thelma Mansfield and Charles Mitchel, who read the news, were swells. They weren't like the local swells, imitating the gentry and acting stuck up. They were middle-class Dublin swells. Most people in Nenagh knew nobody like them. Most people in Nenagh, if they went to Dublin, went for a big hurling match, dutifully drank in bars they knew were owned by Tipperary men, and then came home again.

Thelma Mansfield wasn't like a movie star. She was, like Gay Byrne, Irish but unknowable. The sleekness of her and the fact that she had a job just appearing on television, beautifully dressed, heavily made up and smiling, was a strange, new kind of magnetism. You couldn't imagine her going to the Scouts Hall for a hooley with a ceilidh band and ould fellas playing fiddles and accordions. You couldn't imagine her going to see a showband either. She'd probably be wise to the fact that they were only doing imitations.

Small as I was, I knew that Thelma Mansfield was extraordinarily glamorous and that there was something about her that made people uneasy. My aunt Vera was stunningly beautiful, but you knew why. She had a foreign sort of feeling to her, with her rich, dark hair, wide smile and cheerful eyes. It felt good to be around her because she was so full of life and laughter, and people paid her little compliments about how well she looked. She laughed it off, politely, and picked up a child and hugged him, or told a story about the plans she had for the house she lived in with Tom. You could tell Vera was in love, and a rich, earthy, sweet feeling spread from that. You couldn't dislike

Vera. She was simultaneously beautiful, self-assured, cheerful and loving. Vera was about the countryside, marriage, many children and knowable happiness.

The continuity announcers on RTÉ, like Thelma Mansfield, were not about marriage, children and walking country roads with a tin bucket to get water for washing clothes and cooking dinner. They weren't connected to dark, wood-panelled pubs filled with farmers drinking pints of Guinness and with sawdust on the floor. They'd never sat in such a place and heard an old farmer, indulged after he'd had a few pints of porter, insisting that he would sing "The Old Bog Road." They were about the magic of Dublin hotel bars, brightly lit lounge bars and neon lights on city streets. They weren't housewives, but they weren't workingwomen either, like schoolteachers, nurses or shop assistants in chemists' shops. Their job was to appear on television and talk for a few minutes about the upcoming programs, and there was something sinfully sensual about the kind of job where you got paid a lot of money to say a few words and smile. Once, at Sunday Mass, I'd heard the priest say, twice for emphasis, "A woman's place is in the home." It was impossible to imagine Thelma Mansfield in any home that I knew.

Apart from Thelma Mansfield, the other prominent continuity announcer was Kathleen Watkins. She was less urban and sleek, and people said she was already famous in some quarters for playing the Celtic harp. Then people learned that she was married to Gay Byrne. This was strange. Why did the woman not call herself Mrs. Byrne?

Were all those people in RTÉ married to somebody else on television? There was something peculiar about the idea of Gay Byrne being married to that Kathleen Watkins who announced the programs and played the harp. It made them like characters in a serial drama about the people who worked in Irish television. Putting Ireland and Irish people on television was itself peculiar. It was like suddenly deciding that Irish men and women could be the equal of Hollywood stars. Yet Gay Byrne and Thelma Mansfield truly were stars. They had a shiny sleekness about them that didn't belong on Irish people at all.

Apart from the Gaelic games and the news on television, there was little that was Irish. There were only two weekly dramas set in Ireland. *Tolka Row* was the Dublin drama, about people living on a working-class street in the city. Hardly anybody in Nenagh watched *Tolka Row* because half the conversations on it meant nothing outside Dublin. Nenagh people were annoyed by it. It was ridiculous trying to make drama out of some character in Dublin complaining about the number 24 bus and where it stopped on its route.

It was *The Riordans* that country people watched. Mam was devoted to it. *The Riordans* was a soap opera about Tom and Mary Riordan, who owned a hundred-acre farm in a place called Leestown. Their son, Benjy, was a teenager and expected to take over the farm. Nearby were Johnny and Julia Mac, running the pub. Also nearby was Miss Nesbitt, the rich Protestant lady in the big house. She was the local gentry. There were also a doctor, a schoolmaster, a priest and the Riordan family's farm labourer, Batty Brennan. The priest was in every episode, no matter what the story. The actors weren't television- or movie-handsome. They looked like Irish country people. Tom Riordan was bald and plump, smoked a pipe and annoyingly said "Hello, hello, hello!" every time he entered someone else's house. Benjy was gangly and awkward looking and seemed as ill at ease with the world as any Irish youth.

The drama in *The Riordans* moved at a plodding pace, but that slowness gave it a familiar feel for viewers. The Riordan family dealt with crises big and small. Would Benjy stay on the farm or leave the farm for the big city? Would he take a notion in his head and traipse off to Manchester or Birmingham to work in a factory? It was all fuelled by countless cups of tea, a few drinks at the pub and meals that featured potatoes and cabbage. Around Nenagh, people loved *The Riordans*. You could see Batty Brennan walking down Sarsfield Street on a Fair Day, a stick in his hand to herd the cattle. I watched it, but it wasn't an escape; it was too much like everyday life.

At Easter 1966, most of our favourite programs disappeared for a week. It wasn't just that RTÉ shut down on Thursday night and stayed off the air until Saturday, like it did every Easter. That week, there was an eight-part Irish-made drama called *Insurrection*, which dramatized the Easter Rising of 1916.

Insurrection was strange television for its time and unsettling for a child. The story of the Easter Rising was known to us all, but *Insurrection* told it in an unfamiliar way. In 1916, at a time when the fight for Home Rule and an Irish Parliament had been put on hold because of the First World War, some idealists in Dublin, a motley crew of poets, teachers and labour leaders, had taken it upon themselves to declare war on English rule. One day, they just walked out onto the streets and started that war.

It was no coincidence that they started it at Easter. It was all about sacrifice and being reborn. The Christian Brothers told us that at school. They also told us that the rebels were jeered by the people of Dublin as they proudly marched along the street with guns, made proclamations and promptly took over the General Post Office in the centre of Dublin city. There were scattered uprisings by their cohorts in other parts of the country too, but those were quickly defeated, and it was the men inside the post office who fought and fought. Surrounded, outnumbered and facing certain defeat, they just wouldn't give up. The British army had to bring in heavy guns on ships, up the river Liffey in Dublin, and pound the post office with bombs until it was almost rubble. Only then did the rebels surrender.

In defeat, they were still jeered in Dublin. Many people wanted no part in a bloody rebellion by poets and artists. Then the English made a mistake. The leaders had been put in jail, but that wasn't enough for the English. The leaders were executed. Even the already dying were executed. The Christian Brothers had told us at school about James Connolly, the Labour leader. Even though he was near death in jail from his wounds, he was carried out from his cell on a chair to be executed by a firing squad of English soldiers. That detail was told to us over and over again. The zealous overreaction of the English changed public opinion. Soon enough, almost everyone was in favour of armed rebellion against cruel English rule.

Insurrection presented the events of 1916 as if they were happening now, with reporters interviewing the leaders and their rebel followers. It was like the *RTÉ News* mixed with drama and filled with figures from history giving opinions about the Rising. I saw it, as everyone did, night after night, knowing how it ended but still curious about how 1916 could be turned into something for television. After a few years of American TV shows about cowboys, spies, soldiers and other assorted heroes of the old west and modern America, the heroes of Easter 1916 seemed so ordinary, plain and disorganized. It was only ordinary-looking Irish actors playing them on television. The leaders, those men with exalted names—MacDonagh, McBride, Connolly, Pearse and Collins—whom we'd been hearing about in school day after day, and all the men and women who'd fought and who had created the country, were diminished by the TV screen.

In my Nenagh boy's mind, they had none of the panache of Illya Kuryakin or Napoleon Solo. They weren't cunning or clever. They were bookish, and a bit boring in their obsession. They had none of the wit or sly humour of Bat Masterson. They were men reduced.

After Mass on Easter Sunday, we marched through the

streets. There were marching bands, banners and speeches. The priests were at the front of the parade and at the back too. A priest said we were commemorating the rebirth of Ireland and the rebirth of Our Lord Jesus. A politician said Ireland would only be free when Northern Ireland was free of British rule. The band played "God Save Ireland" and we schoolboys belted out the words.

> *"God save Ireland!" said the heroes;*
> *"God save Ireland" said they all.*
> *Whether on the scaffold high*
> *Or the battlefield we die,*
> *Oh, what matter when for Erin dear we fall!*

After dinner, when darkness had fallen and the excitement of the day had faded, we settled in to watch *Insurrection* on television, and wished that *The Man from U.N.C.L.E.* would come back soon.

PART TWO

THE THREE-CHANNEL UNIVERSE

CHAPTER NINE

A PLACE APART

ON A SUNNY SATURDAY in June of 1967, we left Nenagh forever.

After years of sterling work for Irish Life Assurance in Nenagh, Dad had finally been promoted. He had been summoned to Dublin to meet his bosses. They'd offered him an inspector's job in Leitrim. He'd returned to Nenagh and told Mam. He said, "We're going to Carrick-on-Shannon!" Mam said she'd never heard of it. A few weeks later they went to Carrick for the first time. They had lunch at the Bush Hotel with Michael Hugh O'Donnell, the Irish Life man who ran the northwest area for the company. O'Donnell was a legend for his business smarts, his good nature and his false teeth. Mam sat through lunch transfixed by his teeth rattling like castanets. Then, while

O'Donnell walked Mam through the town, Dad walked quickly down to the post office. He went in and asked someone there what the population of the town was. "There are 760 people living here," he was told. Dad was taken aback and wondered if he'd be able to make a living in such a small place. Mam was pleased to be leaving Nenagh, even for a small, out-of-the-way place.

That Saturday, we all sat in the car outside 32 Sarsfield Street as Mam and Dad said their farewells to Dad's uncle Paddy and the neighbours and friends who had come to wish them well. Dad cried as he shook hands out the window of the car. Mam looked apprehensive. Máire, beside me in the back, looked bewildered. I read a book and tried to ignore it all. It was a children's book about brave Irish rebels and the long struggle for freedom. I was engrossed in a section about the Wild Geese—the Irish soldiers driven from the country to fight in other countries' wars. I had two books on the go, just in case. The other book was a *Man from U.N.C.L.E.* book about Napoleon Solo and Illya Kuryakin going off to Scandinavia to stop THRUSH agents from taking over the world. I wasn't a bit interested in Nenagh's old grannies and retired guards tossing tired platitudes at the departing Doyles.

We left Nenagh and followed the Shannon north for 150 miles. With every glimpse of the river as the road twisted and turned, I tried to imagine what Carrick-on-Shannon might be like. County Leitrim called up nothing in my mind, no images or impressions. It was near Northern Ireland, I knew, and that made it a bit forbidding.

It was evening when we arrived. Dad announced that we were entering the town and I looked around. The few streets passed by in a wisp of time. We were no sooner in it than we were gone from it. Carrick-on-Shannon wasn't so much a town as a village. It was T-shaped, with one long street and one short one jutting off from the long one. At the foot of the T was the bridge over the Shannon. It was a small but open town, a pause in a dramatic bend of the long river. And it was tranquil. There was hardly anyone on the street, and few cars. We swept over the Shannon and out of the town again. Dad said we were going out the Elphin Road, which led to the town of Elphin in county Roscommon. We passed the railway station and kept going. We stopped in an area that Dad said was called Cortober. There was our new house, one of a row of six homes built only recently. Scattered around were a few older cottages, snug behind trees or tucked into a slope in the land.

The first thing I noticed was the quiet. On a Saturday evening the air was still, and only the wind rustling the trees made any noise at all. A cow bellowed long and mournfully from some unseen field and it felt as if the sound was coming from very far away.

The new house was a modern two-storey, three-bedroom home, with a small garden at the front. Behind the house, a ragged garden blended into open fields that stretched for miles to the railway tracks and, beyond that, to the banks of the Shannon. It was open, wild land, soft underfoot and boggy. It looked melancholy, bruised and

beautiful. In the long, slow sunset, the scattered flowers—
tiny bog-bane and marsh marigolds, the white bloom of
the blackthorn—were glimmering faintly in the golden
light. The sound of a train came vaguely through the gathering darkness, and I waited so long for it come into sight
that I was shivering in the garden and Mam called me in to
the kitchen of our new home.

The movers were just finishing off. Furniture was scattered around the house and Mam was anxious to get it in
order. While she and Dad told the movers where to put the
beds, couches and chairs, Máire and I were told to watch
TV, the television having already been set up in the living
room. I turned it on. A familiar RTÉ voice was giving the
weather forecast. The picture was fuzzy, and I turned a
knob to see if it would improve. There, to my astonish-
ment, was another picture entirely and the sound of
English voices. I turned the knob again and yet another
picture appeared. More English voices were talking. I
turned the knob back and forward again and, sure enough,
there were three different channels to watch. There was
the BBC Northern Ireland service, the commercial Ulster
channel called UTV, and RTÉ. We were near the North,
and as the signals drifted, ignoring borders, we were connected to territory controlled by England.

As soon as I got Dad's attention, I asked him about the
TV channels. "That's right," he said. "Sure, Northern
Ireland is only a few miles away. Everyone in Carrick gets
the three channels. Some of the people here watch an
awful lot of the BBC. They say the films are better."

We were soon hustled away from the television set, given something to eat and sent to bed. I was still wondering what tiny Carrick-on-Shannon was like, and I was worried I'd miss my friends in Nenagh. But I knew that if I hated it and all the boys at school ignored me, there were three channels to watch on television. I had a place to go to.

We were lucky to have moved to Carrick in early summer. It was months before we went to school, and Máire and I could ramble the fields and streets until we knew every inch of the area. That summer, I ran wild. There weren't enough hours in the day to explore Carrick and its fields, back roads and crannies. A few minutes' walk up the road was a tiny side road that took miles to meander down to the Shannon. It was eternally silent there, with few travellers ever walking between the high hedges. Partway down there was an apple orchard. Some of the trees had grown wild and reached over the edges. I learned it was owned by the Gree family, Protestant landowners who had a business growing and selling fruit. But there was nothing imposing about the land and orchards they owned. There was no mansion to be seen, no tall stone walls to keep out the peasants. Even the main roads were always quiet, and the fields behind were quieter still. Sometimes cattle grazed there, dolefully plodding across the higher, firmer ground, avoiding the soft patches that yielded to their girth. When it rained they sheltered in a small knot of oak trees and stared at the empty road.

The first thing we discovered is that we were truly miles from the town. To get into Carrick I would walk north along a road that had no pavement, with only empty fields to the left and right. Then I turned right and toward the railway station. The hedgerows grew wild and tall with blackthorn bushes. In some places, alder trees with long spindly branches grew taller than the blackthorn. After rain, the wind blew stinging showers of raindrops from the trees and bushes. The air was always fresh and smelled of wet grass. The people who passed in the occasional car or tractor always seemed to be in good spirits. Every driver blew a horn and waved.

By the railway station, traffic actually began and a pavement started. Going under the railway bridge meant leaving Cortober and entering the outskirts of Carrick, but there was another twenty-minute walk to get to the town, past occasional houses, most of them with long front gardens filled with potato plants. At Tommy Glancy's pub, a long, low building painted in cheerful red and white, the Elphin Road met the Sligo Road, and to the left were the banks of the Shannon. They were dense with tall chestnut trees that, I eventually learned, in fall could cascade hard nuts. Coming home from school on that stretch of road was a game of dodging missiles.

Beneath the trees was a small park, a place with benches to sit on and watch the river drift past. Old men sat there, smoking their pipes, and mothers brought their little children in prams, to sit and watch the river's flow, and an occasional pleasure boat, filled with English or German tourists, would pass and the boaters would wave at the locals lingering on the bank.

Then I'd turn left over the narrow stone bridge and enter the tiny town itself. It only took two minutes to walk up Bridge Street, past a handful of shops and the garda station, to reach the junction with Main Street. Off to the left was George's Terrace, where there was the post office, the court house and the offices of the *Leitrim Observer*, the local newspaper. Just past that, the old jailhouse was being demolished, very slowly it seemed, and a new marina for pleasure boats was being built.

If I turned right and went along Main Street, it took a few minutes to pass more shops, pubs, the Catholic church, the Bush Hotel and the Christian Brothers school, and then the street veered right again and became the Dublin Road, and there the town ended. There wasn't much to Carrick, it appeared, but it had its obvious novelties. For a start, I learned that Carrick-on-Shannon had the smallest church in Ireland, the second smallest in the world, and it had one of the heaviest men in Ireland.

The church was a tiny structure at the crook of Bridge Street and Main Street. The little building was one man's tribute to his wife. When Mary Josephine Costello died at the age of forty-seven in 1877, her heartbroken husband, Edward, had her body embalmed and placed in the care of the nuns, the Marist Sisters, in Carrick. He then commissioned, no expense spared, this little chapel as a last resting place for them both.

The heavy man was Ging Duignan, who owned a pub right at the bridge over the Shannon. Ging was enormous, but he was far from idle. A familiar figure walking briskly around the town or serving drinks in his pub, he was light enough on his feet to be a volunteer fireman. A wit and a scold to people who refused to be cheerful, he was adored.

I soon began to understand that Carrick was a carefree place compared with Nenagh. The people were more casual and relaxed. But it was the open, barren landscape that drew me in. Through the summer days, I tramped through the fields. If I was caught in a shower of rain, I sheltered under trees, sometimes with two or three cows for company, listening to their long sighs as they stood there, and I contemplated the rain falling, watching for the shift of light to the west as the rain clouds drifted off. If it rained in the morning, I stayed inside and read books. In the evenings there were the three television channels to watch. There was something magical in the English programs available from the BBC and Ulster Television.

One night I watched *The Avengers* for the first time. There was John Steed, the dapper English gent in his three-piece pinstriped suit and bowler hat, issuing acid-tongued witticisms as he dealt with bad guys. To me, an English gent in a bowler hat was the oppressor, an anti-Irish, anti-Catholic bigot who took pleasure in hanging Irish rebels.

This Steed man was different. He really didn't seem to care much about Ireland, the Irish or Catholics. It took a while for me to grasp it, but I eventually understood that *The Avengers* was making fun of English gents in bowler hats who carried umbrellas and talked in the clipped voice of the upper class. The joke was on them. In one episode I saw that summer, two gents in their suits and bowlers were meeting an important spy. The spy looked uneasily at the second gent, who was studiously saying nothing. "Is he dumb?" he asked the first. And the reply was, "No, he's British. He wouldn't dream of discussing important matters with you until he's been properly introduced." For months I relished that question and response: "Is he dumb?" "No, he's British."

Mostly, Steed directed his skeptical looks at his sidekick, Emma Peel, and made wildly suggestive remarks that even I understood were racy. Emma Peel, played by Diana Rigg, was majestic. Raven haired, long legged and wickedly haughty, she looked like no woman I'd seen before on TV, in movies or in comic books. She wasn't at all like Agent 99, who drooped in a sort of languid pose and allowed her eyes to rest longingly on Maxwell Smart. Emma Peel was bossy, assured, modern and free. She had an English assuredness and a brazenness that told you it was something modern. The England on *The Avengers* wasn't a frightening picture of tightly wound bigots and oppressors. It was foreign, new and funny.

The town of Carrick itself was almost exotic to the Doyles from Nenagh. We had been used to having as neighbours people named Nolan, Dolan, O'Brien and Meaher. In Carrick the local names were fantastic and foreign to us—Gallogly, Delahoyde, Gormely, Cangely, McGushin and McGahern. There were plenty of Flynns and O'Rourkes too. As anyone in Carrick would tell you, Leitrim was O'Rourke country. The O'Rourkes had been the Gaelic chieftains of the area for centuries, controlling the crossings of the Shannon and the local river trade. They also controlled land that straddled the border with old Ulster, and they had long connections with the O'Neills and the O'Donnells, the two great Gaelic clans of Ulster. With their allies, the O'Rourkes connived to keep the ancient Gaelic order alive in the remote areas west and north of the Shannon, beyond English rule.

At first, I learned smatterings of information about Carrick from the books in the library, but mostly I was sizing up the town and its ways. From the way the Doyles were treated, I knew that there was little snobbery in Carrick. As small as it was, the town wasn't insular and isolated. It had long been open to the river's trade and travellers, and the local people were accustomed to outsiders. Pleasure-boat cruising on the Shannon was becoming popular and Carrick's main business was in tourism. The number of visitors was small, but some of those who came to fish or explore had stayed on, deciding to live by the river forever. Men who had experience working on boats in England, Holland and Germany came to Carrick for work, brought their families and stayed. There were no walls against outsiders.

Unlike Nenagh, the town had never been walled. The English conquerors had given up on it. It was an important river crossing to secure, but the land was open and flat, and the river twisted this way and that. In the early seventeenth century the English had panicked and fled Carrick to build a walled town, four miles downriver, called Jamestown. It was where the English army garrison was, and for decades they only ventured warily into Carrick. It was later, in the eighteenth century, that Carrick and its surrounding townlands became a stable place to govern, and the centre of administrative power was established.

It was a town blessed by a spirit of openness. The river seemed to take away the bitterness and bile that so often cement small towns. Even Mam and Dad were astonished by Carrick's treatment of the tinkers. I was surprised too. In Nenagh, I'd grown up terrified of the tinkers. Some called them travellers, and officially they were called itinerants, but to most people they were tinkers. These were Gypsy people who lived in caravans and tents, wandering endlessly around Ireland. They set up home wherever they could find land they could use. They were called tinkers because, in the old days, many were tinsmiths. They were mysterious people to town dwellers and farming people alike. They were horse dealers or casual labourers, and they begged. The women dressed in old wool shawls and the men were often long haired, bearded and unkempt. In Nenagh, they'd been the absolute lowest form of life, mistrusted, loathed and kept out of shops. The pubs wouldn't serve them drink, the guards moved them off the streets if they begged, and homeowners feared that their houses would be burgled if tinkers were loitering on the street. Nobody in Nenagh actually knew or spoke to the tinkers, except to hire a few to do rough labour for a day or two. If I saw them on the street in Nenagh, I didn't want to look at them. They smelled like animals and they talked a strange mixture of English and Irish in a hard accent. They were a drifting, different people.

Once, I'd asked Mam why the tinkers didn't have a proper house like everybody else and lived in tents at the side of the road. She told me that nobody knew who the tinkers were or why they lived that way, but some believed they were descended from people who had been thrown off their land during the famine and had been wandering the roads ever since.

In Carrick, where they had a permanent campsite near the site of the old workhouse that had been turned into a hospital, tinkers were welcome in the pubs and treated with kindness and respect in the shops. They were entrenched in the town's population, not outside of it. They were usually called by the more polite term, itinerants, and sometimes local people called them travellers, though they hardly travelled at all. They were just there on their site, always the same families, and they went about the town as if they belonged there. Some itinerants scavenged on the town dump, picking out what they could fix and resell.

When we moved to Carrick, Dad brought a big box of his golf balls with him. They'd accidentally been left for the garbage collection and disappeared. One day, not long after Dad had realized they were gone, he heard that some itinerants were selling golf balls in the town. Indeed they were, and half the town's golfers had already bought them. Dad admired Carrick people, especially the pub owners and shopkeepers, for their tolerance of the itinerants and the fondness they showed toward them. He mentioned it a few times to people in the town as something that had struck him as a newcomer. But he stopped mentioning it. It wasn't something peopled talked about. It was nothing to note or be excited about.

CHAPTER TEN

"AN INDOLENT AND
UN-SELF-RELIANT PEOPLE"

SOME PEOPLE IN CARRICK talked about ghosts. They didn't mean monsters like the fiery carriage that was supposed to race through Nenagh on some nights of the year, driven by a headless creature who grabbed people and took them straight to hell. There were some places in Carrick that people said gave you a strange feeling, a lonely feeling, if you lingered there at night. The ghosts were crying children who could be heard even when everyone was safe inside and tucked up in bed. Once, in a shop, I'd heard a woman ask the shopkeeper how his mother was keeping. She'd heard the mother wasn't feeling well. The shopkeeper said that his mother was only lonely, after being out walking. "She said she heard the crying," he said.

The thing is, when you're ten years old, you're curious

about things that are hinted at by grown-ups. You want to know, but you don't want to ask stupid questions. You want to know for yourself, in your own way. In the end, it was Theresa Lee who told me most of it. Mam and Dad had made friends with Mrs. Lee and her husband, Paddy, who lived a few minutes' walk from us in Cortober. Mrs. Lee was a retired assistant schoolteacher, a kind, brisk woman who had spent decades teaching young children. She'd never made it to university or a teacher's training college, so she'd never become a full-fledged schoolmistress. But she'd had enough education for the time to be allowed to teach in a small town. She was full of opinions delivered with certainty and sometimes asperity. She had come to welcome the Doyles to Cortober and Carrick, and to the little stretch of road where we all lived. Mrs. Lee loved children and believed in educating them gently but constantly. Often, if Mam and Dad were out for an evening, it was Mrs. Lee and Paddy who minded Máire and me. We'd stay in her kitchen by the fire and she'd talk and banter with us all evening. She'd ask if we knew the names of the flowers and the trees in the fields. If we didn't, she'd tell us. She told us that if we got stung by the nettles that grew in the hedgerows, the best cure was the sap from a thick reed that grew near the Shannon's banks. The first time I tried her cure I was amazed. After rushing through brambles that had hidden stinging nettles, my knees were covered in bright red swellings. I hurried down a field, pulled up a hard, thick reed from soggy ground and saw the thick liquid that covered its roots. I smeared it all over one knee that was throbbing with pain, and in seconds the pain eased. It was a balm, a secret among people who lived there, and I loved sharing the secret.

Often of a night when Mrs. Lee looked after us, she made boxty for us. Boxty was a potato cake much loved in Leitrim. Mrs. Lee would say to us, until we knew it by heart, "Boxty on the griddle, boxty on the pan, if you don't eat boxty, you're not a Leitrim man!" She cooked it on a griddle over the fire and served it to us hot, with butter running all over it. It was served to us as though it was a great delicacy. Mrs. Lee said it was important food in Leitrim.

It was after eating boxty one night that I asked Mrs. Lee about the ghosts that some people said were hanging around parts of Carrick town. Mrs. Lee scoffed. "It's not ghosts," she said. "It's old feelings. It's the famine that people are afraid of." She paused a long time before she asked me what I knew about the famine.

I told her that I knew there had been a famine in Ireland because somebody related to Mam's people had been thrown off their land and people were still angry about it. I knew that there was a potato blight and that some people starved to death. Mrs. Lee told me I should read about it. But she said she'd tell me what she knew, because she was a Carrick woman and because the famine had been bad in Carrick.

She said I shouldn't be afraid of ghosts, and that if I knew the past, I could enjoy the present and look forward to the future. Then she told me, partly in her own soft way and partly like a schoolteacher, that Carrick was once a place of unspeakable horror. The little streets I walked to school, to go to church or to buy sweets at Flynn's grocery had once been crowded with thousands of starving, half-naked people, many of them children, trying to get help from the workhouse during the famine of the 1840s. Most of them died in the town. Carrick had been a giant graveyard. It had a past drenched in death and sorrow.

The land around Carrick was mostly bog-like and bedraggled. That I could see. But Mrs. Lee said that back then, almost all of it was owned by English landlords, many of them absent in London. The Irish slaved as tenants on small leased holdings. As the nineteenth century progressed and the Catholic population grew, their holdings grew smaller as land was parcelled out to successive generations. In most of Leitrim, around Carrick, little could grow except the potato. It was what kept the peasants alive. When the potato crop first failed in 1845, there was no other source of food and a lot of people died. When the blight struck again in 1846, and again in 1847, famine swept across the entire country. The only option for some people was the workhouse. Workhouses had been built as homes for the utterly destitute. The landlords paid a small tax to subsidize them and most resented it. The workhouse was inevitably a forbidding place where living conditions were as harsh as possible. Families who entered the workhouse were separated by gender and kept apart. They were sent out to do hard labour and had to work to earn their meals.

The workhouse in Carrick catered to several dozen parishes in the region. The population of the area it covered was 66,000. But it was a small building and could house only a couple of hundred people at most. During the winter of 1845, a few hundred died of starvation in the Carrick area. The workhouse was full of those who had barely survived. In 1846, tens of thousands were starving. The countryside was filled with wandering families in search of food of any kind. As the land was picked clear of berries and anything else that could be eaten, those who could walk came to Carrick-on-Shannon. The workhouse couldn't hold them all, and the entire social system collapsed. Typhoid and dysentery were rampant inside the institution. Hundreds of those inside, dying and near naked, were released into the town. Disease spread. Families huddled in the streets under rags and died where they lay. In the winter of 1847, crowds of those strong enough to act tried to lay siege to the work-house, and failed. That long winter, the only sound heard in the town at night was the wailing of the dying.

In the countryside around Carrick, almost everyone died. At first, landlords routinely ordered tenants evicted for the non-payment of rent. The famished hordes who couldn't eat and therefore couldn't work were thrown out of their hovels. Most were too weak to travel far. They lived in ditches and died in ditches.

The Great Famine was general throughout Ireland, Mrs. Lee said, but few places suffered worse than Carrick. Every field for miles, every bend in the road, every ditch held ghosts. I shouldn't be frightened of them, for they were the memory the land kept of the people. It was a powerful, old feeling that could never be banished.

Strangely, Mrs. Lee told me, what happened in Carrick during the famine was even known in England. There had been a fuss about it. But she laughed when she said it. It was known, she said, not because of the death and horror seen in the town but because the management of the situation had been so notoriously haphazard that it was reported to the House of Lords.

A local landlord accused the workhouse administrator, Captain Wynne, of impropriety. The landlord was outraged by the amount of money he was obliged to pay for the upkeep and running of the Carrick workhouse, and when rumours reached him that Wynne was having an affair with a local, impoverished woman, he complained to the authorities. It wasn't the mass deaths of the starving that caused him to complain, it was Wynne's relationship. Theresa Lee said the story was a farce, but a relevant one. Her people knew the details, all the mad English arrogance of it. She told me that the English government's man in charge, a toff named Trevelyan, had said that the famine was a punishment from God for "an idle, ungrateful country and an indolent and un-self-reliant people."

A century and a decade after the famine, English tourists came to Carrick in their cabin cruisers, floating up the Shannon, entranced by the beauty of the river and the lonely, desolate land that surrounded it. They moored their boats at scenic places and watched the always-changing light or they waited through the showers of soft rain for the sky to clear, taken by the silence and struck by the distinct sound of a single curlew calling out over the water. They came into Carrick and were greeted, and no one told them why the countryside had the beauty of desolation, the feeling of loneliness. It wasn't worth dwelling on that pain. That was left at the back of the mind, in a remote place only God and Carrick people knew.

CHAPTER ELEVEN

A PLACE NEAR AND FAR

IT WAS THE ULSTER channel UTV that intrigued me first. The news programs were often unerringly similar to RTÉ's, with their focus on farming and agriculture. The accents of the news readers and reporters were just a slight variation on the accents of Carrick people. The stories and events took place in Irish counties, in Fermanagh, which was only a few miles away, or in Tyrone or county Down. But suddenly, out of nowhere, there would be news about the royal family or parliamentary events in London, stories that were never heard on RTÉ. It seemed to me that I was watching a strange, made-up version of Ireland, an Ireland created by somebody in England.

One Saturday, we all set out for Enniskillen, the nearest large town in Northern Ireland. Mam wanted to see it and do some shopping, maybe pick up some things that weren't available in Carrick. Máire and I wanted the sweets and chocolate bars that were advertised on UTV but couldn't be bought in the South. Dad was just interested in seeing Enniskillen, his Irish Life work having taken him close to the border on many occasions.

We drove across the border at a small crossing where a police officer merely came out of a hut, glanced at the car and waved us on. The countryside looked similar to Leitrim but there was an air of prosperity about the place. The fields were more lush, the houses more solid, and there were more of them. There were more cars on the road and everything seemed to move a little faster.

In Enniskillen we toured around the shops, bought our sweets and a few groceries and stopped at a restaurant for lunch. As we headed back to the car, Dad decided that he wanted to buy an umbrella. He'd had a fine sturdy umbrella in Nenagh, but he'd lost it somewhere on his travels around Leitrim. He saw a big shop that seemed to specialize in raincoats, Wellington boots and all the necessities for surviving in the rough country weather. Mam and Máire wandered off to buy ice cream and I went with Dad. We entered the neatly organized shop, with its racks of coats, rows of boots and other items in display cases. Dad looked around for umbrellas. A shop assistant, a tall burly man with a fussy air about him, descended on us.

"And what are we looking for?" he asked with a peculiar mix of local accent, English-style formality and a faint touch of obsequiousness.

Dad explained that he was after a large, sturdy umbrella. He glanced around as he explained, looking for what he wanted. I watched the shop assistant. As soon as he heard Dad speak, the polite interest left his face and he glared at us. I shrunk into Dad's side.

"Can you afford a decent umbrella?" the big man barked at Dad.

"I think I can," Dad said, with a small laugh. He continued to explain the type he was looking for and mentioned the one he'd lost after buying it in Dublin years before.

At the mention of Dublin, the shop assistant rose to his full height and snorted. Fury became visible on his face and contempt was obvious in his tone. "That sort of umbrella isn't sold here. That type of umbrella is used by farmers in the South to herd pigs along the road. We don't have that sort of item here. We don't supply items for pig farmers. You'll find items for pig farmers in the South. Not here."

He stared hard at Dad and Dad stared back. I was terrified. I'd never heard such hatred. I tugged at Dad's sleeve. "Let's go, Daddy. Let's go home now."

"Go back where you came from," the shop assistant snapped and turned away.

As we walked to the car, I clung to Dad's hand, suddenly seeing Enniskillen as a dangerous place. That man hated us because we were Catholics from the South. Could people tell that just by looking at us? It felt as if we were in peril just walking down the street. While we hurried along the street Dad murmured, partly to himself and partly to me.

But he spoke in Gaelic, not English. As calm as he was, I knew some old instinct had been summoned up inside him. *"Tá se as a mheabhair,"* he said. "That man is out of his mind." We never went back to Enniskillen.

I discovered that there was a sweet calmness about Carrick all year round. On the long winter nights, when a chill wind brought hard rain over the low Leitrim hills to land on Carrick, the pubs—of which there seemed to be dozens—were full but quiet. In winter, Leitrim men drank deep from their beer and were silent. They were seeing out the winter, waiting for spring and the warmth of the sun on the river. The people and the place were one, placid and unperturbed.

Out in a field behind our house one afternoon, I came across a small, distinctive arrangement of stones. I knew they marked something, but I didn't know exactly what. I wanted Mrs. Lee to come and see it, but she wouldn't traipse that far into the fields. She said she knew what it was. It marked a grave and most likely it had something to do with what had happened in 1798. Surely to God, she suggested, in her schoolteacher's way, I knew what had happened in 1798.

I'd read all about it. In the spring of that year, rebellion swept across Ireland. The United Irishmen, a group of mainly Protestant young men—the only educated youth in Ireland at that time—were inspired by the French and American revolutions to fight for an end to English rule in Ireland. The country was simmering. Colonial rule had become corrupt. The peasants were paying tithes to

English lords and facing harsh justice if they were in arrears. Eventually, rebellion broke out in a scattered fashion across the country. But the English rulers in Dublin had anticipated war and reinforced the occupying army. The United Irishmen called on the French for support. Amazingly, and in the spirit of the times, the French came.

French ships landed on the west coast of Ireland in September 1798. There were just eleven hundred French soldiers ready to fight to make Ireland a republic. Under the command of General Humbert they marched east, gathering local recruits on the way. In Leitrim, Humbert dodged the massing English forces and crossed the Shannon near Carrick. The recruits grew into the thousands. Entire families—men, women and children—joined in, most of them armed only with pitchforks. They were gripped by something from far away—an idea that people could simply rise up and defeat their oppressors.

The French and their ragtag Irish forces kept going, blithely heading for Dublin. They didn't know that the army gathered by the newly installed lord lieutenant of Ireland, the Marquis Cornwallis, had grown and grown in size, and fifteen thousand English troops were ready to drive them back to the Atlantic.

In a town with the strange name of Ballinamuck, which in Gaelic means the Mouth of the Ford of the Pigs, some fifteen miles from Carrick, the French soldiers and Irish peasants collided with the well-armed and ruthless army of England. To say they were defeated would not do justice to the scale of the slaughter. The French were rounded up and held as prisoners of war. The Irish were shown no mercy. All those who were injured were massacred in the fields where they fell. Those who fled were hunted down and killed. The field leading to the banks of the Shannon was filled with the dead. Some, who were thought to be Irish ringleaders, were taken to Carrick-on-Shannon to be executed.

In Carrick, they were to be hanged and their bodies put on display to show that the firmness of English rule should never be challenged again. In the old court house, the building beside the post office where I had opened a savings account and put in a shilling every week, a few dozen of the Irish were held. The English commanding officer devised a method for deciding who would be hanged in the doorway to the street and who might be hanged away from the crowd's eyes. He created a lottery system. Into a hat were thrown pieces of paper that either were blank or had the word "Death" on them. The prisoners who drew the paper with "Death" were taken instantly to the door and hanged.

The whole story was a shock to me. It had happened, like the famine, in the fields where I played. I was smitten with the idea that, once upon a time, the bright, sunny world outside Ireland had sent soldiers to come to Ireland and free us. But in Carrick, it looked like we didn't need to be set free any more. We already were free. Everybody went about their business without worrying about the English oppressor and battles against English soldiers. Yet I knew that something from the old fights would remain in

Leitrim. After a day travelling through the hills of Leitrim and Cavan with the local Irish Life men, Dad would tell us about the people who lived on remote farms near the border, and a few of the old-time fighters he'd met. "Some of them are real rebels," he said. "They're true IRA up there. They haven't lost a bit of the spirit. You'd think it was back in the 1920s. That's the old men, anyway. Maybe the younger ones are different. But some of the old men are very hard Republicans." It didn't surprise me to hear it. If the land held the memory of the people, then the people surely kept memories of what had happened on the land.

CHAPTER TWELVE

FREE AS THE BREEZE

WE THRIVED IN CARRICK. We weren't bound in by anything.

After a few months at school in Carrick I'd become an altar boy. I cycled to and from the small Catholic church very early in the morning to serve at the seven o'clock Mass. I did it in all weathers, enjoying the solitary ride down empty streets, even in the pouring rain and the freezing sleet that sometimes swept over the town. I was ten and paying attention to the roads, the fields, the trees, the Shannon river's curves and turns. The history of the place had opened up to me. I could wander away from home without fear of bullies or being watched by other Doyles, free to watch, look, listen and savour where I lived.

I savoured the mornings when I cycled to serve Mass and the winter weather was calm but cold. There was a fringe of silver frost on the dark green scrag grass in the fields and a white trim on the ditches and hedgerows when the dew fell. Nearer the town there was often a mist on the river that enveloped the streets, thickening the air and carrying the sweet smoke of peat turf being burned in the fireplaces of the early risers, and it mingled into the river mist to make Carrick a silent, self-enclosed place.

If I wasn't serving Mass, Máire and I would sometimes get a lift to school with Mr. Swendon, a neighbour who'd moved from England to work for a pleasure-boat company. A gruff man with a broad Lancashire accent, he was prone to driving his van at high speed, and we'd arrive at school dizzy from the wild ride and Swendon's barely comprehensible running commentary on the peculiarities of Carrick and Ireland. "This is all right, this is," he'd say, thumping the side of the van. "I likes this van here, but I can't get it serviced, can I? Takes too bloody long. Take this van to the garage here and some chap tells me to come back next week. He's waiting on a part to come on a train. Train comes four bloody times in a day. Where's the bloody part? Lovely here in Carrick, but everybody works bloody slow. Be the next century before you can get your car fixed as fast as you can in England. They teach you that at school? Do things slowly? I shouldn't wonder!"

He was right. At the Christian Brothers school, the teachers seemed to have been sent there and then forgotten. The brothers were older, gentle, lazy and forgiving.

They talked about fishing on the river and tried to engage the boys in the study of Shannon fish when we should have been learning math or science. Of an evening, the brothers could be seen going in groups to the tiny local cinema, lining up for ice cream, passing the time of day with the locals and talking among themselves about the films they'd seen.

In Carrick it was easy to make friends quickly. There weren't cliques or gangs in the schoolyard. I was invited to other boys' homes to play or to watch television. Sometimes it was soccer we played. There were soccer games on BBC and UTV and I loved them. Nenagh had been obsessed by the Tipperary hurling team and its glorious history. There had been a famous Tipperary hurler named John Doyle, from the town of Holy Cross, and I'd grown used to men saying to me, "John Doyle of Holy Cross! Do you know who that is, young boy?" I did, but I didn't really care. It was my name, not just some old fella who used to play hurling before I was born. Soccer was English and new to me. Huge crowds swayed on the stands and roared when someone scored. The game was fast and slick and it was about using a simple skill with your feet, not about being big and burly. I'd known I'd never make a Tipperary hurler because I was too small, too shy and not used to crashing into other people. Kicking a soccer ball and running with it was a liberating, unfettered game. There was a famous soccer player from Northern Ireland, George Best, and everyone knew about him. He looked like a pop star but he talked in a soft Northern accent, and he was shy. You could tell from the way he looked at the ground when he was being interviewed on television. If we played soccer in Carrick, someone would shout, "Go on like Georgie, the Belfast boy." Nobody said soccer was an English game, or "a garrison game," as I knew they did in Nenagh.

At home on winter afternoons we watched English TV programs. Mam, Máire and I had become addicted to *Crossroads*, a drama set at a motel in Birmingham. We'd never seen anything like it. The characters were not distant American figures living in New York City or California. They were ordinary people working in a hotel or a newsagent's, dealing with weather like ours and daily disappointments like ours. Yet there weren't priests or politicians there to scold them. They married and divorced, their teenagers became pregnant without being married. They didn't look glamorous or sleek. They looked like the people in Carrick-on-Shannon.

In 1968 we were utterly absorbed in a new TV drama airing on the BBC. *The Railway Children* seemed so close to our lives. The physical resemblance between the setting and our own town was instantly obvious. On *The Railway Children*, the Faraday family, nice middle-class people, had to leave their home in London because their father had been arrested and wrongly convicted of being a spy. The mother took the children away to a remote little house in the country. She couldn't afford school for them, so the children ran wild through the area. They lived near a railway track, made friends with the station master and had many adventures associated with the trains. They learned about the trees and the flowers and were rarely disturbed by adults or anybody else.

We too lived in a remote area with a train track winding its way through the fields that stretched from the end of our back garden. We watched the trains go by every day. We often wandered down to the station to see the train stop and to watch the passengers alight and the packages be gathered up and put on old Ned's horse and cart to be taken into Carrick. We were just like those English children in so many ways and we savoured every moment of their adventures. Like every boy who saw that series, in England or Ireland, I fell immediately in love with Jenny Agutter, who played the brave, beautiful young Bobbie. She was the eldest of the Railway Children and always ready for adventure or to take charge in an emergency. We identified deeply with the Railway Children, English though they were. There was no difference at all really, if you were eleven years old.

And then, one day that year, on the television news, there was a shocking report of riots in Northern Ireland, that place a few miles away. Angry faces filled the screen, talking excitedly about people's rights. Some of those faces were bloodied. There was a terrible, ominous sense of something sleeping in history having been awakened by a rifle crack and a scream of agony.

It came like a sting because for ages everything had been playing out in a pattern on the news. There seemed to be changes everywhere. People were fighting for their rights and getting them. It was unstoppable. For a year or more, the TV news, especially on the BBC, had been reporting on the civil rights movement in America. Everybody admired the bravery of black people marching for an end to discrimination. "Aren't they the working people of America, like the Irish often were," Dad said. "And it was an Irishman who began that whole movement for the blacks in America. John F. Kennedy started that. They only want a decent life. More power to them." When we saw those news reports from America, Dad and Mam tut-tutted about the furious white people shouting abuse at the dignified blacks marching in the street. The pictures of the police with whips and attack dogs shocked us all.

It was obvious to anyone that those same television reports had inspired the Catholics in Northern Ireland. They were marching too. It had been going on for months, and *RTÉ News* gave it extensive coverage. In the North, they copied what they saw on television in the same way that we children in Carrick tried to be like the Railway Children. In Northern Ireland, the Catholics also called themselves the civil rights movement. They wanted housing and jobs. They said there was discrimination against Catholics. On television we'd seen them marching in the thousands in Belfast and Derry, singing "We Shall Overcome," just like the black people in the South of America. Some held signs and banners that said "One Man, One Vote." This I didn't understand at all. Couldn't everybody vote in Northern Ireland? Or did Catholics not have the right to vote, like the old days in Ireland under English rule?

Dad told me that it was all about local elections for town and city councils. Only those who paid property tax could vote. Not many Catholics were wealthy enough to own property, so many couldn't vote at all, and even if a Catholic did own a house, only the person who actually paid the tax could vote. If a house had a husband and wife and sons and daughters old enough to vote, only one person in the house could vote, the person who paid the tax. Dad said it was criminal what powerful people did to keep down the working man.

And he told me something else I didn't really understand at all. Companies or rich people who owned several houses or business could have more than one vote. They might vote six times if they paid tax on six properties. Only some Protestant mucky-mucks were rich enough to have six votes, he said. Catholics never got to be that rich. They were always held back, denied good jobs in the civil service, never allowed into the police force, and some of the Protestants really, really hated Catholics. They devised ways to keep them down all the time. Dad saw it as another case of the working man being denied a fair chance. We never mentioned the man at the shop in Enniskillen, but I remembered him.

When the civil rights marchers were on the TV news, row and row of them walking arm in arm down the streets, I felt like cheering. Everybody in the South was proud of them, standing up for their rights. But that one day, the singing of "We Shall Overcome" and the dignified marching had stopped and we all saw what had been done to the Catholics. The news had been on the radio for hours and people wanted to see it.

And there it was, on the TV screen, the awful scene of fighting and chaos that made my stomach feel empty and my head feel dizzy. The police had decided to stop a march. Big men in uniforms were swinging sticks at people with banners that said "One Man, One Vote." You could see that some of the marchers were bleeding on the ground. Other people were throwing bottles and stones—not at the police but at the marchers. Men in suits and ties and wearing glasses, men who looked like schoolteachers or office workers, were pleading with the police to stop. You could hear a man yelling, "For God's sake." But it didn't stop. The batons swung, the people screamed in terror and ran helter-skelter. Some sat on the roadside, crying like children who'd fallen and hurt themselves. But they were grown-ups, not supposed to cry. A woman in a headscarf, who looked like somebody's mam going to the shops for groceries, sat crying. You could see the blood flowing down her face. A policeman ran by her, swinging his baton, trying to catch a man who was running away.

The TV cameras were jerking this way and that. You could hear the RTÉ reporters shouting, their voices showing they were afraid that they would be hit too. The *BBC News* played the same footage, and I could tell from the quiet voice of the news reader that he was shocked. He seemed to be warning people that they would see pictures that would frighten them.

After that, week after week, everybody wanted to see the news. The Protestants, who called themselves Unionists because they were proud of their union with England, started marching too, led by a big man named Ian Paisley, who was always on television. You could see the foam on his mouth as he ranted about Catholics and waved his arms in the air. The nastier he was about Catholics, the louder the cheers. He said the enemy was the Roman Catholic Church. He said the Pope was the Antichrist. He said there was a problem of housing for Roman Catholics in Northern Ireland only because Roman Catholics bred like rabbits and vermin. He said the Lord's anger against the corrupt Roman Catholic Church would soon be seen.

At home in bed in Carrick I had bad dreams about Ian Paisley. I dreamt that he would come to Carrick with the man from the shop in Enniskillen and try to kill us all. One night I got up and wandered down the stairs after a nightmare. Dad got up and asked me if I was sick. I didn't want to tell him I'd had a bad dream about Paisley, but I did anyway. Dad said Paisley had a nightmare about Paisley too. He said Paisley was the most frightening man he'd ever seen. But Dad said Paisley was like Peter Cushing in the horror films on television. He seemed to be evil incarnate, but he was only acting. The end of Paisley was coming, he said. Times were changing.

At school that fall, the brothers in Carrick often talked about the trouble in Northern Ireland, and it wasn't just in history class. The proclamation of the Easter 1916 Rising hung on the wall of the classroom. A map of Ireland beside it showed that Northern Ireland wasn't really Ulster and that some counties in Ulster had been left out of Northern Ireland. It was a sore point. The Protestants said they lived in Ulster but Ulster was an old province of Ireland, trimmed of some Catholic counties to suit them when Ireland was partitioned. Brother Glynn said a united Ireland was inevitable now that the civil rights people had started protesting. He said the government in Northern Ireland would come to its senses and give Catholics their civil rights. He said the whole world had seen on television what was going on in Northern Ireland. Brother Glynn was old and sounded tired, not angry, when he said this. He spoke as if he had seen it all before.

For a while the marches stopped. On TV there were reports about "concessions," and the man in charge of Northern Ireland, Captain O'Neill, talked in a reasonable voice about maintaining peace. He seemed like a nice man, Captain O'Neill. You could tell people trusted him a little bit because he looked and sounded like the bank manager. He had lovely manners. He was dignified and a gentleman. He wasn't like Paisley at all.

That quiet winter we all watched the variety shows on BBC and UTV. The best was hosted by Cilla Black and called *Cilla*. Everybody in Carrick watched on Saturday nights. Mam said Cilla was a Catholic from Liverpool and there was discrimination against her in England. Now we all talked about who was Catholic in England. Cilla was funny and silly and lovely. Every week she would go to people's houses and just barge in and look at their furniture and the photographs on the wall. She chattered away to them in her Liverpool accent and they stood around smiling at her. You could tell they loved her. Lulu's show was the other one we watched, but it was more about pop songs. It was called *Happening for Lulu*. Mam liked Lulu too, but she preferred Cilla. Mam knew all about the English girl singers from reading about them in magazines. She said Lulu was from Glasgow and that her real name was Marie Lawrie. She said she was a Glasgow Catholic. Nobody on the English shows talked about being Catholic or Protestant. It was something you had to guess if people didn't tell you who was who.

After Christmas, there was more trouble in Northern Ireland. People said Captain O'Neill was only codding the Catholics, telling them fibs to keep them quiet. The Catholics said he hadn't given them real civil rights. O'Neill had said on television that he'd heard enough about civil rights and wanted to hear more about civil responsibility. The civil rights people had been joined by a group called People's Democracy, who wanted to show that the civil rights marchers weren't alone. Most of them were students from the university in Belfast. The People's Democracy was going on a big march, all the way from Belfast to Derry. The start of the march was televised on the BBC, UTV and RTÉ. The protestors sang "We Shall Overcome" as they walked along the roads. There weren't many of them and they were mostly young people, but at every village and town some locals would join them and their numbers swelled.

After school and before dinner on a cold day in January of 1969, Mam asked me to bring in the washing from the clothesline in the garden. It was so cold that the sheets and Dad's shirts had frozen stiff. They felt like they would break if you folded them. I was gathering up the stiff clothes when Mam called me inside urgently. "Look at this," she said, pointing at the news on TV. "It's like there's a war going on now." A crowd of Protestants had attacked the marchers with stones and bottles, and beaten some of them with sticks. Some people were lying on the ground, curled up in a ball as they were being kicked. The screaming was awful. There didn't seem to be any police involved. It was just people fighting people. The name of the place where it happened was mentioned again and again—Burntollet. It was, said the television reporters, an "ambush."

After that, the situation in Northern Ireland seemed to get worse every day. There were riots and petrol bombs being thrown in Belfast and Derry. On the BBC and UTV it was called Londonderry, but on RTÉ it was Derry. Everybody knew the geography of Derry from watching the news. The street names became familiar to us from accounts of riots and barriers and blockades.

The star of the Catholic side was Bernadette Devlin, from the People's Democracy movement. She was a student with long dark hair; she wore miniskirts and talked with a hard Ulster accent, like a fire was inside her. The way she moved on TV, pulling her long hair back behind her ears, holding a microphone and giving a big smile when she finished talking, she could have been a pop star like Cilla Black or Lulu. She was all energy and movement and anger. Everybody adored her.

During the next few months, there were constant riots in Derry as the Catholics in the Bogside slum refused to let the police into the area. Over and over, RTÉ showed the sign in the Catholic area that said "You Are Now Entering Free Derry." Bernadette was always there, throwing stones, fighting back. The cameras always found her. She helped teenage boys smash up the pavement for stones to throw at the police. Her hand kept going to her hair to pull it back behind her ears. She wore no coat even though it was cold and the police were using water cannons on the protestors. She had such strength and rage. She was Ireland itself.

Every week the rioting seemed to become more intense. In the British election that April, Bernadette Devlin was elected an MP, the youngest ever. She was only twenty-one years old. Captain O'Neill resigned. Another man replaced him, but nobody seemed to be in charge. It was one riot after another.

Then the focus moved to Belfast and the riots there. RTÉ said that Protestant gangs were trying to drive Catholics from their homes. The BBC just said there were riots. UTV said the police were trying to calm the situation. On RTÉ we saw long sequences of footage, without commentary, of the riots at night, petrol bombs being thrown into Catholic homes and people fleeing. Dad said there was going to be outright war inside Northern Ireland. It had already started. It was as plain as a poke in your eye.

That year, the Americans sent men into space and the astronauts walked around on the moon, and people in Carrick saw that but they hardly talked about it. The day after Neil Armstrong walked on the moon, there were more riots in Belfast. Catholic families escaped from their burning homes in the night and you could see women carrying pictures of the Sacred Heart as they ran down the street. I saw one woman clutching the picture to her side as she ran, with Jesus' face and the compassion in his eyes, as Mr. Daly has described it to us. The TV camera showed the Sacred Heart bobbing up and down as the woman ran, and then the woman's face, rigid with fear. Protestant gangs and men called the B-Specials, auxiliary forces to assist the police at riots, were said to be behind it all. Some people on TV said that the plan was to drive the Catholics out of Northern Ireland forever. Nobody was just talking. Everybody shouted and screamed.

The prime minister of Ireland, Jack Lynch, went on RTÉ to address the nation. He said the Irish government and people would not stand by and just watch what was happening in Northern Ireland. I wondered what he meant. It must be time for action, for Ireland to fight back. Everybody expected that, but maybe he couldn't say that out loud because he'd give away the plan. Maybe what he said was only vague words to cover up the action that was coming.

Two nights later, Mam woke Máire and me in the middle of night. In an excited but hushed voice, she told us to come to the window of the front bedroom and see what was happening outside. We stood in our pyjamas and, half asleep and a little afraid, we looked out on the road, usually silent and empty at night. Irish army trucks were slowly going by, dozens of them, one after the other. It took hours for them to pass. We could see the soldiers in the back of some of the trucks, with their green berets, not saying anything, just staring out at the road.

We thought Ireland was invading the North to save the Catholics and take back Ulster. There would be a war between England and Ireland again. On our road it looked like there were hundreds of troops heading for the border with Northern Ireland. Maybe on other roads leading to the North there were hundreds more green trucks with more soldiers heading off to war. It was impossible to get back to sleep after that. The thought of war to reclaim the North from Britain was exciting and nerve-wracking.

The next morning we listened to the radio anxiously, waiting to hear the news about the invasion. But the news never came and the invasion never happened. The Irish army had moved to some border posts and set up field hospitals for Catholics who were fleeing Belfast and Derry. They were helping, not fighting.

Dad wasn't there to see the Irish soldiers pass along the road in Cortober, heading for the border. Dad was in Dublin. Irish Life had transferred him there, and in a few weeks we would all be living in Dublin.

PART THREE

AND NOW FOR SOMETHING
COMPLETELY DIFFERENT

CHAPTER THIRTEEN

THE CULCHIE

One wet October evening in 1969 I was watching
television alone when I saw something that made me
laugh out loud. I couldn't stop. I was cackling and banging
the arm of the chair. Mam came in from the kitchen to see
what was so funny. She glanced at the screen and saw what
looked like an arts program on the BBC. Somebody was
being interviewed and both the guest and the host of the
program were talking in typically posh BBC-style accents.
Mam gave me a look that told me she thought I was being
peculiar and went back to the kitchen.

It was, I told her later, a spoof. You see, this BBC interviewer was talking to a famous film director about his
films, except that the interviewer kept getting stuck on
the film director's name. He was called Sir Edward

something-or-other. The host was asking if he could call him Edward. That was fine. Then it was a question about the possibility of calling him Ted. Then the interviewer started calling him "pussycat" and Sir Edward something-or-other got annoyed and just walked out. But he came back when the interviewer fella apologized. Everything was going smoothly again. But as soon as Sir Edward started talking and got into his stride answering the questions, the host fella glared at him and said, "Oh, shut up!" It was craic—that Irish word that meant fun and sarcasm done with gusto.

Mam said it sounded like a *Carry On* comedy, but it wasn't. Every skit on the show was angry as well as absurd. They were attacking rules and authority with an almighty rage. It was called *Monty Python's Flying Circus* and it was immediately clear to me that some very, very angry and sarcastic people were behind it. It popped up on the BBC out of nowhere. In Dublin we could get four channels, including the new BBC2, so I could see dozens of odd shows that came on late in the evening. There were chat shows, comedy shows, sports shows and documentaries from all over the world. A lot of it was eccentric. You never knew what you'd find. It could be something about Northern Ireland or something about the U.S.S.R. Shows came and went quickly and they started and ended at peculiar times because neither BBC channel had advertising. Programs could start at 9:55 p.m. or 11:03 p.m. If it was rude and involved what I soon realized was the BBC2 specialty, showing women's breasts, it was usually on after ten. After Mam and Dad had finished watching the news on RTÉ and shook their heads about events in Northern Ireland, they would head for the kitchen for tea or a drink, and I would change the channels and keep watching.

The first Monty Python program I saw that October night was called "Whither Canada?" but Canada and where it was going were never mentioned. I knew the idea that there would a discussion about Canada was droll because everybody would turn it off. I would probably have changed the channel too. That was the first joke. The faces and voices of some of the performers on *Monty Python's Flying Circus* were already familiar to me. They'd been on many of the skit shows we'd seen from the BBC or UTV in Carrick. But this show wasn't jolly, gently funny or wacky like those ones. These men seemed to be in an awful rage, particularly about the BBC. A lot of what they did was to mock the BBC seriousness and the BBC rules and traditions they obviously found ludicrous. You only saw how pretentious the BBC was when it was mocked on the BBC itself. There was a bit about famous dead people and the way they died. It was a spoof of what the BBC often did on Sunday evenings, with programs about long-dead saints and figures from history. As Monty Python saw it, droning about long-dead saints was absurd.

There was a vaguely Irish quality to the humour of Monty Python, that trick of turning things on their head with a savage twist and just leaving them there, for all to see their patent absurdity. But there was something specific about Monty Python's comedy too. It was all about attacking rules, proper behaviour and the standard way of doing things. They mocked the upper class, the middle class and the working class. Everything was ridiculous to them. These men were seething with fury about rigid ways of seeing, talking and behaving. I needed it and relished it.

We had come to Dublin in the summer of 1969, at the same time as British troops were arriving in Belfast. A few days after Jack Lynch had given his speech on TV, it wasn't Irish troops who poured into the North. It was British soldiers, arriving in the hundreds. They were there to restore order. At least that was what all the British politicians said on TV. At first there was great relief. Dad said it was Protestant gangs and the police who were causing all the trouble. The British army was there to put a stop to it. They had no quarrel with Catholics in Belfast and Derry. On RTÉ and the BBC news, we'd seen the troops being given cups of tea by housewives in the Catholic areas of Belfast. Everybody was smiling. Some women gave the soldiers tea in china cups and some gave them flasks of hot tea they could drink on their break. The women were pleased that the British government had sent in the army to stop the petrol bombs raining down on their homes and angry Protestant mobs screaming at them to go live somewhere else, among their own kind. Everybody knew that some Protestant gangs were trying to clear out Catholics from certain areas, house by house. They didn't want Catholics living near them.

When the British army came and politicians from London kept going to Belfast to have meetings, there was hope that something would truly change. Every day on the

TV news, the British politicians were making promises. They said they would ensure that there was fairness in allocating housing in Ulster. They said the local governments would be reformed. They said the B-Specials would be disbanded and, eventually, local people, both Protestant and Catholic, would make up the police force. But under the surface you could tell something else was happening after the British army arrived. When the Irish army hadn't invaded to protect the Catholics and claim Northern Ireland, some Northern Catholics had taken up the fight themselves. It wasn't petrol bombs and stones being thrown any more. Shots were being fired on the streets of Belfast. On the TV news and discussion programs there was talk about the Irish Republican Army being reactivated. The news showed footage of men with rifles and handguns, shadowy figures behind walls and barricades, aiming their guns at the British troops. At the same time, Protestants were shooting at Catholics. All the British soldiers had guns and could shoot at anybody.

It was eerie and uncomfortable to watch it happen. Those people who had been on the civil rights marches looked so ordinary, like anybody you'd know, and I didn't want to think about people who looked like us being shot dead just walking down to the shops or coming home from work. Watching RTÉ and the BBC, it looked, and felt, like another war of independence was beginning. The IRA, an army from the distant past and made up of old men with long memories, was emerging from the burning streets and from behind the barricades of burning cars and rubble. Their guns and ammunition had probably come from other old men living high in the famine-ravaged hills of Leitrim and Cavan. Dad told me that people had whispered about guns buried in the fields, hidden but never forgotten. You never knew when the fight for Ireland against English rule would start again. And now it had.

In Dublin, though, on our new street, it barely mattered. Dublin was very different from Carrick-on-Shannon. To me, it was more terrifying than Belfast or Derry. It was a shock, and worse, a fist-in-your-face kind of shock.

We had moved to Raheny, a suburb on the north side of the city, about five miles from the centre. Our house was number 95 Avondale Park. There were only 101 houses in Avondale Park, and we were near the end of the cul-de-sac where the street turned in on itself and ended. That was the first thing I noticed—the cul-de-sac. There was no way out. Instead of open fields at the back, we had a tiny lawn surrounded by high walls. At the front was another tiny lawn, and across the narrow street, instead of quiet, empty roads and more empty fields, there sat a triangle of grass, grandly called "a park," where children played. At its far end was a wire fence and on the other side of the fence, a filthy stream trickled slowly down toward Dublin Bay and the sea. On the other side of the stream was another wire fence, this one topped with sharp barbed wire. That fence marked the perimeter of a private girls' school, Manor House, which had a big field where the girls played field hockey. Beyond that was a busy road where cars and trucks passed endlessly.

At first, Raheny was strange and frightening. Avondale Park was welcoming to Mam and Dad but hard to penetrate for a child. It was tightly knit and steeped in its own rigid rules of hierarchy and prejudice. It was solidly, savagely middle class, but it was lower middle class. There was no worse class in Ireland then. Everybody was trying to escape the taint of working-class existence, accent and attitudes. If you were twelve years old and had spent your short life so far in the fields of Leitrim and a small town in Tipperary, you hadn't a clue.

On my first morning in Dublin I set up an elaborate toy I'd been given years before. It was a matter of constructing a long track for little battery-operated cars to race along. I set it up on the narrow cement pavement from the front door to the gate out onto the street. The idea was to alert other boys on the street that I was there. The cars and the tracks would attract them, I hoped. It was hours before anybody came along. The first boy who did looked at the cars for a few minutes and then at me. He asked me where I was from. I said we'd moved from Carrick-on-Shannon in Leitrim. He said he'd never heard of it. A minute later, one of his pals came along. The first boy smiled at him, cocked his head toward me and said, "He's a culchie. From somewhere in Leitrim." Then they both laughed. The second boy stared at the cars and at the track and looked at me with a smirk. "Howya, Benjy," he said.

I had no idea what to say. Benjy on *The Riordans* was as removed from me as he was from these two Dublin boys. Still, as far as they were concerned, I had cow dung dripping from my shoes and I was used to travelling around on a tractor. It was my accent that gave it all away. The two boys, and probably their families too, were instantly sensitive to accents. They could tell whether someone was from the upper or middle class and who went to a posh school. They could tell whether somebody was from the south side of Dublin rather than the north side. Everything hinged on fixing a person inside the tricky Dublin class system. But culchies were easy. All culchies were stupid and had no notion of what Dublin was about. They all lived on farms and stank of manure. They were slow witted and poor. They had the wrong name for everything.

"Culchie" was the name all people from the country were given in lower-middle-class Dublin. It didn't matter if you were from the tenements of inner-city Cork or the most remote farmhouse in the Kerry mountains. You were still a culchie. Being from Dublin was important. Being from anywhere else in the country made you a nobody and a figure of fun. Mam and Dad were culchies too, but they could probe this new Dublin world with far more confidence than Máire or I. One reason Dad had bought the house at 95 Avondale Park was that he'd gone next door to talk to the neighbour when he had inspected the house. A lovely, friendly woman named Kathleen O'Reilly had greeted him. Kathleen was from Donegal and married to Pat, a true born-and-bred Dubliner. Kathleen talked fondly of Leitrim and country people, and Dad had decided she would be a good neighbour.

Sometimes people admitted that they were originally from somewhere else, or that their parents were. Sometimes they didn't, even if Dad found out later that the man who claimed to be a Dubliner had been born on the banks of the Shannon near Limerick and hadn't been to Dublin until he came to get a job in the city. It was just easier to say you were from Dublin, if you didn't have an accent that marked you as being obviously from somewhere else. At least you were better than somebody who could be taken for a fool just arrived from the bog somewhere. It was very important to be better than somebody else.

By living in Avondale Park you were automatically better than somebody who lived in St. Eanna's Park, where there were Dublin Corporation houses that people didn't own. They only paid rent to the Corporation. Many of the fathers there worked for Dublin Corporation, driving buses, fixing the roads or even sweeping the streets. But even if you lived in Avondale Park you weren't as good as the people who lived on the Howth Road, the main thoroughfare that linked the inner city with the old fishing town of Howth at the northern edge of Dublin Bay. Avondale Park was a tangle of a street off the Howth Road. Houses on the Howth Road were bigger and better and were owned by civil servants, doctors, dentists and accountants. It was a huge step up from Avondale Park.

If you lived in Avondale Park you weren't quite as good as people who lived in Mayfield, the more open, tree-lined estate that sat beside Avondale Park and was a turn left, instead of right, after you left the Howth Road. In

Mayfield, there were more trees, and the gardens, front and back, were slightly bigger. Some of the houses were detached, and even the semi-detached ones were a few inches wider than the houses in Avondale Park. That meant the living rooms with the TV sets and the record players were a little bigger. If you lived in Avondale Park you lived in stark, sullen daily envy of people who lived in Mayfield. Families who lived in Mayfield sent their children to schools in Sutton, which had a nicer-sounding name than Raheny. Raheny was a bit of a step down from Sutton. In Sutton all the kids were definitely middle middle class. There weren't any working-class children out there with their rough accents and wonky ideas that the best job you could get when you left school was putting on a uniform and driving a Dublin bus. When I lived in Raheny, we hardly ever met anybody from Sutton. We only heard about them. We barely saw people from Mayfield. We rarely spoke to them and they didn't go walking down Avondale Park.

And then there was the territory north of the Howth Road. The streets up there were just the same as Avondale Park or Mayfield and the people there observed the same small, subtle gradations of class among themselves, but beyond their streets was what some people called Apache Territory. The fields north of the settled estates had been bought up by Dublin Corporation and the county council and were being turned into huge estates for the working-class families who were moving out of the inner city. The place was called Kilbarrack. Some homes were finished already, but it was mostly acres of half-built houses, half-finished streets and no shops or other amenities. And that meant the Kilbarrack kids had plenty of space to roam and play. Sometimes they crossed the boundary into old Raheny, where they shouted, stole things and made sarcastic remarks. They were feared and loathed. Old Raheny lived in terror of them, the hordes from the inner-city slums suddenly let loose in the sprawling suburban streets.

They were reputed to wander in gangs, damage cars, trample on flowers and steal from gardens. People said they really should have been moved somewhere else by the Corporation or the council or whomever decided to put them on the edge of Raheny. People who had paid good money for homes in Raheny and maintained them as nice middle-class homes had rights too. And one of those rights was not to have your property values lowered by the council deciding to move thousands of working-class people into your area. Those people were used to living in tenements. Most of them hadn't had a house before. Put them in a place that was still half countryside but close to nice homes, and they'd naturally go wild. Hadn't anybody in authority thought of that? They'd be close to nice middle-class homes with cars and televisions and record players and all sorts of gizmos that they weren't able to afford. They'd envy and hate and steal, wouldn't they? It stood to reason they would.

Culchies, Kilbarrack and Corporation houses. That's all I heard about my first few months in Dublin. Everybody was always on the verge of being upset about something.

Everybody was looking for ways to be superior. Nenagh had nothing on suburban Dublin. But *Monty Python's Flying Circus* stabbed at the heart of pretension and snobbery. It was a relief to learn that other people, even if they were actors and writers in England, working for the BBC and hating it, were just as angered by the snobbery, rigidity and rules that seeped into every aspect of existence. *Monty Python* was like manna to me. I was awed and amazed by Dublin. Smarting from insults and ignominy, I was ready for rage. I was almost a teenager.

CHAPTER FOURTEEN

DUBLIN BOYS AND GIRLS

Mr. Ingoldsby was in charge of Scoil Assaim, the St. Assam's senior school for boys in Raheny. I went to Scoil Assaim for the final two years of primary school. From the first day, I knew that this was going to be vastly different from going to school in Carrick. For a start, everybody seemed to talk in another language. The language was Dublin slang, and for me it was new words and phrases to learn every day.

No boy called Mr. Ingoldsby by his full name. He was Ingo. Mr. Craydon, the terrifying maths teacher, was Craydo; homework was called "exercises" by the teachers but "eccer" by the boys. Complaining was "giving out." The bathroom was "the jacks." Someone's house was "a gaff," most houses were "a kip," girls were called "moths" (pronounced "motts") and everybody's mother was called "the old dear," "the ould wan" or "the ma." All boys' names were shortened or lengthened. Anybody named Anthony was Anto, Declan was Deco, Myles was Myleser. Instantly, I was Doyler, if I wasn't "the culchie." Most words were preceded by "bleedin'," as in "I'm not going to the bleedin' jacks in yer man's bleedin' gaff 'cos his bleedin' ould wan is there and she'll be givin' out." To be embarrassed was to be "mortified," shortened to "morto," and to be really embarrassed was to be "scarlet." An eejit was a "sap" and the words "arse" and "hole" were interchangeable.

It wasn't hard to learn the dense slang of schoolboys, but I had to be careful to get it right. If you didn't get it right you were a sap, and just another culchie. There was pride in using the most aggressive phrasing. I soon noticed that the boys had an almost fanatical devotion to colourful expressions of hunger. At lunchtime, when the boys were hungry for something to eat and heading for the fish and chips shop—the "chipper"—devouring their sandwiches, called "sambos," or racing home for a meal, the phrases became intense. "I could eat a baby's arse through the bars of a cot," one would say. Another would counter with, "I'd eat a farmer's arse through a blackthorn bush!" A third would up the ante with "I could eat a nun's arse through a convent gate." Unused to the language and still largely without friends, I didn't dare enter the competition. I just listened cautiously. This was about hunger and famine. It was rural Ireland talk, really. An avid watcher, and now with an accent that set me apart, I was well prepared for staying quiet. At the back of my mind I noted the intensity of the expressions of hunger and wondered. Did they learn these phrases from their fathers and mothers, who'd learned them from their own parents?

There were countless words for being drunk. These were mostly featured in stories about older brothers or fathers who had been seen coming home from the pub, or the "boozer." To be drunk was to be locked, langered, paralytic, fluthered, footless, motherless, mouldy, gee-eyed, shellacked, banjaxed, scuttered, sozzled and stocious. Most of these words and phrases were working-class slang, and the boys in St. Assam's school only used them to act tough. They weren't working class at all. I knew their parents were anxious for them to be as middle class as possible. It was all a con.

Adapting to the language and attitudes of the boys at St. Assam's was tricky enough, but the schoolwork was also a trial. It was soon clear that, by Dublin standards, the easygoing brothers in Carrick had taught me hardly anything. Mam and Dad were informed that I was behind in every subject except Irish. There were schoolbooks I didn't have and math principles I didn't know and I was completely backward in science. This wouldn't do. The big drive at St. Assam's was to prepare boys for the entry exams for good secondary schools. As far as I could see, all parents were obsessed with the secondary schools their boys could enter. There were the famous, la-di-da ones such as Belvedere and Gonzaga, where the boys wore uniforms, played rugby and, according to the talk, automatically became part of the country's elite. Just by attending

Belvedere or Gonzaga you could get any job you wanted. Then there was the famous O'Connell's School, run by the Christian Brothers in the north end of the inner city. O'Connell's was famous for its motley mix of students from all backgrounds. It wasn't elitist but it had very high standards and had produced many boys who went on to university. Mam and Dad decided, after being told by the teachers at St. Assam's, that I was at such an academic disadvantage that I should aim for O'Connell's School. It was easier to get into, but hard work after you got in.

Because I was considered backward in so many subjects, the teachers scrutinized me. Being almost fluent in Irish gave me a small advantage with some teachers, but it marked me as an obvious culchie with the other boys. They believed that only people in remote rural Ireland had the slightest knowledge of the Gaelic language and in Dublin it was completely useless, for saps only.

After the relaxed style of the brothers in Carrick, Dublin teachers were ferocious. The maths teacher, Mr. Craydon, continually set me tasks above my knowledge level to determine just how backward I was. Once, when we had completed an assignment in class, he assessed the answers while we sat there, quietly. When he got to mine, he saw a muddle of wrong answers. He said, "Doyle!" and when I looked up at him I saw a metal stapler flying at my face. I dodged it just in time and it smashed against the wall behind me. That was Craydon's specialty. For punishment, we were supposed to be sent down to Ingo's office to be hit with a leather strap, but Craydo and other teachers had their own methods. Craydo kept an array of objects on his desk to be flung at you. The duster he used to wipe clean the blackboard was his favourite, and you could only hope that it was the soft side that hit you on the head or in the face, rather than the hard wooden side. Sometimes he just threw what was nearest his hand. We all kept an eye on where the heavy metal stapler was sitting. Once, having wandered away from his desk, he whipped his car keys out of his pocket and flung them at somebody.

If Craydon's flying objects had to be avoided in the classroom, gangs of belligerent boys had to be avoided on the way home after school. Loosely knit gangs from certain streets or estates would form in the schoolyard. These weren't the legendary savages from Kilbarrack. They were only middle-class hardmen out to prove something. Sometimes they'd decide to pick a fight with boys from another street. Sometimes they'd decide to try to hit every boy who wore glasses. Sometimes they'd decide to pick on the culchie. If they singled me out, they'd first try to make me say something so they could mock my pronunciation. Then the pushing and shoving would start. The important thing was not to be pushed onto the ground, where you'd be trapped and one of them might fail to resist the temptation to kick your prone body.

The first time it happened to me, I was pushed and shoved, yet I stayed on my feet, saying little. They grabbed my schoolbag and threw my books around the street. That caught the attention of a teacher passing in a car. He stopped, rolled down his window and told everyone to pick up the books and get moving. The gang scattered and I retrieved my books, dodging traffic. There was little I could do, being new and not yet having a group of friends to protect me. But on the following Saturday afternoon, I saw one of the gang walking toward me on the street. He was on his own and kept his eyes averted from me. I did the same, but just as I passed him I swung out my fist and landed it square on his nose. He groaned and swore, and his knees buckled under him with the pain and shock as he tried to run. I said to him, "You're not so tough on your own, are you, you thick Jackeen?" He never came near me again, on the street or in the schoolyard, but there were dozens more who wanted to bully somebody. I had decided on my tactic. I was like Illya Kuryakin. Wait. Watch. I wouldn't be bothered to fight groups of the bullies. I'd try to remember their faces and, when I met them alone, I'd let them know that revenge was inevitable.

Soccer saved me. In Dublin every boy was soccer mad. It didn't matter if you were working class or middle class, you still followed soccer intensely and played it at every opportunity. Nobody thought that I would know anything about soccer. Culchies generally didn't. They knew about Gaelic football and hurling, but soccer was for city boys. To know a lot about English soccer was sophistication itself to twelve-year-olds in Dublin. I didn't have the fanatic's knowledge that the others boys at school had developed, but it wasn't hard to figure it out. Manchester United had the best team in the world. Georgie Best was the greatest player in the world. I knew that already.

Georgie Best was from Belfast and that wasn't quite as good as being from Dublin, but it was close enough. Everybody collected pictures of him and picked up English soccer magazines to see more photos of him. In Dublin, Georgie Best wasn't just a player. He was a god. He played with the ease and skill of a soccer magician. He had long hair and long sideburns, and women loved him too. He was often in the papers, for going on a date with Miss World or getting thrown out of some nightclub because somebody had started a fight with him. He always looked like a fella who should be singing in a band. He was a playboy, the papers said. If he didn't keep scoring goals for Manchester United, he'd get the sack because he was too interested in women and boozing. He was a rebel.

Almost everybody followed Manchester United, not just because they were winners. They had won the European Cup in 1968, the first English team to conquer Europe. But it was something more complicated about Manchester United and their popularity in Dublin. I studied the team's history closely, just to be in the know. The story of Manchester United was a story of tragedy and triumph. Many of the team's young players had been killed in a plane crash in 1958—the Munich Disaster, it was called—which created a lot of sympathy for the team. At a time when English soccer clubs hired only local players and scoffed at outsiders, Manchester United had scoured Ireland for promising youngsters and the club didn't care that they were Irish and Catholic. There were loads of Catholics in Manchester, apparently, people who were as devout as Irish Catholics. Nobby Stiles, who played for United and was from Manchester, was such an old-fashioned Catholic that he wouldn't eat meat on a Friday. It said so in the Dublin paper. Manchester United's men were bigger than English prejudice. They were going to be the best club in Europe and they weren't going to do that by only hiring local Protestants. In Dublin, they were called Man United, and that meant something too. They were about unifying people by being better, more stylish and more sophisticated than all the other clubs.

All the boys watched *Match of the Day* on BBC on Saturday nights. A game was shown that had taken place that afternoon and, although we all knew the result of the game, we watched avidly, especially if Manchester United was playing. Georgie Best floated around the field, waiting for the ball and then showing off his skills, twisting this way and that past the defenders, his long hair flowing behind him. The crowd in the stadium roared him on and I did too, at home. I felt part of the crowd in the English stadium, cheering on the man from Belfast, and when they sang their songs, I wanted to join in. The boys and men in the crowds at the games in England looked just like people in Dublin, except that they were right there, watching the game. They didn't have to wait to see it later on television, and I was jealous of that. But I was glad the BBC was available, to show me Georgie Best scoring goals and being the best player. I felt a tingle of excitement watching those English soccer games, something that never happened when Gaelic games were shown on TV. Even the theme music from *Match of the Day* was thrilling. The only music you heard at the start of a Gaelic game was the Irish national anthem.

If you followed Manchester United, you could talk to other boys. They always wanted to know which team you supported and who was your favourite player. They wanted you to despise other teams and other players. Some boys took an independent stand and insisted on following Leeds United or Chelsea. Leeds was the team nipping at Manchester United's heels. They were winners and played a rough, hard game. Leeds also had Johnny Giles as a star player, and Johnny Giles was from Dublin. At one time he played for Man United, but he didn't like the set-up and he went off to Leeds, where he helped the team start winning. If you followed Man United, the only Leeds player who was any good was Johnny Giles. If you followed Leeds, you had to admit that Georgie Best was good, but you had to say that he wasn't a tough guy like the Leeds players.

The Leeds shirt was all white, which showed that they didn't go in for fancy nonsense with colours and designs on their shirts and shorts. They were just hardmen, kicking and tackling and winning at all costs. Boys who followed Chelsea followed the club because it was glamorous. Chelsea was in London and the players were brilliant but casual. They won sometimes, but they played as if they didn't care. Their followers were snooty about every other team. It was an attitude. In London the Chelsea area was associated with fashion and pop groups. It was about attaching yourself to something more fashionable. It was about being closer to England. Hardly anybody talked about Northern Ireland and what was happening there. The point was to admire England and the English.

At St. Assam's and in Avondale Park, loners and misfits came to be my friends, boys who'd been wounded by saying the wrong thing in the schoolyard and mocked for it, or had an abiding interest in things that were scorned by others—reading books, studying trains, collecting stamps. They drifted toward me, spotting another outsider. They didn't care if I was a culchie.

And then there were girls. In Carrick, we'd been innocent, too young yet, in a town of relaxed, country attitudes, to be interested in girls and sex. In Dublin, boys of my age were years ahead. Some had girlfriends and claimed to be busy most evenings French kissing and feeling them up in lanes or in the big St. Anne's public park. A pretty girl was "a ride"; there was an obsession with girls who had breasts or "monster tits." A vagina was "a gee" or "gills." It was all a foreign language to me.

The older girls from the Manor House school were the ultimate objects of desire. The nuns at Manor House, The Poor Servants of the Mother of God, were strict and that added to the girls' allure. The girls were sized up for their legs, breasts and arses. Mid-afternoon, when their school day was finished, they'd appear on the streets like flocks of exotic birds, in their pale blue uniforms of long skirts and V-necked sweaters. The tall, gangly ones, with their skirts swaying, looked like Victorian ladies out for a stroll,

absorbed in their own conversations and completely indif-
ferent to schoolboys loitering on the street and looking at
them. They had a haughtiness that was impenetrable.
Some smoked cigarettes as they strolled along, one arm
holding the cigarette and the other across the bosom.
They'd roll up their sleeves to catch the small bit of colour
that might come from the watery sun, or they'd sit on the
bench by the bus stop, their long skirts hitched up enough
for the sun to reach their legs. They didn't pay attention to
anything or anyone but themselves.

I asked other boys if they'd seen *Monty Python's Flying
Circus* on the BBC. None had, and it was another year
before the series caught on. The shows they watched constantly were the English comedies like *On the Buses* and
The Liver Birds. The vaguely dirty jokes of *On the Buses*
were memorized and repeated, especially if they involved
knockers, knickers or tits. For a while, the only common
ground in taste for television shows was *The Dave Allen
Show*. Allen, an Irish-born comedian, would sit in a chair
and tell weird, absorbing, long-winded jokes that sometimes touched on the differences between the Irish and
the English, sometimes attacked the Catholic Church
and generally had something to do with the wantonness
of certain women.

One evening that long winter of 1969, I was at home
alone, watching Dave Allen spin his gossamer-thin stories,
when the doorbell rang. When I answered I was surprised
to find Maria Cullen, a teenage girl from down the street,
standing there smiling, with a cloth bag rolled tightly in

her hand. Maria Cullen was about sixteen years old. She was tall and beautiful and had an abundance of light brown hair. She was one of those girls who could be seen in Raheny with other schoolgirls in their uniforms in the afternoons, hanging around, ignoring schoolboys and enjoying the attention from passing men in cars or trucks. She'd never spoken to me, and I was sure she didn't know I existed.

She nervously apologized for disturbing me and told me, in a rapid, rehearsed way, that her mam had forgotten to order coal and the coal was being delivered the next day, but in the meantime they'd run short and her mam had sent her to ask if we could spare enough coal to light a fire for the evening. I babbled back at her. "That's grand. No problem at all, isn't it fierce cold for the night, sure we have loads of coal in the back, come in, come in." I sounded like somebody on *The Riordans*. While she waited with a smile of embarrassment frozen hard on her face, I went to the back shed and filled her bag with as much coal as it could hold. She thanked me and left as fast as she could.

I told Mam and Dad when they came home. They exchanged looks. It took me a few minutes to grasp the meaning, but I heard Mam muttering about those poor Cullen people, trying to keep up appearances when there was a rumour that the father was out of work, and now it seemed the rumour was confirmed because they had no money to heat the house. They'd probably sent the girl to our house because we were new and less likely to make much of the request, or because we were country people and used to such things. It was only then that I grasped the terrible shame that Maria Cullen had suffered, coming to ask me for coal on a cold winter's night. It would be years before Maria would even look at me again.

CHAPTER FIFTEEN

IT'S NOT UNUSUAL

LATE ON A DAMP SATURDAY afternoon in the winter of 1970, I sat on the number 29 bus in Raheny village waiting to go into the city centre, or "town" as everybody in Raheny called the centre of Dublin. I was going to buy yet another textbook that I needed, one that other boys at St. Assam's already had. I'd dawdled at home watching *Grandstand*, the BBC's all-Saturday-afternoon sports program. I was less interested in the racing results and the occasional news flashes from soccer stadiums around England than in the show's never-ceasing movement, its commitment to covering everything. All that effort, with cameras, phones and countless reporters across England delivering bits of news to satisfy people watching at home or, more likely, standing in the smoke-filled bookie's shops in cities across all of England, Scotland, Northern Ireland and the Republic.

I was the only passenger on the bus and I listened to the conductor and the driver talk out the few minutes of their break. They'd paid no attention when I got on, had forgotten me, and they had no reason to notice me now. A small twelve-year-old schoolboy in an anorak, sitting alone, staring out the window, gloved hands clasped together on my lap, for the warmth that was needed in the damp, foggy chill of Raheny on a darkening Saturday. It was the short-back-and-sides haircut that would have marked me as a schoolboy. Like everyone else at St. Assam's I'd sat in Peter Duffy's barbershop to have my hair sheared. It was a dismal, smoky, cold room and it took forever because Peter Duffy always let an adult go first if one came in, even with four schoolboys waiting, reading ancient, grubby copies of *Beano* and *Hotspur* comic books as they waited on the bench. When he finally put you in the chair and wrapped a greasy towel around your neck he didn't even speak. He just made the electric razor go *vroom-vroom* for a second and started shearing. We all came out looking the same.

The style was for longer hair, but if you were still in primary school you had the short-back-and-sides and there was nothing you could do about it. So I sat there, anonymous, a kid with too-short hair, dark and fine Ahern hair though it was, with my ears sticking out and an old plaid wool scarf of Dad's wrapped around my neck. The bus conductor, who was doing most of the talking, had long, lank hair falling over wisps of sideburns on his pinched face. I had only been in Dublin a few months, but I already knew his type. In his early twenties, he looked like he was wound tight with constricted energy, dying to get out of the busman's uniform and act the man about town. He was skinny, pale and almost chinless, with a pointed, crooked nose. I knew the cruel Irish phrase for his type, "*scrioba leis an grinneall*," the scrapings of the pot. It meant he was the last-born of a large family and had emerged weak and pale, as if his mother and father no longer had the strength to create a strong-featured child. I'd never have said that phrase out loud, but I knew it. I knew this conductor too. He was often on the route and I'd seen his technique. He was a devil for pouncing on young women for their fares when the bus was moving fast. He'd descend on them, with a vague smirk on his face, and sway above them as the bus moved and bounced. As they fumbled for the change to pay the fare, he would look down the front of their dresses or coats, trying to catch a look at their breasts.

I sat silent and still on a back seat, and listened to the conductor talk to the driver, an older, bulkier man.

"Are you going to the hop?"

"What fuckin' hop?"

"Up at the Ierene. The busmans' dance."

"I will in me hole. The Ierene is full of culchies."

"Ah go on. It's only a shilling in, if you show your busman's card. Loads of women."

"Culchie women. Who's playing?"

"The Indians."

"Not those fuckin' eejits dressed up as red fuckin' Indians. That's for fuckin' culchies."

"Ah but—the culchie women, now. They're mad for it. Randy, they are. Give 'em a few jars and they're fuckin' gaggin' for it."

"Sez who? You and your fuckin' shorty friends."

"My arse. You shoulda seen 'em goin' for Maccer last month. One bird took off her knickers and threw 'em at him when he started singing 'Delilah.' It was at the end of the dance. He was telling his mates he could sing better than yer man in the band, so one of the mates dared him to sing to the young wans. They were meltin' for him. I was pissing meself. When Maccer got her knickers he shoved them down his trousers."

"Who the fuck is Maccer?"

"Ah ya know him—Tony Mac from up in Harmonstown. A big, wide fucker, with the long sideburns. He looks like Tom Jones. That's why yer culchie one threw her knickers at him."

"Are you seriously telling me that some young one took off her fuckin' knickers and threw them at him?"

"I seen it meself. He was well jarred. He threw out his arms and started singing 'Delilah.' The voice on the fucker. He was louder than the fuckin' band. The culchie birds were gapin' at him. Then one of them threw her knickers at him. Like I told ya. True as I'm sitting here."

"I'd pay to see that all right. But I'm not going near the fuckin' Ierene. There's a smell of Benjy off that fuckin' place."

I was a good boy, but this was information worth storing. It was better than being a culchie who didn't have a clue. I knew about Tom Jones from television. Tom Jones had been the top man on TV for a while and he had everybody talking. Opinion was divided on his salty humour, but it was only the old grannies with their rosary beads who didn't like it. In Dublin, Tom Jones was adored. There was a whiff of raw sex about him. A lot of people thought it was all made up, for publicity, but everyone knew the stories about women throwing their underwear at him. Imagine that. Women throwing knickers at yer man, the big Welsh bruiser, and him famous for being able to lower fourteen pints down his gullet before he'd go on the stage to belt out songs and swing his hips for the women.

I knew it helped that Tom Jones was Welsh, not English, and he never tired of saying it. Watching Tom Jones on television was like watching a rude joke go on and on. It was about some sexually uninhibited world that existed somewhere else. But if you believed the lads at school and now the bus conductor's boasting, there were certain women, right there in Dublin, drunk on Baby Cham in city centre dance halls, who'd fling their underwear at some fella just because he looked like Tom Jones.

The boys at school said Tom Jones had a reputation for being able to shag like a lion. I had only a vague idea what that meant. It was hard to tell if those stories about Tom Jones were real. They seemed outlandish in Raheny, where the lounge bars at night were full of mams and dads talking about their children's entrance exam for some posh school and where the same people's moody, middle-class daughters were standing outside the chipper, giggling and refusing to even look at the young fellas trying to get their attention. You never heard people talking about sex. There was schoolboy boasting and then there were grown-up people who used Tom Jones as an excuse to come at these things sideways.

There was nothing about sex on Irish radio or television, or in the newspapers. Hints about sexual carry-on came only in the English Sunday papers, with their stories about randy vicars, sex-mad pop stars and skirt-chasing soccer players. It was ironic that these stories came in the Sunday papers. In Raheny, Sundays began with the parade to mid-morning Mass. Hardly anybody drove, not because they didn't have cars but because the walk was an opportunity to parade your family and the clothes on their backs. The church in Raheny was the Church of Our Lady Mother of Divine Grace, a spectacular structure in the centre of the old village. You could see it for miles, and you were meant to. It looked like an exaggerated version of the ancient Catholic churches dotted around the Irish countryside. It even had a tall bell tower beside the entrance, and the doorway itself was a semicircular opening placed under a triangular thing that soared upwards. I compared it with the old church in Nenagh, which had been deliberately designed to be bigger than the castle. The Raheny church was the same thing, I knew, only more modern. It was brazen.

On Sundays, from the nearby streets and estates, the parishioners came. A plethora of mothers in Jackie

Kennedy suits and coats, their children bathed and brushed for Sunday in their once-a-week outfits, shoes polished. The dads were in suits and narrow ties, and the rich, important dads had Crombie overcoats. After Mass came the ritual of Sunday dinner, prepared by the mams while the dads had a pint at the Raheny Inn, the Cedars or the Manhattan Bar. The mothers cooked, coaxing the children to lay the tables, all the while making mental notes of who had been wearing what at the church and whose husband hadn't turned up for Mass, not because he worked a job that required a Sunday shift but because he was too shattered from the Saturday-night drinking.

Two sounds battled in many houses on Sunday afternoon. The radios would be tuned to RTÉ for an hour-long news program that covered all the big stories. If the radio was left on, there followed loud, frantic reports of Gaelic games from around the country, delivered by men with hard country accents, their voices going up and down in the sing-song style of RTÉ radio announcers as they blared out clichés about the hard Cork men or mighty Galway defences. Meanwhile, TV sets were tuned to BBC or ITV for the Sunday-afternoon staple, a *Carry On* film, the arch comedy of plummy voices and Cockney accents crashing and cackling together, and the inevitable limp-wristed "ooooooooooh" of Kenneth Williams as he was shocked by some brawny man or bosomy woman. If it wasn't a *Carry On* film, it was ancient comedies about doctors and nurses, or maybe the antics if the St. Trinian's private school girls causing mayhem.

I was twelve, lonely and lost, still adjusting to Dublin. Sundays were torture, with the all-day clash of voices and opinions and attitudes. The radio, with its endless noise of rural Irish voices, all of them excited about events and games that meant nothing among schoolboys in Dublin, was an irritation. In fact, it was an embarrassment to be caught paying attention to those voices and the hurling or Gaelic football games taking place in Cork or Limerick or Galway. Those games were for old men and culchies.

By contrast, what was on television was English and breezy. The zippy comedy, slick innuendo and farces were already old, but I could see they were lazily inhaled in Dublin. Sunday nights were especially worth looking forward to. RTÉ aired *Rowan & Martin's Laugh-In*, and everybody was talking about it. The catch phrases were repeated in the schoolyard, on the bus and in the bars. *Sock it to me. Beautiful downtown Burbank*. When Goldie Hawn appeared, all gangly legs, blond curls and giggle, you could almost feel the hot, sweet breath of America cutting through the grime and grey sulk of Dublin. In America young people were angry. I knew that. There was Vietnam and all the protests. Richard Nixon was the president and a lot of people hated him. *Rowan & Martin's Laugh-In* was making fun of staid old American politicians and the conservatives who supported them. But it was a sunny kind of sarcasm. The young people on the program were trying to be free and different, but they already knew they were different. They were young and beautiful and couldn't care less. From the perspective of Dublin they glowed golden.

In Dublin, England and America seemed closer than they had in Carrick. People didn't talk about the North, as they did back there. It wasn't that it was remote. Belfast was only two hours from Dublin on the train, or two hours' drive up a straight road, but nobody wanted to pay much attention to it. Worrying about the North was under the surface, like a fear you didn't want to admit was gaining on you.

One day in May of 1970, we were late getting off to school. The radio was on in the kitchen and Mam and Dad were trying to catch the news as Máire and I packed our schoolbags before hurrying out. Something had happened, but it was difficult to get a picture of what, exactly, was going on. I could tell from the puzzled look on Dad's face. People had been fired from the government. They might be arrested. But who was it? It couldn't be true that Charles Haughey and Neil Blaney, two ministers in the Irish government, had been fired. It seemed as though it had something to do with the North.

Máire and I walked up the laneway to the Howth Road. There was a house on the corner there and everybody knew that somebody important lived in it, somebody in the government, we knew, because sometimes you saw the big official car parked outside. That morning there were guards everywhere. Garda squad cars were parked helter-skelter around the road, surrounding the house as best they could. A bus going out toward Howth pulled up at the bus stop opposite the house, and some people got off, but the bus didn't move on. You could see the driver and everybody on the bus staring out at the house on the corner. Then a guard, a sergeant or somebody senior from the look of him, came bursting out of a car and roared at the bus driver to move on. Then he stared up and down the road, daring anybody to stop and gawk.

It was the talk of the schoolyard. Charles Haughey, the minister for finance, a local hero who lived like a lord in a North Dublin mansion, had been thrown out of the government. According to the prime minister, Haughey had been trying to import arms to send to the Catholics in Belfast and Derry. Haughey had Neil Blaney, the minister for agriculture, working with him. It was Blaney who had the house on the Howth Road. There was a crisis and the government was split. You couldn't throw two ministers out of the government for trying to help the Catholics in the North. Boys in the schoolyard repeated what their parents were saying—Charlie Haughey would win the day. He had the money and the power. Some said that the prime minister was an eejit, trying to reign in men like Haughey and Blaney. They were tough men. Some boys spouted what their fathers said, that there would be a civil war over this, that the guards and the army would side with Haughey and Blaney and push for Irish intervention in the North. Others said it was all a cod, that Ireland couldn't afford to make the English government angry. If Ireland interfered, the English would stop our exports to England and the country would collapse. Men like Haughey and Blaney should be more interested in building factories in Ireland and creating jobs for people. They were mad to spend money buying guns and ammunition and trying to ship them into the North. What happened to the Catholics in the North was their own problem. Dublin people wanted jobs, not guns and riots.

The excited arguments went back and forth, but I could sense that the dominant view was against Haughey and Blaney. In Raheny, England was too close to seem evil. Nobody really wanted to do battle with England. There was a fear about the stability of Dublin and nervousness about Ireland becoming unravelled by the actions of Republican figures like Haughey and Blaney. Nice middle-class people didn't need to be embroiled in all that trouble, petrol bombs being thrown, riots on the streets and soldiers everywhere trying to keep the peace. I'd seen it in the fury of the garda sergeant who had marched angrily down the Howth Road and told people to keep moving. He didn't want any fuss. He wanted order maintained. Most people did.

Besides, in the schoolyard we had so may English heroes we could hardly hate the English, their government or their soldiers. Just at the time when Haughey and Blaney were charged with running guns into the North, we were gripped by the English soccer team's trip to the World Cup in Mexico. We all collected the coins you got at the Esso stations, the ones with the players' names and heads on them. We begged our dads to go to the Esso station for petrol. The England team had won the World Cup in 1966 and now the best players from the home of soccer were making the long journey to Mexico to play against their old enemy, the Germans, and then the Brazilians, the team that played the fanciest soccer in the world.

The 1970 World Cup had us mesmerized from the moment it started. What was happening in Dublin ceased to matter. The games were aired late at night, but we were all allowed to stay up and watch. On the BBC we could see live games from places named Guadalajara and Puebla-Toluca. A little country like Ireland had no hope of going to the World Cup, so, of course, we cheered for England.

What happened in those few weeks of late-night games, played in the blazing sun of Mexico's cities, changed forever the perspectives and dreams of every boy watching in England and Ireland. The World Cup was a stage, the grandest, most international stage ever created. The first game broadcast was Brazil versus Czechoslovakia, and we were stunned by it. The Czechs scored first. When he scored the goal, the Czech player just kept going, following the ball into the net. He slid to his knees, his arms raised in triumph, and then he did an amazing thing—he blessed himself. Every Catholic boy in Ireland was expected to bless himself ten times a day, for the angelus bells or when passing a church or a graveyard. It was stupid and boys in Dublin just didn't do it. Here was this soccer player making the sign of the cross as he almost burst with joy on a distant Mexican field.

What happened next was magical. The Brazilians were legends, but written about in newspapers, not seen in the flesh or on television. The Brazilians were untroubled by

JOHN DOYLE

the Czech goal. They just took up the game's tempo and
began playing the rhythmic, samba-beat soccer that most of
the world, and certainly those of us in Dublin, had only
ever imagined. They danced with the ball. They caressed it
with their feet. They smiled as they played, enjoying
the slickness of their own movements and the roar of the
crowd as they created an intricate movement that baffled
the Czechs. They scored over and over again. Once, a long,
passing ball floated through the air and Pelé raced toward
it. He took it down on his chest and in one movement he
volleyed it toward the Czech goal and scored. The ball had
never touched the ground. It was ballet and it was beautiful. After seeing that, few of us could sleep. The first game
of the World Cup was more than a game of soccer to us. It
showed us something sublime, and we were giddy with it.

In school the next morning, Ingo came to talk to us. As
headmaster he had to say a few words about boys staying
up late to watch the World Cup. It wasn't good to be coming in to school exhausted. But then he asked us if we had
seen the Czech player make the sign of the cross after scoring that goal. He reminded us that Czechoslovakia was a
Communist country and such religious gestures were for-
bidden. He told us that God and the Catholic Church
meant more to the player than the game. It was God he
thanked for scoring. We all listened, but what we remembered afterwards wasn't the speech about Catholics and
Communism. It was that Ingo had watched the game too.
Ingo was as gripped as we were.

When England played Germany, I cheered for England,

like all the boys in school. We all absorbed the news in the papers and the reports on television about it. It was traditional English skill and resilience up against the old enemy, Germany. England had beaten Germany in the final of the World Cup in 1966. As far the English were concerned, it was necessary to keep beating the Germans over and over again. The English weren't fancy players, but they had a special dedication. Bulldog spirit, the papers said.

The game was a torture to watch, especially late at night, because it went into extra time. The English had been struck by a disaster just before the game. The great goalkeeper Gordon Banks had been taken ill. His replacement was Peter Bonetti of Chelsea, a schoolboy's favourite because he was tall, skinny and spectacular when he leapt to catch an incoming ball. He did well for a while and England was ahead 2–0 with about thirty minutes to go. I watched, tired and elated, and knew I'd soon be going to bed, certain that the English heroes would advance.

But in minutes, everything changed. The English manager began taking players off the field, to save them for the next game. It was a terrible, terrible mistake. The Germans roared back and the game was soon tied 2–2. You could sense the panic in the TV commentator's voice. England looked tired and unsure in the Mexican heat. Nobody was saying it out loud, but every Irish person was thinking it. Maybe English arrogance had defeated them again. They'd underestimated the enemy. They'd be defeated by their own complacent attitude. When Germany won 3–2, it was like old England had collapsed.

We kept watching after England was defeated, and it was the Brazilians we loved, in their canary-yellow shirts. Their celebrations were as memorable as their goals. They jumped and beamed with delight. They danced, with their hips swaggering. But it wasn't like Tom Jones swaying his hips to suggest quick sex with a woman who had thrown her knickers at him. It was a smiling physical thrust to indicate they'd scored and won with pleasure. They didn't smirk. They didn't glare at opponents. They looked like they were possessed of some easy joy.

During the summer of 1970, I had to do homework every day. I was so far behind in my studies that I needed to catch up and I had been set essay and math problems to work on all summer. It was a maddening, dispiriting grind, and I despised it. But in those hours when I wasn't forced to study, I ran to the little patch of ground in Avondale Park and played soccer with the other boys. We tried and tried to play like the Brazilians. We jumped in the air and attempted acrobatic overhead kicks. We tried to keep the ball moving constantly, not to slow it down while we considered options. To hell with the British bulldog spirit. We wanted the yellow Brazilian shirts on our backs and we wanted to play with a smile. We weren't English and we didn't have to play like them. Tom Jones and the British ethos just evaporated for us.

CHAPTER SIXTEEN

NOTHING RHYMED

The Liver Birds WAS ABOUT TWO girls, Beryl and Sandra, who were sharing a flat in Liverpool, and it was great craic. Beryl was working class and loud. She was a bit thick, but funny and a tomboy, and you kind of liked her. She followed the Liverpool soccer team and got depressed when they didn't play well. Sandra was more posh but she was only claiming to be posh, really. If she got excited or angry her accent changed and she sounded just like Beryl, dropping her *h*'s and prattling away until she realized she didn't sound posh any more.

Sandra was much more obviously sexy than Beryl. She had a big bosom and looked good in little skirts or tight jeans. The show made fun of Beryl and Sandra and their clothes. They'd wear skin-tight jeans with big flares at the ankles and they'd wear clogs because that was the fashion. The two of them would hobble down the stairs and out into the street trying to look sexy and fashionable, but their faces told you they weren't enjoying it. It was hard walking in clogs. I'd seen a fella who looked like a hippie wearing clogs. He was on Grafton Street in Dublin and it had been raining for ages. When he turned the corner onto Suffolk Street he started slipping all over the place. I knew clogs were the fashion but they made the man look like an eejit.

The best parts of *The Liver Birds* were the funny bits where Beryl got excited about something and it didn't work out. One time, Beryl got mad at a fella who said she didn't really know anything about soccer. So she organized a game between all the girls she knew and all the boys. Sandra didn't want to play, but Beryl made her anyway. Sandra played with a crash helmet on her head. She had figured out that players head the ball and they can't use their hands. She said, "Don't some blokes kick the ball with their heads?" And Beryl gave her a look. Sandra said she didn't want to get her hair messed up anyway, because she'd spent loads of money having her done to look good for some fella who might be playing at the match. The boys won the game but they all loved Beryl and Sandra for giving it a go.

Liverpool was only over the water from Dublin. It was so familiar that nobody needed an explanation about the show's name or needed to be told that it was a pun on the giant metal birds on top of the Royal Liver building in

Liverpool. Beryl and Sandra were lively girls, and the old pronunciation for Liverpool was "Lyverpool." A boat left from the North Wall in Dublin for Liverpool every evening and took just a few hours to get there. On winter nights when it was foggy and still, in Raheny you could hear the foghorn from the boat. Loads of people followed the Liverpool soccer team, or Everton, the other team in the city. Liverpool was full of Catholics because lots of Irish people who had left Ireland for England had stopped in Liverpool and didn't go any farther. Lots of people in Liverpool even had Irish names.

The Liver Birds wasn't about posh and stuck-up people in London. It was about people who weren't far away. You could imagine Beryl and Sandra living in Dublin and their mam and dad worrying about them, two girls living in a flat on their own. It wasn't like trying to imagine Bat Masterson wandering around Nenagh. I could easily see Beryl and Sandra on Grafton Street looking for fashionable clothes and running for the bus home. But no girl in Dublin was named Beryl, that was sure. It was a very English name. The other difference was that Beryl and Sandra didn't always talk about getting married, the way every young woman of their age in Dublin did. They were more interested in fun for themselves than in talking about weddings and children. Beryl was Catholic and Sandra seemed to be Protestant, but they never mentioned what the priests were saying about contraception. In Dublin that's what women were talking about all the time. There was a woman named McGee who had children but her doctor said her health would suffer terribly if she had another child. The woman had gone to court to demand that she have access to contraception on medical grounds. Contraception was outlawed in Ireland, and the Church was dead set against any form of contraception being allowed. Everybody, especially women, was watching the case of Mrs. McGee very closely.

On *The Liver Birds*, Liverpool seemed like Dublin, with lots of people being famous for their jokes and their funny attitudes. People on the show talked about the Beatles all the time, and even though everybody knew the Beatles had broken up, it was like Liverpool was a place with loads of musicians and poets and comedians. Sandra kept saying, "You're so basic, Beryl," but you knew she was happy that Beryl was such fun. Often at the end of the show Beryl and Sandra would sit in their bathrobes having a cup of tea, talking about their jobs, families and boyfriends. That's when you could really see that Sandra was the sexy one. She was always clutching the robe so that it didn't open and you could see her bosom just sitting there under her nightie.

Dennis Gavin was in my class at school and he said that yer woman Sandra was a nympho. He said if you were in England you could get magazines with yer woman who played Sandra in the nip. She was randy for men. He claimed he had read it in some magazine his brother sent him from England.

Gavin was a messer. He was stupid and never stopped looking for attention and causing trouble. If there was a patch of new cement laid on the pavement anywhere in Raheny he had to go and write his initials in it with a stick from an ice pop. Sometimes he also put his hands in the wet cement. He'd take you miles to see his initials and his handprints in the cement.

He was older than the rest of us but he was held back in class because he was thick. He liked to call me a culchie, and I knew full well that he did it because once he'd seen me flinch after being called a culchie. After he'd seen that, he wouldn't stop. There were times when he called me "Nenagh pig" because he knew that culchie had stopped working as an insult and I was used to it. There were times when the other boys even got fed up with Gavin going on about culchies. He looked like a culchie himself and they told him so. He was tall and broad across the chest with a huge arse on him. He had bright red hair and until he opened his big mouth to start talking in a Dublin accent, you'd swear you were looking at an eejit from the bogs.

Gavin was touched, he wasn't the full shilling at all, but he was sly as well as thick. He would say things out loud that nobody else wanted to talk about. He'd get away with it because people thought he was mad and didn't understand what he was saying. Gavin had one brother, who was older than him and living in England. Nobody knew where his father was and nobody was brave enough to ask him. He said his brother sent him home filthy magazines with pictures of women in the nip, gagging for a ride. He said his brother had magazines from Sweden with pictures of women in the nip licking a fella's prick, but there was no way his brother was going to send that back to Dublin in the post because they'd all get arrested for having pornography.

He said he was going out with Mary Keane. Most of us knew who Mary Keane was because she lived near the school and she had blond hair and was gorgeous. She didn't look sexy, with a big bosom and long legs showing off under a short skirt. She just had this aura of gorgeousness about her. Apart from the natural blond hair and the very pale skin, she had blue eyes that were so bright they shone. Once, when I was on the number 29 bus coming out of town, Mary Keane sat down right opposite me. She tossed back her blond hair and I could see she was wearing a long scarf draped around her neck and shoulders. She looked amazingly elegant, like a film star, but she was only Mary Keane from Raheny. She smiled at me, a big warm smile, as if she knew me, and I couldn't believe that she'd even remember seeing me before. I was mortified. It was hard to believe that she was going out with Dennis Gavin. She looked like she was seventeen, but Gavin was only thirteen, even though he was big enough to look older.

It was impossible to know what to believe about Dennis Gavin. He was a great source of information about things that nobody wanted to talk about, but he was everywhere and sometimes he was nowhere. One night Dad had been at the Cedars for a pint with somebody from work, and as he was driving down the Howth Road he saw a young fella running along the pavement carrying a bus stop sign. Dad couldn't believe it for a minute, but it really looked like the lad had torn the entire metal pole out of the ground and was legging it with the big pole under his arm. Dad pulled over the car and asked him what he was doing. The young fella looked at him and started asking questions back. He just kept saying, "Who are you? Who are you?" over and over again. Dad gave up and told him to leave the bus stop where it was, and he drove home. The next day he described the young fella to me. He asked me if I knew him. I knew it was Gavin, but I didn't say so.

After school, three of us walked down the Howth Road to where Dad said he had stopped the night before. Sure enough, there was a bus stop sign in an odd place, just stuck in a hole in the pavement, leaning over into the road. A bit farther down the road there was a hole where the bus stop used to be. Nobody could figure out why Gavin had done such a thing. If Gavin got up to that sort of carry-on late at night, you knew he was a bit mad but you also knew he was up for anything. Maybe it was true what he said about going out for walks with Mary Keane and kissing her.

After I talked the one time with Gavin about *The Liver Birds*, he wouldn't stop going on about it. He said when the school holidays came—except that he called them "the hollyers"—he was legging it over to Liverpool with some money in his pocket and he was going to look up yer woman Sandra, the nympho, and he was going to give her a good ride. His theory was that you could ride any bird if you had rubbers. They had no fear of being up the spout with a baby, so they'd give you a ride. He said the reason birds in Dublin would never give fellas a ride was that there were no rubbers. But he had it from his brother, who brought rubbers back to Dublin when he came home, that if you went out with a bird in Dublin and gave her a few drinks and then you told her you had rubbers, she'd give you a ride. But only if you had the rubbers.

Dennis Gavin was an awful gobshite when he got going. But even if he was an eejit and a bit touched, I had the feeling that some of what he said about girls was probably true. All the boys at school and in Avondale Park were afraid of girls. Only the ones who had older brothers and from that knew how to flirt with girls could really be going out with anybody. Everybody knew you couldn't buy rubbers or any kind of contraception in Ireland. It was against the law. On *The Liver Birds*, you assumed that Beryl and Sandra were on the pill even if they didn't talk about it all the time. They were nice girls but they were always looking for boyfriends, and they didn't talk about not having sex until they got married, and they never argued about whether the Church was right to ban contraception. The contraceptives were available to them in any chemist's shop in Liverpool. In Dublin the shopkeeper would get arrested for selling them.

One day *RTÉ News* reported a story about a group of women from the Irish Women's Liberation Movement that took the train to Belfast and bought condoms there. The reporter called the contraceptives "condoms," not rubbers. Then they got the train back to Dublin and waved the condoms around at Connolly Station. They even waved them in the faces of the guards who were standing there. Some of them even blew up the condoms like balloons and held them up in the air for the television cameras. The leaders spoke passionately about the need for women to have access to contraception and how important that was in a free and democratic society, which was what Ireland was supposed to be, they said. Some of the other women off the train were standing there breaking their sides laughing at how stupid it was to make balloons out of condoms and wave them at the guards who were too embarrassed and outnumbered to do anything about it.

The scene was comical and you knew, watching it, that the evil thing the Church was always going on about, and what the priests called "artificial contraception," was just some bits of rubber that you could blow up like a balloon. It was like the Church making a big fuss about the toys that little children played with. The story about the condom train was repeated on RTÉ many times over the next few days. It was used in the roundup of the week's news and then it was used for discussion programs about the Church and the government's policy on artificial contraception. After I'd seen it a few times, it was still funny but I kept thinking about what Gavin had said about girls being willing to let fellas have what they wanted as long as the fella had a rubber. It wasn't a group of men who went up to Belfast on the train to make a show of how stupid the contraception laws were. It was women. It was women who wanted the right to buy contraceptives in Ireland and have sex without becoming pregnant.

It also seemed odd that they had gone to Belfast to buy their condoms and to make a point. Nobody ever went to Belfast from Dublin, because they were afraid of the trouble there. At the same time, the government and other politicians were always saying that the North was really part of Ireland and it was not a separate country at all. And here were these women going on the two-hour train trip to Belfast to buy condoms and bring them back because you couldn't buy them in the Republic. The guards were supposed to arrest them and confiscate the condoms but they were afraid to do that because there were so many women and the television cameras were recording everything and they knew they'd look stupid.

Gavin said he had never seen the story about the condom train. But like all of us he had seen the news stories on RTÉ and the BBC about the women's liberation movement in England and America. In those places the stories always seemed to be about women burning their bras. According to Gavin it was great news for fellas who wanted a good look at women's knockers. He said he'd keep an eye out for women's libbers in Raheny and he'd keep the rest of us posted.

I knew there was a big difference between what was happening in England or America and what was happening in Ireland. It was obvious from the scenes of the TV news and the programs on the BBC that in other countries the women's libbers burning their bras were doing something symbolic. They wanted more freedom and they didn't want to be held back by old ideas. They wanted the same jobs as men and they didn't want to be told that they couldn't achieve something because they were women. They'd had the pill for years and weren't planning to spend the rest of their lives as wives and mothers. In Ireland, the women's libbers were years behind. When they appeared on television they debated with the Catholic Church, not just with politicians. And the priests didn't only argue with them about contraception. They told the women's libbers that of course women should stop working if they got married. That was the rule in the civil service in Ireland and in most companies. I heard a priest on a program on RTÉ say that it wasn't right for a married woman to have a job when there were men with large families to support who needed that job. When a woman said that in other countries there were many women working in important jobs, the priest just smiled. What was happening in other countries didn't interest him. People in other countries envied Ireland, according to the priest, because Ireland wasn't connected to all of these changes that were making people miserable.

In my house the issues of contraception and jobs for women were discussed sometimes, usually after a TV program. Dad admired the working-class Dublin women who worked, especially those women who had a stand in the open-air market on Moore Street, in town. They were tough and witty, full of jokes, and some of them could swear like a docker. They reminded him of the hardy women he'd grown up with in Nenagh. Mam was in favour of women having contraception if they shouldn't have any more children for the sake of their health. That poor Mrs. McGee, having to go to court to get something that any Christian person would give her. And that woman Mary Robinson, who was helping Mrs. McGee's case, was an honest, educated woman doing the decent thing. Neither Mam nor Dad was sure about letting married women with children have jobs. It was terrible to see a man thrown out of his job and on the dole when he had children to support and educate. It wasn't fair to have a married, well-off woman sitting in a job when a man was looking for work. It was what everybody thought in Avondale Park. You couldn't keep up with the changes that were going on in the world, but Ireland would always be different.

Dennis Gavin talked a lot about girls but it was hard to tell if he knew anything at all. The one thing he did know about was pop music. Only a few of the boys paid much attention to it, and only if their older brothers and sisters bought records and followed the charts in England, but Gavin was an avid follower of *Top of the Pops*, the weekly Top Thirty show on the BBC. Part of the show's attraction was Pan's People, a gaggle of leggy dancers who performed when a band, usually an American one, couldn't appear on the show. They wore short skirts or long flouncy dresses that always seemed to go up in the air during their routine. And when the camera was on their faces, they'd make these inviting smiles and pouts that suggested they were up for anything. They had names like Andi and Dee-Dee, names that no girl in Ireland ever had, and everybody wondered what they got up to with the pop musicians before and after the show.

One day, Gavin brought the news that a fella who'd been on *Top of the Pops* and had a song on the charts was Irish. According to Gavin, Gilbert O'Sullivan, a peculiar-looking fella in a cloth cap and a woolly sweater like you'd see a kid wearing in Ireland, was really named Ray O'Sullivan and he was from Waterford. Ray O'Sullivan's song was called "Nothing Rhymed," and it stuck in your head because it was sad and it was about being confused by the world and by your mam and dad. I'd heard it loads of times and liked the line that said, "Today, nothing rhymed," and it always made me wonder about the fella who sang it.

I was thirteen and sullen, and nothing made sense except my own feelings. Dennis Gavin's endless talk about girls and sex and rubbers and the way he talked about *The Liver Birds* was all hard to understand, but it was there to be heard and thought about. None of it made life in Dublin easier. Being Irish in Dublin seemed a maddening, confusing thing to be. It wasn't being Irish like I was used to thinking of that, which meant being proud to be Irish, being suspicious of the English and knowing the Irish language. In Dublin all of that was drifting away. It was like something between being Irish and being English.

I was watching *Top of the Pops* often then, because it was good to know about bands and singers and songs and not only know about soccer teams and players. You were ordinary if you knew about soccer teams but you were part of the special crowd if you knew about pop songs. There were no Irish pop stars that I knew about, except yer man Ray O'Sullivan. It was in England that they made the songs you sometimes heard on the radio. I loved T. Rex when I first saw them, just the two fellas singing this song called "Hot Love." The singer was small, with black, curly hair, and he looked like a woman, the way he shook his hips and could hardly be bothered to say the words to the songs. The other fella was tall and stocky and just sort of stood there, playing the bass guitar, making the beat for the other fella to sway along with. It was all about giving some woman hot love and that's all there was to it, but it sounded so sexy and easygoing, in a way that nobody on the streets of Dublin could match. It was maddening to have it on the television but hardly ever on the radio. You had to watch *Top of the Pops* to hear the song again.

The summer of 1971 was drifting away in warm days and English pop music. We didn't have a record player in the house, so I set out one day to find one. Brian Lambert came with me. Shy and completely uninterested in sports, he fell into friendship with me because he'd spotted another isolated boy. He never called me culchie and couldn't care less where I was from. He had a transistor radio and listened to the BBC Radio pop channel, the pirate channels and Radio Luxembourg, the pop channel that you could get in Ireland late at night. He knew all the songs and the names of the bands and singers. We pooled our pocket money and went into town in search of something we could use to play records. All the new record players were too expensive, so we began looking in second-hand shops in the back streets and alleys. Eventually we found a battered old machine that played records but had no speakers. It had to be hooked up to a radio for us to actually hear the sound. We bought it and took it home. Brian's mam would not allow him to take apart the radio, so we took it to my house and took the back off an ancient radio that had come from Nenagh with us. We were delighted with ourselves. We haunted second-hand shops for old records and bought old scratched 45s by forgotten English bands, for pennies. We watched *Top of the Pops* and any English program that might have pop musicians performing. School and the troubles in the North seemed far away.

One August Sunday I stayed up listening to Radio Luxembourg and got up late the next morning. The radio in the kitchen was tuned to RTÉ at top volume. "It's internment," Mam said. "They're locking people up. Putting them in camps. It's all Catholics. The North is going to explode." By early evening, when the first pictures appeared on television, the full extent of what was happening was clear. The British government had introduced internment without trial in the North and the army had invaded Catholic areas in Belfast and Derry to arrest anyone they thought was linked to the IRA. At dawn, tanks and armoured cars had smashed through barricades and soldiers had burst into the tiny row houses of the Catholic ghettos. Men and boys were dragged from their beds and taken away. There were no arrests, no charges and no lawyers pleading for their release. All those old rules were gone. People were disappearing from their homes, from work and off the streets. They were being taken to camps in the countryside and locked up. On the television news, mothers wept and wept again as they described the soldiers charging into the house, screaming and tearing everything apart before dragging a husband or a son from bed and into the back of a truck. The cameras showed the damaged homes and the streets full of women at their doorsteps, silently numb or shrieking with fury.

The stories they told were raw, filled with detail, and they stayed in the mind for long after. One woman said that she had been in bed with her husband when they heard the front windows and door being smashed. Soldiers burst into their bedroom. The woman said she had picked up her baby girl, who was screaming with terror in the cot. A soldier hit her with his rifle butt, knocking her to the floor with the child in her arms. Her husband told them to stop and said he'd go with the soldiers if they left his wife alone. He asked to be allowed to put on his shoes, but another soldier hit him with a rifle and dragged him down the stairs. He was dragged barefoot through the broken glass of the smashed windows. The woman said the floor was covered in blood and every piece of furniture was in smithereens. She spoke calmly, her Northern accent giving her story a sing-song rhythm, like she was a child talking in a sleepy voice. That night, the news showed people in Belfast and Derry taking to the streets. The riots lasted all night. A priest was shot dead while trying to give the last rites to a man dying on the pavement.

The tension rose and rose. You couldn't wish it away with pop songs and thinking about the new soccer season that was starting any day. Within days, there was another song on the radio all the time, "The Men Behind the Wire."

Armoured cars and tanks and guns
Came to take away our sons!
But every man must stand behind
The men behind the wire.

Through the little streets of Belfast,
In the dark of early morn,
British soldiers came marauding,
Wrecking little homes with scorn . . .

Not for them a judge or jury,
Nor indeed a trial at all,
Being Irish means they're guilty
So we're guilty one and all.

I knew it wasn't going to be on *Top of the Pops*.

CHAPTER SEVENTEEN

WHERE ARE YOU FROM?

NOBODY IN MY CLASS at O'Connell's School had heard of *Monty Python's Flying Circus*. It was very disappointing.

I'd got into O'Connell's by the skin of my teeth. I'd performed well in most subjects in the entrance exams but I'd almost failed the maths test. Dad talked about it with the brother in charge of the exams and the brother said they didn't want to put me in the A class with the boys who got the top marks in everything, but they also didn't want to put me lower than the C group or I'd be stuck in the company of young fellas who had no brains at all, who couldn't be bothered and were probably going straight into some trainee program for plumbers or on the dole as soon as they were old enough. It was the Irish-language results that got me into the C class, and the brothers were determined to use it. Eventually they put me on the Irish-language debating team.

Going to O'Connell's meant a long day and a long journey. The school was in the heart of the old north side of Dublin's city centre. It was on a side street off the North Circular Road, always called the Norrier, and getting there meant a bus journey and then a long march through blocks of Corporation apartments and narrow streets of tiny working-class homes. The day started before nine and ended after four o'clock. In winter it was dark going to school and coming home. Each day the bus sat in rush-hour traffic and we schoolboys sat in the bilious light of the ancient, diesel-fuelled bus, talking idly about the brothers, soccer and what we were going to watch on television. For a while, I didn't care if I was watching television shows that nobody else watched. I had someone to watch *Monty Python* with, and that was my uncle Martin. Nenagh had followed us to Dublin.

First came Martin Ahern Junior. Martin had got married the year before, to a tall, glamorous Limerick woman named Helen. He'd only been courting with her for a while, but she was mad to get married and Martin was for it. Her family owned a small business in Limerick and Martin drove a van for them. But, inside a few months, there was trouble in the marriage, the family and the business. Whatever happened was never made known to Máire and me. We just knew that Martin's marriage had ended and he was coming to Dublin to stay with us for a while. Martin's situation caused an awful commotion in

Castlecranna. It was unheard of. Nobody ever openly acknowledged that a marriage was over. There was no divorce in Ireland because nobody needed it. Everybody who got married stayed married. If it happened that a married couple split up, the husband had the sense to go to England. That way, everybody could accept the story that he'd gone to England for work, and there was no fault in that. If he never came back, it was never mentioned.

Some of the relatives were outraged at Martin. I knew this from the many phone calls to and from the country and the stress that Mam was obviously under, trying to help Martin but not aggravate people who thought he was just too much of a carefree boyo to stick to a marriage. Mam told Martin to come to Dublin and stay with us, and promised that nobody in the house or the street would pass judgment on him.

At first, Martin was a peculiar presence in the house. He was quiet and melancholy, like a man waiting for an injury to heal. He had little money and sat in the living room or went for long walks all over Raheny. If he had the price of it, he'd stop in a pub for a pint and nurse it for hours. He'd read an evening newspaper that somebody had left in a pub and bring it home with him, a little contribution to the household. At mealtimes, he talked to Dad about hurling or Gaelic football, but you could tell his heart wasn't in it. Martin was famous for his mischief and his jokes, but the humour had seeped out of him. Dad slowly tried to coax him into looking for work, telling him he didn't begrudge him the roof over his head or the few pounds for a pint, but he should be thinking about getting something, to take his mind off his troubles. Martin nodded and sighed.

I knew he'd worked at many things, from the building trade, as everybody called the construction business, to bar work and driving trucks and vans. Over the years he'd worked in Nenagh, Limerick, in Dublin for a while, and he'd even spent a few years in London before he got fed up with being Irish in London. He said it was better to be from Australia or New Zealand if you lived in London. The Aussies and the Kiwis were the best for a laugh. He'd spent too many long nights sitting in bars in Kilburn and Camden Town talking to Irishmen who had nothing to talk about except being Irish.

I liked Martin. Mam put another bed into my room. He smoked all bloody night, which he wasn't supposed to do, according to Mam's rules. He'd start to tell me a story about going to a club in London, the Bag O'Nails, where the Beatles used to drink, and I'd fall asleep listening to his low whisper. If I woke up again, he'd be gone from his bed, downstairs, restless, moving from a kitchen chair to the living-room sofa, reading anything he could find. He read my soccer magazines as avidly as I did and knew the names of pubs in London where soccer players drank.

I also knew he'd rather watch the BBC than RTÉ. Television brought him out of himself. He'd sit with me and watch any English comedy, even stupid ones such as *On the Buses* or *Queenie's Castle*. His eyes lit up a bit when he saw Diana Dors, middle aged, blond and buxom, shrieking away on *Queenie's Castle*. He told me I was too young to know it, but English girls were the best fun, they'd give you a great feeling after being in Ireland. All the women in London were gorgeous, he told me, and the look on his face meant that I was supposed to know he was laughing at me and with me at the same time.

I loved meeting him when he was out for his long walks around Raheny. He wore his one battered blue suit and a white shirt, with no tie. Over that, he wore a big country-man's overcoat that came to his knees. His shoes were shiny, patent leather, the kind that fellas wore for a night at a dance hall. I knew he'd come to our house with only one bag and he'd just grabbed a few bits of clothes, but he looked different, entirely himself, walking around Raheny. One day, I met him when I was coming home from school. I was walking from the bus stop with Cormac Green, who lived in Avondale Park and said his dad was an engineer. Everybody knew his dad wasn't really an engineer but some kind of technical fella who made a living working with engineers. You could tell that Cormac Green's mam had told him to say his dad was an engineer because it sounded better. He was always going on about the school he was going to. He'd got into Belvedere and he thought he was great. He talked about playing rugby, and how he was being taught by Jesuits, not Christian Brothers. I was saying nothing back to him, when I saw Martin Ahern coming along the road. I stopped and Martin said, "Howya, boss?" Cormac Green looked at him, the coat, the suit and the sly smile. Martin looked at Cormac and said, "Where are you from?" Cormac said,

"Avondale Park." Martin snorted. He adopted a country-man's pose of elaborate grace on meeting a stranger. I could sense the demon in him. It was in the pose of him on the street, his great Ahern head and dark eyes taking in the road and the sky, before he pounced. "And where's your father from?" he asked with intense sincerity. Cormac said, diffidently, that he didn't know. Martin stared at him for a second and said, "Are you a bit thick?" Before Cormac could say anything back, Martin looked at me, winked and said to nobody in particular as he walked away, "I'm from the arsehole of Tipperary, and I don't give a fuck!"

The first true sign that Martin was recovering came on an autumn evening. Himself and myself were watching the end of *Top of the Pops* when the doorbell rang. I knew it was probably the Mormons. Everyone in North Dublin lived in dread of the Mormons calling. They were all over Dublin, travelling in pairs. It was always two fellas in dark suits and they looked big, American and earnest. You'd see them on the bus, side by side, talking to each other in whispers. Their mission was to go door to door in Dublin and try to convert people. They'd arrive at the door and when you answered, they'd ask politely if they could have a minute of your time to talk about God. People were unnerved by them. They didn't want to be rude because the Mormons were Americans, but they were notoriously difficult to get out of the house once you let them in. They wouldn't budge until they'd read the Bible to you and made you promise to attend a meeting about becoming a Mormon. Most people knew eff all about being a

Mormon. They only knew about the Osmond family, who were Mormons and who were on the charts all the time, the whole clatter of them. With their big white smiles and sweet voices, they were always so wholesome, saying they didn't do drugs and they didn't touch a drop of drink. At the time Martin got out of the chair to answer the door, little Jimmy Osmond had just been on *Top of the Pops* belting out an awful song called "Long Haired Lover from Liverpool."

Sure enough, it was the Mormons at the door. I could hear the American accents. The next thing I heard was Martin inviting them in. I went to the living-room door and peered into the hall. Mam emerged from the kitchen. Dad came out of the dining room, where he'd been doing his Irish Life accounts. Máire had been upstairs in her room and came halfway down the stairs. Everybody was amazed that Martin had invited them in.

"I have great respect for youse and your work," Martin announced, in a serious voice, to the smiling Mormons. "But I don't want youse wasting your time knocking on this door. The people here are decent people. But youse should know this," he said, and allowed a pregnant pause to hover in the crowded hall. "These people here are Communists," he shouted. "All the Doyles from Nenagh are Communists. Every man jack and one of them." The Mormons' smiles disappeared and they began backing out the door. Mam was as startled as they were, but the sight of her waving her tea towel in dismissal they took to mean they were being firmly shooed out. She closed the door behind them and gave Martin a deadly look. Dad said, "Jaysus, Martin, but you're an awful man!" Martin didn't stop laughing for hours. Later, Dad took him out for a pint.

One wet morning, not long after, Martin arose early and went to the shed at the end of the little back garden. He rooted around among the tools and put the biggest shovel aside. We watched from the kitchen window as we ate our breakfast. Martin came in and said he'd be borrowing the shovel for a while. Then, after he'd had a mug of tea, he set off with the shovel. I saw him when we were going to school. He was marching down the Howth Road. He carried the shovel in his hand as he strode along, his bare head taking the rain and his overcoat flapping behind him. He was going to look for work and he found it, using that shovel on a building site. We were all delighted.

The best time to watch television with Martin was after he'd been working and then had enjoyed a pint at the pub or a bottle of Guinness with Dad after dinner. He had no time for American programs at all. Shows like *Hawaii Five-O* were good for five minutes, according to Martin, and he meant the first five minutes, when the mystery was set up. After that, it was all the same, he said. He'd spent so much time in England and worked with so many English bosses that he delighted in the mocking of their rules and regulations. He'd sit, splayed in an armchair, and watch English comedies intently, savouring the jokes, giggling until he went red in the face. One night as we watched *Monty Python* a sketch ended and, over the BBC logo, a voice announced, "Now on BBC television, a choice of viewing. On BBC2, a discussion about censorship between Derek Hart, the bishop of Woolwich, and a nude man. And on BBC1, me telling you this." Martin exploded into laughter. He couldn't move in the chair. His face went redder and his chest moved in a mad rhythm as he laughed and tried to catch his breath. I began laughing too. According to Mam, we could be heard from one end of Avondale Park to the other.

At school, the boys had been talking about *Casanova*, a drama on BBC2 that was pure filth. It was all about the life of yer man Casanova and all the women he'd slept with. According to the boys, the women ran round in the nip and at least once an episode some gorgeous young woman would sit up in bed showing off her knockers. Sometimes yer man Casanova got busy feeling them up. This was too good to miss. I watched *Casanova* with Martin over a few weeks and it was an eye-opening experience, in more ways than one. Casanova had been arrested in Venice by the Inquisition and put in a tiny, filthy jail cell. He'd annoyed the priests and the bishops by having lascivious books and declaring that he was an atheist. In his little cell, he remembered all the love affairs and seductions he'd had. To be sure, at regular intervals he was in bed with a woman and she'd sit up, showing off her knockers to the camera. But most of the time it was Casanova talking and arguing with people about religious dogma and the rules of the aristocracy and the Church. Martin sat there with me the first time, enjoying the fun that Casanova was having with giggling girls. As soon as Casanova got a woman into a bedroom, Martin would say, "Oh boys, this is going to get unsavoury. You'd better tell the priest in confession about seeing this carry-on."

But as the drama unfolded, Martin looked at me and said, "Sure, this isn't dirty at all." He thought for a minute and said, "It's about yer man's notions, not the women. He's saying there's no God, religion is all a cod and people would be better off loving sex than loving God, the Virgin Mary and all that." Martin was right, and the fact that he'd explained it made it more interesting to watch. In a scene near the end, Casanova was old and banjaxed from all kinds of ailments. His hands were like those of an old woman with arthritis. There was a young woman he was interested in and he talked his way into feeling her up. His withered hand was on her breast and he had this look on his face, a look of utter joy. It was uncomfortable to watch, in a way, this old man feeling up a young woman, but it wasn't really embarrassing because Martin was there and he knew the program was about Casanova being a rebel in his ideas, not just some fella who was always chasing girls.

On the last Sunday evening in January of 1972, Martin was in the living room watching TV and dozing off. I was in the kitchen finishing my homework. The radio was on and the sound was low. Mam and Dad were in the dining room, having a drink with the O'Rourkes, friends from Leitrim.

I was writing out a translation of an Irish poem when, even with the ancient radio only murmuring sounds, I heard the distinctive, staccato sound that preceded a news flash. I listened as a news reader, speaking in a slow, serious tone, said that there were unconfirmed reports of shooting at a civil rights march in Derry, that the British army had opened fire on the demonstration and that some people had been seriously injured. It was the phrase "opened fire" that halted me. After a minute, I went into the dining room and told Mam, Dad and the O'Rourkes what I'd heard on the radio. They were too busy enjoying themselves to pay much attention. I wasn't much of a news carrier. But they hadn't heard what I'd heard—the sound of that man's voice.

I told Martin and he said there had been no news flash on television, but he'd switch over to RTÉ. I went back to the kitchen. Within minutes there was another report. This time, there was the voice of a reporter on the phone from Derry. He was panicky, shocked, his voice quavering as he told what he'd seen. The British army had opened fire and kept shooting. There were people dead. There were bodies all over the street. Then the O'Rourkes were leaving. I said nothing until they'd gone and then I told everyone to come and watch RTÉ. We waited and waited for the report.

It was terrifying to watch. There was footage of Derry in the rain, bodies on the ground. A priest was seen crawling toward one of the bodies. He waved a white handkerchief in the air. You could hear the rifle shots coming and coming. You could hear someone wailing, a sound that made your heart sink, as the bullets kept flying. The cameras tried to give a bigger picture and it was even more awful. You could see that some of the bodies on the street were lifeless, unmoving, dead. The priest tried to keep the white handkerchief in the air even as he bent down to murmur the last rites to the dead and the dying. There was silence and the sound of another bullet hitting concrete, with a whining after-sound. Nobody spoke as we watched. Not a single word was said. The reporter advised that there might be as many as twelve people who'd been shot dead. You could feel the gloom and despair that emanated from the pictures on the television screen. Everything had changed.

On Monday Dublin was quiet. Nobody knew what to think, but you could tell they were waiting. On the news that night we all learned that in the House of Commons in London, the man in charge of the army in the North, Reginald Maudling, had said that the army had only responded when they were attacked with petrol bombs and gunshots. Bernadette Devlin, who had been in Derry that Sunday, reacted with fury. We all listened to the description of her racing across the floor of the House of Commons to hit Maudling in the face, tear at his hair, scratch his cheeks and shout "Murdering hypocrite" over and over again. When Bernadette talked to the TV reporters, her face was ashen. She could barely speak, such was the pent-up fury in her. She said there was nothing she could say. And everyone watching knew she was right. The North wasn't about politics now.

As I entered the gates of O'Connell's School the next morning there was chaos. An older student, a sixth-year who was close to leaving school and going to a job or university, was standing on one of the gate pillars. He was giving a speech to the crowd. Hundreds of boys had gathered around him. The boy on the pillar said that what happened in Derry needed an answer. He shouted that the Irish people had tolerated for long enough the actions of the British army in Northern Ireland. He was going hoarse. There was something about the way he stood there. You could tell he wasn't self-conscious at all. He wasn't acting, and he meant every word of it. Spittle flew from his mouth. His face was pale with rage. He called on everyone to take to the street and march to the British embassy. He said we had to give an answer on behalf of the dead in Derry. Two Christian Brothers stood and watched him. They didn't move to stop him or tell him to shut up. They didn't try to shoo the boys into class. By the look on their old faces, you could tell they approved. The morning light was grey. The air was sullen. Someone shouted, "Up the IRA!" And then everybody cheered. The two brothers looked on silently.

In class, when we finally went inside, the teachers were subdued. None of them wanted to broach the topic and none of them wanted to avoid it. Mr. O'Higgins, the history teacher, told us it was Bloody Sunday. That's what it would be known as. He said the first Bloody Sunday had happened just a few hundred yards from where we were sitting. It was in 1920 during the War of Independence. On a Sunday morning, Michael Collins had sent IRA men to assassinate British agents in Dublin. Several were shot dead in their homes in the morning. That afternoon, the British army made sure there was a reprisal. Armoured cars went to Croke Park stadium when it was full with thousands of people watching a Gaelic football game. They drove onto the field, aimed their machine guns into the crowd and started firing. Fourteen people, some of them children, were shot dead. Mr. O'Higgins said the British army did it to let every Irish person know that they considered all the Irish, every man, woman and child, to be the enemy. It was what armies did when they couldn't see the enemy they were fighting. The British army was trained to fight in battlefields and they didn't know how to deal with real people. They attacked everybody. They had done it again in Derry. He said terrible things would probably happen. There might be riots in Dublin, but we should stay at home and not be part of the trouble.

By lunchtime we knew that the school was almost empty. Half the boys had gone on a march to the British embassy, following the boy who'd stood on the pillar and the one who'd shouted "Up the IRA!" The brothers told us to go home. I wanted to follow the crowd of boys who were speaking for the dead in Derry. But I was reluctant. I was too young, and I saw that when some of the younger boys started to follow the older crowd, a brother shooed them back. He said young boys should go home to their parents before they went anywhere near the British embassy. He said the next day would be a day of mourning and all the schools would be closed. Everything in the country would be closed while Ireland mourned the dead.

At home, all we did was watch the news on RTÉ and

the BBC. After the news report on the BBC, Mam changed the channel. We all had the same feeling, that it would be sickening to watch British programs after what had happened. It had been confirmed that thirteen people had been shot dead. Thousands of people had gathered on the street outside the British embassy in Merrion Square. There was no rioting, but you could tell from the pictures on TV that the mood was ugly. People were stone faced, spitting out words in interviews. "There was no need for that. Innocent people dead on the street. It was only a march for civil rights." Mam watched and got more agitated all evening. She announced that she would join the march to the British embassy the next day. Dad said it might be foolish. There could be petrol bombs and the guards might use their batons on the crowd. Mam was having none of it. "I hate the English," she said. "They're killing women and children in Ireland. This is our country. I'm going."

Martin said nothing. He stared gloomily at the television and sighed. Eventually he said, "It's a time when you wouldn't know what to do with yourself." When the late news came on the BBC and a British army officer was interviewed, Martin jumped out of his chair. "I'm not listening to that fuckin' bastard," he said as he went. The next afternoon, Mam went into town to join the march. I said I wanted to go too, that there would be boys from school there. Both Mam and Dad said no, it wasn't a time for children to be in the city centre. Mam was going with other women, they were leaving their children at home.

Dad stayed at home, doing his accounts and occasionally emerging to see if there was any news on TV. Soon after Mam left and before she'd even reached town, we knew that she wouldn't be anywhere near the British embassy. The crowd on the streets of Dublin was so large that it stretched away from the embassy for miles. Martin went out and got the afternoon papers and we all pored over the pictures from Derry and from Dublin.

The crowd at the embassy, when we saw it on TV that night, had gone wild. Stones were thrown at the windows. There was an explosion and the front door fell open. The guards standing outside just walked away. The crowd poured inside and tore the building apart with their bare hands. Screams of rage were heard as every piece of furniture and paper in the building was torn apart. Then petrol bombs rained down on the front door. The crowd seemed to stand back and watch as flames went high into the night. There were shouts of joy from the crowd, and I felt like cheering too. Some people placed black coffins on the steps of the burning building and then walked away. Mam came home very late and said that everyone in the crowd was talking about boycotting the British. At the airport the workers were refusing to refuel planes from Britain. In other places, workers were refusing to unload goods from England, and some shops were taking English goods off the shelves. It was good to see people taking action, she said. Nobody cared about the embassy going up in flames. Good riddance to them all. I knew she was right. Not even *Monty Python's Flying Circus* could find humour in what had happened.

CHAPTER EIGHTEEN

SPOT THE BALL

THERE WAS A PROBLEM with *Upstairs, Downstairs*. Everybody enjoyed watching it but nobody wanted to talk about it. It was about them, the Brits. Worse, it seemed to celebrate the lives and la-di-da attitudes of the English upper class, those people whose attitudes to Ireland and the Irish were the source of the whole problem. When you thought of Reginald Maudling, who got slapped in the face by Bernadette Devlin, you could imagine the dozy, snooty Maudling on *Upstairs, Downstairs*, having dinner with the Bellamy family and the whole lot of them complaining about the Irish.

Everything was in the context of hating the Brits then. The country had gone mad and raw feelings were on the surface. Paul McCartney released a song called "Give

Ireland Back to the Irish," and though it was banned on BBC Radio, it seemed to be on RTÉ Radio every few minutes. You'd hear people singing along with it. Everybody said that Paul McCartney had great sympathy for Ireland because he was from Liverpool and that made him half-Irish to begin with. Anyone could tell from the way the Beatles had carried on that there was a bit of Irish in them. And look at the Liverpool soccer team, with loads of Irish players over the years, and every second week there was a boatload of Irish lads going over to watch Liverpool play. Even if it was only *The Liver Birds* that you watched on TV for your information about Liverpool, you could tell that there was something Irish about the town and the people in it.

The only English show you could watch on television and not feel regret or embarrassment about was *Match of the Day*. It was all soccer, and wasn't that innocent? Anyway, if you were a teenage boy or a man at all in Dublin and you didn't know what was going on in English soccer, you'd have nothing to talk about. But even that became part of the resentment against the British government and army. It was Irish players we looked for and cheered, wishing and willing them to play harder and faster than the English. Manchester United was in decline. Georgie Best was always in trouble, and stories about his escapades filled the English Sunday papers. I wondered if they were picking on him because he was Irish. There must be English players who got drunk and were in a fist fight with some girl's boyfriend. But you never read about *them*.

Watching *Upstairs, Downstairs* was different, though. This was the upper crust, the crowd who sat in their big houses in London with their servants and played games with Irish politics. Besides, it was set at the turn of the twentieth century, when Ireland was under English rule, and that made people uneasy. Richard Bellamy was a typical Brit, who was supposed to be fair and honest and a practical man. But you could tell he got sentimental only about his family. Not the servants or anybody else. And the son, James, was a tosser. The moustache on him and the glad eye for the girls. You could see him as the kind of English eejit who'd be up on a horse using his whip on some unfortunate Irish person. Mind you, it wasn't so bad looking at Lesley-Anne Down, who played Lady Georgina. There was a touch of the hussy about that young one. She was used to showing off her body, you could tell by the way she walked around in them long dresses. She was used to having men look at her.

The thing about *Upstairs, Downstairs* was that once you started watching it, you realized it wasn't glorifying the upper-crust Brits at all. It was about the servants and the terrible lives they lived. Dad loved Gordon Jackson as the butler Hudson. He like the way Hudson had to act one way with the Bellamys and adopt another attitude with the staff below stairs. He had to be subservient to one set of people and domineering with another. Dad told me to note the way Gordon Jackson acted with his eyes, his face expressionless. In truth I'd myself noticed that *Upstairs, Downstairs* seemed be about what was going on under the surface. The servants had a false jollity and often competed with each other to be the best, most important servant in the house, but in reality it always emerged that they were servants, not free people. They followed blindly, never questioning what their master said. There was something to be learned from that.

I was shocked the day one of the older brothers at O'Connell's School made a reference to *Upstairs, Downstairs*. Brother Mahoney said the program was very accurate in its depiction of the time. The references to politics and other matters were dead-on, he said. The writers had everything correct. I supposed that the brothers were allowed to watch it because there was no sex in it and there was never a rude joke. Although what they made of Lady Georgina was another matter. Maybe they knew half the boys in the school were thinking about her in the nip when she sashayed around in her long dresses and looked out at some fella from under the big brim of her hat.

Mostly, the brothers were dead set against English things. After Bloody Sunday, they wouldn't let us play soccer. Once a week we were put on a bus and taken to some fields at Clontarf where we were supposed to play games and gets loads of exercise under the supervision of one of the brothers, most of whom were so fat that they could barely make it up the stairs in the school without being red in the face. One week, that spring of 1972, we were out on the field before Brother Day had his shoes off. We were well into a game of soccer, with some fellas being Manchester United and other fellas being Leeds, when

Brother Day came out and started roaring at us for playing soccer. He told us it was an English game and a garrison game and we should be ashamed to be playing it. He stood there, his hands on his hips, and gave us a speech about the mercenaries who played soccer for money when there were decent Irish men playing Gaelic football for the love of the game, no money involved. He ordered us to play Gaelic football and be quick about it.

We did it sullenly, deliberately messing up and acting like we didn't know the rules or we'd forgotten how to score. We glared at Brother Day's back every time he turned away from us. He got the idea, but there was no stopping him. He roared at us for pretending that we didn't know how to play Gaelic. He told us to stop and made us run laps around the field until we were exhausted.

The following week, when we were standing outside on the street with our gym bags, waiting for the bus to take us to Clontarf, we made a plan. It was Eamon Quinn, known as Eamo or Quinny, who came up with it. "Fuck this for a game of darts," he said. "I'm not going out to that fuckin' field to play fuckin' Gaelic just because that fuckin' sack of shite thinks we all have to act like we're fuckin' culchies. I'm getting on that fuckin' bus all right, and then I'm getting off it. Me brother did it last week. Are youse with me, lads?" We were. On top of his ability to insert "fuckin'" into every possible part of every sentence that came out of his mouth, Quinny was a good leader. We trusted him.

The bus came and we all trooped on, making sure to sit at the back. As soon as Brother Day got on, he started talking to the driver, making small talk, like he always did. Quinny got up quietly and opened the emergency door at the back of the bus. We all followed him out and ran, as quietly as we could, down a lane and away from the school. The bus took off, with only a few scaredy-cat fellas sitting at the front of it. About ten of us had escaped and we knew that was too many for Brother Day to make a fuss about it. He'd be outnumbered. Anyway, as Quinny said, maybe the stupid, fat sack of shite would-n't even notice we were gone. Somebody asked Quinny what we were doing to do now. If we just went home, our mams would know we were home too early. Quinny said we'd go to the pictures. There was a Hammer horror film showing in the cinema on Talbot Street and there were tits in it. If you waited long enough, two of the young ones in it took off their tops before yer man Dracula had a bite of their necks. His brother had recom-mended it. We marched over to the cinema and spent two hours watching a Dracula film and, yes, near the end, there were tits on display. Then we got a bus home.

The Christian Brothers continued to disapprove of boys playing the garrison game of soccer, but in the months after Bloody Sunday, the mood in Ireland shifted. There was still hostility toward the British government and army, but people were made uneasy by the actions of the IRA. Six months after Bloody Sunday, Belfast was stunned by twenty-two bombs exploding inside two hours. It was the work of the IRA, and although warnings had been given, it seemed that so many hoaxes were used that the IRA deliberately caused total confusion to inflict as many casualties as possible in streets, bars and restaurants. Nine people died and hundreds were injured, and on the TV news the devastation was starkly visible. People called it Bloody Friday. A few days later, the tiny village of Claudy, in county Derry, was blown apart by car bombs planted by the IRA. Nine people died there and five of them were Catholics. This wasn't what people in the South expected. They were angry at the British army. Seeing ordinary people killed by car bombs made us all uncomfortable and apprehensive.

I didn't have Martin to join me while watching TV any more. He had gotten his own flat. He still came on Sundays for his dinner or to go out for a pint with Mam and Dad. But Nenagh was still following us to Dublin. No sooner was Martin out of the house than Paddy and Lizzie moved to Raheny. Mam and Dad had their hands full helping them out. I didn't know what was going on, but as far as I could tell, Paddy was making his living doing competitions in the Sunday paper. It had started a few years earlier in Nenagh. The shop had burned down and Paddy was saddled with a lot of debt to his suppliers. He'd been doing a competition in the Sunday paper for years, one that had a five-hundred-pound prize. Paddy won and was able to pay off a lot of his debts. He decided it was worth pursuing as a way of making money.

The competition he concentrated on was Spot the Ball. There was a photo of a soccer game in the paper, but the ball had been erased from the photo. You had to guess, from the way the players were placed, where the ball was, and put an X there. The X nearest the centre of the ball got the prize money. There was a Spot the Ball competition in one Irish paper, and several others were carried in the English papers. The prize money was much bigger in the English papers. Paddy went to a shop on a Monday and the shopkeeper would give him tons of unsold Sunday papers. He took it so seriously that he got architect's instruments to make sure he covered every scintilla of space in the photo with X's that would be near the centre of the ball. Paddy began winning money like nobody's business. The thing was, as far as Paddy was concerned, the money he won was nobody's business at all. If he could keep his name out of the list of winners in the following week's paper, he would. Sometimes it just said "P. Doyle, Dublin," and that could be any Paddy, Peter or Philomena Doyle in the city.

When they sold the house in Nenagh and moved to Raheny, they bought a newly built house up in Foxfield, near the border with Kilbarrack. It was a corner house with a big front garden that stretched all the way around the side of the house. Paddy decided that he was going to have the best-looking lawn in Foxfield and he started studying how to get a good lawn. Somewhere he read that if you planted some crops in the ground for a year before you put in a lawn, the nutrients would give you brilliant grass. So Paddy planted potatoes, onions and cabbages all over the front and side of the house.

It was the talk of the area. Dennis Gavin was in heaven. He brought people for miles to look at the front garden filled with potatoes and cabbage plants. "Culchies! Culchies!" he'd roar and jump up and down with delight. He was roaring "Culchies!" one night when a guard walked down the street and told him he'd feel the toe of his boot up the hole of his arse if he didn't shut up and quit bothering decent people. Gavin told the guard that it was a well-known fact that all guards were ignorant culchies who'd been hired into the guards by some fella dragging raw meat through the bogs to lure them out of the bog holes they lived in. Then he legged it up the street and over the fields into Kilbarrack, where he felt safer. Or so he said, anyway.

It was no use talking to Gavin about *Upstairs, Downstairs*. He was fixated on *The Partridge Family*. According to him, he watched it for tips about what girls liked. All the girls were going mad for yer man David Cassidy, and if you could figure out what was so effin' special about that Yank, you'd have it made. The songs were shite but the young one who played Laurie Partridge, Susan Dey, was effin' gorgeous. Gavin said he wanted to crawl up that little dress she wore and if he got up there he'd die a happy man.

I kept watching *Monty Python*, even the repeats. It was easy to enjoy it again. It turned out the fellas on *Monty Python* hated the British army too. In sketch after sketch, they'd make fun of idiotic, barking army officers. In one program, an officer kept interrupting the show to denounce it. One sketch made their scorn for the entire British class system, including the army, abundantly clear. In the Upper Class Twit of the Year Competition, moronic, titled gents moved around like stupid saps trying to do the most basic things. About one of them, the cackling commentator said, "He's in the Grenadier Guards and can count up to four!" In the end, these twits were so stupid they either shot themselves or shot each other. I watched, awed by the implied ridicule of those British army barbarians who shot dead innocent people in the North. Those Python boys knew exactly what they were doing. Sometimes the show was ferocious, and the police arrived and arrested the actors at the end of a sketch. No wonder, I thought while watching it. The comedy was an assault on everything that made the Irish angry at the British establishment.

CHAPTER NINETEEN

DEATH, CHAOS AND COMEDY

IT WASN'T UNTIL I LEFT O'Connell's School and went to Sandymount High School that I finally fell in with boys who knew and loved *Monty Python*. After three years in O'Connell's, I'd done well academically but I was deeply unhappy. The brothers bullied and bullied. I'd spend the long day at school there and often have to go out at night to talk in a Gaelic-language debate for the school. I was either tired or tense all the time. If I got sick, and I was regularly ill, I'd take ages to recover, and eventually Mam and Dad realized that I just didn't want to go to school there.

The country was sick too. A strange blend of radical-ization and lethargy gripped Ireland. Everybody had been galvanized by Bloody Sunday, and anti-British feelings ran high. The IRA was being tolerated and, as Protestant paramilitary groups emerged in the North, it seemed that a guerilla war was going on, with the British army in the middle of it. On the Protestant Unionist side there were the Ulster Defence Association, the Ulster Volunteers Force, the Ulster Army Council and the Ulster Vanguard. It was impossible to keep track of them. In Dublin, they were all called just "them," the Protestant Loyalists who hated Catholics. When a couple of Loyalists were interned, after hundreds of Catholics had been rounded up and put in internment camps, the Loyalists went on strike in the North. They brought the place to a standstill for ages. It was a message about who was really in charge in the North.

For a time, it was difficult to get BBC or ITV coverage of events in the North, or to see any British TV at all. The miners had gone on strike in England, and, combined with the international oil crisis, the effect was to bring Britain to its knees. Electricity was available only intermittently in most of Britain, and the TV channels would broadcast for a few hours and disappear. When they reappeared, they were mostly airing repeat programs. Nothing new was being made because nobody could get to work or use electricity. English newspapers were only six or eight pages long, as the government imposed a three-day workweek. There was satisfaction in that. The English were working three days a week and spending the rest of the time sitting at home in the dark.

But the oil crisis began to affect Ireland too. Unemployment rose, prices skyrocketed and people who had been passionate about the North began worrying about their jobs and their future. Some IRA men and their leaders had been jailed in Dublin. In response, the IRA stole a helicopter and brazenly flew it into the exercise yard of Mountjoy Jail. Three IRA men got into the helicopter and were flown away. One of them was the chief of staff of the organization. People in Dublin were amazed by the daring of it and most of them just laughed about it. They were frightened by the bombing campaign in the North but had a sneaking admiration for the ingenuity of the prison escape.

At the end of a school year at O'Connell's, when I'd passed the exams with good marks, I was moved to Sandymount High. Máire had already been going there since she left primary school. It was one of the few schools in Dublin that had both boys and girls in the same class. Nuns or Christian Brothers didn't run it; in fact, there was no religious affiliation at all. It was a small school on the south side of the city, and I'd get there by train every morning and back by train every afternoon. The days were shorter than at O'Connell's, but best of all, it was a school for misfits, rebels and the children of parents who wanted nothing to do with priests, nuns or Christian Brothers.

Cormac Caffrey, known as Joe 90 because of his resemblance to a puppet on television that wore thick, black glasses, was one of the first friends I made. He adored English comedy and had old recordings by the radio comedy troupe the Goons at home. He could sing the nonsense songs from *The Goon Show* and perform the entire "dead parrot" sketch from *Monty Python*. He smoked cigarettes constantly and moved at a very slow pace. One cold winter day he turned up at school wearing an ancient sealskin overcoat that belonged to his grandmother. He looked like an eccentric old gent, and he loved it. He wore the coat for years. Sometimes we stopped calling him Joe 90 and called him Geezer instead.

Shay Byrne was a genius. His father worked as something in the National Library, and Shay had both a photographic memory and a gift for languages. He spoke Gaelic better than the teachers or anyone except some old fella down in West Cork who had been born to it. He ignored television and films. Occasionally he read a book. Mostly he was interested in music and in particular Leonard Cohen and Neil Young. We all suspected that he was writing songs himself, but he never performed any. We wondered how somebody so clever could be so shy about a thing like that.

Mick Mulcahy was the class subversive. A year older than the rest of us, he'd returned to school after spending a year working. He was a serious student because he'd worked in a factory and knew he'd be stuck there forever if he didn't get back to school and study hard. He was also gay, and open about it. At Sandymount, neither the teachers nor the other students were going to care about that. If he'd been openly gay in any other school, he'd have been beaten, expelled or both. Mick's contributions in school were bizarre and thrilling to us. He had a habit of seeing a gay subtext in everything, whether it was Shakespeare or a history class about the Easter Rising of 1916. According to Mick, Patrick Pearse was gay and several of the men involved in the Rising were his lovers. That's why they were so attached to each other and interested in spilling their blood for Ireland. He told us about Saint Sebastian and how he was a gay martyr. He said Pearse had the same motive, being shot for Irish freedom. The teachers largely ignored Mick when he put forward his theories, but the rest of us were stunned. Many of us had come to Sandymount after years of Christians Brothers and priests as teachers and we'd never heard anything like it. In fact we'd never met anyone who was openly homosexual and who talked casually about who, among the stars on television or in pop music, was gay or lesbian.

It was also Mick who took us drinking. He knew bars that would let us drink even if we were underage, because the bars were almost private clubs for gay men. The owners or the staff were gay and tolerated teenage boys drinking there because, if the boys were gay, they wanted them in the bar and not cruising public toilets to meet other gay men. We'd sit in an old, obscure bar with Mick in the afternoons, drinking half-pints of Guinness and gazing around us, dumbfounded by the number of people who were there. It was like a bar nearing closing time, crowded and noisy with loud talk, but it was only late afternoon on a weekday. Then we spotted a man sitting up at the bar with his arm around another man. He was familiar to us all. A sports broadcaster on RTÉ, he was on television almost every week, his loud voice booming away in a rural accent about hurling or Gaelic football. He was the epitome of the rural Irish male, and here he was in a bar full of gay men. Mick told us about a politician named Maurice, well known to all of us, who was often in the bar. Everybody in the bar knew him as Doris. This wasn't the sort of information we could go home and tell our parents we had learned at school. They probably wouldn't believe us anyway.

Mick was part of a bohemia that existed far outside of school and that included writers, artists, designers and actors. He was very aware of Dublin's literary culture and he passed his knowledge on to us. He enjoyed our attention, and we all knew that. There were few places where a young gay man could be at ease in Dublin, and Mick loved to be the centre of attention among boys whose eyes went wide as he told us his stories and theories. We admired his bravery too, although we didn't tell him. Being a homosexual man in Ireland was a dangerous thing. Everything to do with homosexuality was outlawed. It was illegal to have many of the books and magazines that Mick possessed, and he and his friends took risks every day of their lives. Nobody was agitating for rights for gay men. No politician would go near the issue. A Christian Brother back at O'Connell's had said once, during a rant, that homosexuals were going straight to hell. He wasn't certain, but he was pretty sure they were all excommunicated as soon as they engaged in a homosexual act.

Mick and his friends lived in a secret world, but it was an exciting world, and it made much of what we learned in school about writers and artists seem much more vivid and sexually charged. Irish poets and playwrights whose work we knew was venerated became lurid figures to us, because Mick knew gossip about their affairs, both gay and straight, and the layers of meaning that were buried under their seemingly innocuous words and phrases. He told us that an entire chapter of the greatest novel ever written, James Joyce's *Ulysses*, had taken place a few minutes' walk from where we went to school, down on Sandymount strand. It was a stretch of the seashore that we all knew, bleak when the tide was out, and when it was in, there seemed to be only elderly people there, staring off into the greyness of Dublin Bay. Mick said the chapter involved the main character, Bloom, masturbating while he watched an ordinary Dublin girl, a shop girl, lift her skirt to him. He also said that Ulysses was really a gay novel about two men meeting in what was obviously an unconsummated homosexual relationship.

To me it was liberating to hear these things and see a different Dublin unfold in front of me. The Christian Brothers at O'Connell's School had tried to make us patriotic Irishmen, but they wanted us to be middle class, good candidates for the civil service with a keen interest in Gaelic games. They didn't approve of boys going to films, watching television or even going to the theatre. There was lasciviousness in those things. They were correct. At Sandymount and thanks to Mick Mulcahy, Irish writing was a seething world of excitement. While the country became surly and burdened by the weight of the North, and politicians sullenly kept to the Church's teaching on sex, contraceptives, divorce and all sorts of personal freedoms, the bohemian past and present underworld of Dublin opened up.

It was an invigorating place to visit, for all of us. For a start, we assumed that members of Dublin's bohemian world, especially gay men, were all having sex. None of *us* were. The lack of condoms was a barrier, as Dennis Gavin had declared in Raheny. The situation was becoming comical. Mrs. McGee had finally won her case in the Irish Supreme Court, and the government knew it had to do something about making contraception available to some people. A scheme was eventually devised that might accommodate the court decision while stopping short of clashing with the Church's teaching. Contraception would be available to some people in some circumstances. A bill was presented to Parliament, but at the last minute, the prime minister, Liam Cosgrave, felt that as a devout Catholic he would have to vote against his own government's bill. And he did, crossing the floor to vote with the Opposition. As soon as he did so, several members of his own government followed him, fearing his wrath. The government's bill was defeated, thanks to the action of its own leader. It was back to square one.

One of the novelties at Sandymount was the Friday-night open house for the students. Every Friday evening we were welcome to return to the school to listen to records, watch television or do anything we wanted. Because there were both boys and girls in the school, it was a way for us teenagers to socialize without having to go to the discos and dance halls that catered to teenagers in the city centre. Even the shy ones, the eccentrics and misfits, could feel at home in the tiny school premises of an evening, talking to people we'd see every day, or doing whatever pleased us. It was at those Friday evenings that Shay played Leonard Cohen and Neil Young, pointing out that they were Canadian, not American. "Listen to this," he'd say, before dropping the needle on a Neil Young record, and as we listened to the strange, pain-filled voice, he'd explain all the references to us.

One Friday in May 1974, as Máire and I were leaving home to get the train back to the school, we heard a news report that traffic had snarled in the city centre and there might be some sort of major accident. We left anyway, sure that whatever was happening would not affect the trains. As the train moved slowly through the city centre, all windows open to the spring air, I noticed first the absence of cars and buses moving on the street. Then I heard the sirens. Then came the sight of smoke. A strange smell drifted up from the streets. The train crawled through a station and paused on a bridge, leaving us looking down on the street. There was death there. The shop windows were all broken, litter bins had been thrown about, and some cars were sitting in peculiar positions in the middle of the street, mangled, as if a giant hand had squeezed them in a half-hearted way. Guards leaned over to look at people who were sprawled in the street. Ambulance workers moved around quickly, while everything else seemed to move in slow motion.

By the time we got to the school we knew what had happened. Three bombs had exploded at about five-thirty, just as rush hour sent thousands of people hurrying to buses and trains. The bombs had exploded at the north end of the city, the southern end and in the middle. Dozens of people were dead and hundreds, perhaps thousands, were injured. People going about their shopping or hurrying home from work had been blown to pieces on the street. By whom didn't matter. The war in the North had come to Dublin. I remembered the words of Patrick Pearse that had been drummed into me years ago in Nenagh: "Life springs from death, and from the graves of patriot men and women spring living nations."

It was all nonsense now. I'd read enough and seen enough to know the pattern of Ireland, and the country was closing in on itself again. All that had happened, the internment, the riots and Bloody Sunday, had happened in Ireland, but not on our doorstep. Now the dead bodies were in Dublin. What had started so long ago when I'd marched in Nenagh to celebrate the anniversary of 1916 had led to this, and it meant a looming blackness. We were all trapped in this darkness and there was no light, no escape. All the dead around the city gave answer to the petty arguments about what it meant to be Irish and suspicious of the Brits. The reality transcended the impact of the images from television, whether it was the terror of Belfast or the trite, polite politics of *Upstairs, Downstairs*.

CHAPTER TWENTY

BLIND DRUNK

DURING MY TIME AT University College Dublin, the top show was *The Muppets*. The Swedish Chef was much admired and imitated. The two old codgers who sat in a box during *The Muppet Show* were role models to students. Sarcastic, twitchy and apparently the worse for drink, they were like us, endlessly deriding all that passed before them.

Mind you, up at UCD, the teachers didn't encourage much interest in television. Television was irrelevant, unless, of course, the teachers themselves appeared on it. Many did, and that made it relevant for both the recognition it gave them and the fees they earned. About half of them seemed to be on RTÉ several times a week, hosting programs or pontificating about the state of the country. It was a time of ample and abundant pontification. Statler and Waldorf, the two hecklers on *The Muppet Show*, were ideal for the Ireland of the time.

At UCD the teachers were engaged in their own civil war of words, bickering in class, in magazine articles and on television about Irish nationalism. Some blamed W. B. Yeats and others just blamed RTÉ for showing footage of riots and mayhem. They wanted attention for their opinions, and many cared little about the students they taught. Everything was about the drama that was Ireland, a country sucked into self-analysis about republicanism, the roots of violence in the North, the possibility of a compromise there and the debate about whether it had all started going ominously wrong when Patrick Pearse had walked through the doors of the General Post Office in Dublin in 1916.

There was little to be cheerful about. In Dublin, the bombings in 1974 had traumatized the population. The city felt cut off, and was wary of Republican sentiment. Members of Sinn Fein stood outside the General Post Office on O'Connell Street and handed out leaflets about the Republican struggle in the North. Sometimes passersby would tell them to go to hell or back to Belfast. They wanted none of the Northern trouble that had wreaked havoc in Dublin. It was just like 1916, I knew. The ordinary people of Dublin had jeered the men who fought in the Easter Rising, and now they heaped scorn on the Sinn Fein men who talked in that accent that gave people the creeps.

In the North, the IRA had declared a ceasefire, but the Republican movement had split into factions and engaged in a bloody civil war among themselves, and the Unionist paramilitaries continued anyway, assassinating Catholics on the road, at home and in bars. If a Catholic was shot dead on a Monday you could be sure that by Wednesday a Protestant would be killed somewhere. The IRA, or some part of it, carried out a bombing campaign in England. The Labour government was devoid of ideas about how to create peace in the North. In England, people whose working lives were endlessly disrupted by bomb threats and the sight of buildings being blown to pieces with innocent people inside came to loathe all the Irish. In Ireland, some factions of the IRA took to kidnapping people, and foreign businessmen were moved about the country with armed escorts. Factories closed. Tourism declined dramatically. Nobody wanted to visit or invest when the horrors of Northern Ireland were seeping like a stain across the border and into Irish towns and cities. It was a darkness of isolation. Every guard you saw on the street looked tense, waiting for trouble. It felt like nothing good would ever happen.

I was just past my eighteenth birthday when classes began for my first year at UCD, in 1975. Hardly anyone from Sandymount High was going to UCD. Mick Mulcahy had gone to Trinity College, on the basis that it was nearer his home and, being in the centre of the city, close to his stomping ground of bars and clubs where gay men congregated. Most of the others had gone straight into jobs or left to work in England. Those who found jobs in Dublin were working to save money to leave. One of the boys worked for a month, and as soon as he had enough money to take a ferry to France, he went. He was washing dishes in a Paris restaurant and was delighted with it. Ireland had the highest unemployment rate in Europe. The jobs, the fun and the money were elsewhere.

Being young and foolish, I studied English, philosophy and history at UCD. These were popular courses, and the lectures were attended by hundreds of students crammed into vast lecture halls. The campus was a sea of teenagers carrying books and opinions. After school, university was supposed to be a liberating experience, but the truly liberated were the teenagers from the country who were suddenly set free in Dublin. There was no student housing on campus, and all the students from the country lived in flats in Ranelagh, Rathmines, Churchtown and Clonskeagh, the Dublin suburbs known as "flatland." In flatland they lived two, three or four to a flat, but they were rarely there. The campus was filled from early morning to midnight with thousands of students taking lectures and seminars, studying in the library and drinking in the huge campus bar.

A few months after I started at UCD, Dad was transferred again, this time to Carlow, a prosperous town about an hour's drive from Dublin. Máire and I were in a flat, like all the students from the country. I fell in with a bookish set of country boys. They were my kind, blessedly free of the stultifying attitudes and snobbery of the Dublin suburban schools. Eddie Kennedy from Roscommon was devoted to Russian authors and creamy pints of Guinness. Morgan Flannery from Kerry decided that the best thing about University College Dublin was the number of books by American Beat writers in the library. While we were meant to read Shakespeare, he stuck to Kerouac. When Eddie first met Morgan, he said, "Where are you bunked down?" Morgan said, "I'm up in Churchtown, in an attic with a fine view of the church itself." Eddie lowered most of his pint in a single swallow and asked, "And what's Churchtown like for women, Morgan?" The answer was, "'Tis bleak, Eddie, damn bleak." Morgan had decided, early, that Dublin women were atrocious, not like Kerry women at all. His mission was to find the rare Kerry woman who was attending UCD, and seduce her. He asked every girl he met where she was from.

Joe Gormely, from near Carrick, had spent years drinking his mother's vodka and he wasn't going to start drinking pints now. He carried miniature bottles of vodka on his person at all times. He wanted to be a writer, studied Graham Greene closely and decided that the Catholic theme would make him a fortune in Ireland if he could get the first of his novels written.

Most of the country boys arrived at UCD less in hope of being stimulated by lectures and seminars than in hope of being left alone. Nobody called them culchies at UCD. For a start, there were too many culchies, and if you insulted one, you'd never know when a whole crowd of them would descend on you outside the bar, aggrieved and determined to deposit some Dublin jackeen in a hedge for the evening. At home they'd been peculiar boys, greatly taken with poetry, plays or novels and sidelined by their lack of interest in Gaelic hurling or football or in finding a factory job. They wanted to read, see French and Italian films, watch television programs they knew weren't good for them and talk about it all over pints of Guinness. UCD was full of them, teenage boys with wispy beards and pale faces, traipsing around in tweed trousers and sturdy shoes, eyeing Dublin girls and hoping they would be impressed by the book of Chekhov stories snug in the jacket pocket and carried everywhere, or by the copy of J. P. Donleavy's banned book, *The Ginger Man*, that was hidden back at the flat. They weren't. Neither were the country girls, who marched around the campus in gangs, wearing jeans, sensible shoes and layer upon layer of wool sweaters.

The place was full of priests. In every department there were priests who were lecturers. The philosophy department seemed to be composed entirely of priests. The first one we met was a Jesuit who taught in the English department and was in charge of welcoming the first-year students to the university and giving them guidance. Hundreds of us crammed into a lecture hall on our first day, and the priest gave us practical advice about attending classes, using the library and preparing for exams. It being a priest doing the talking, we half expected him to give us advice about keeping company with students of the opposite sex, but his one piece of non-academic advice was that we shouldn't drink in the afternoons. It was roundly ignored by some of us. We drank like fishes, haunting the student bar morning, noon and night. Outside of classes and studying, there was little else to do.

As students, we fell in on ourselves, as we had to. We ignored the North and cultivated a sort of Irishness that was of our own imagining, but borrowed from our mams and dads. We said "feck" all the time because our parents did, to avoid saying "fuck." We discussed and hated the gombeen mentality in Ireland—the gombeen men being the businessmen who would do anything to make money. We idolized Brendan Behan, Flann O'Brien, Patrick Kavanagh and all that generation of Irish writers who had been stuck in Ireland during the Second World War and the 1950s, never breaking out of the isolated culture of inward-looking complaint. We listened to traditional Irish music. We collected and told endless stories to each other about drinking. Back in the days when all the pubs shut for Good Friday, two Dublin lads had taken the notion that the licensing laws were more relaxed in county Wicklow. They took a bus to Wicklow, but, not wanting to be stuck in Wicklow if there was no chance of a drink, they stayed on the bus and asked out the window for advice. They saw an ould fella walking down the road with the look of a man going for a pint. "Hey," they called to him. "Do you know where two lads might get a drink here?" He sized them up. "I don't," he said with emphasis, and the bus started to move off, heading back to Dublin. Just then, the ould fella pronounced, "But I know a place where three lads might get a drink!" We loved those old and ridiculous yarns.

We were in a kind of limbo and we knew it. Privately contemptuous of the Ireland we lived in, we could do little to change it. The North, with its endless cycle of bombings and killing, was real. The horror it had afflicted on Dublin was real. Ghosts haunted the streets where the bombs had exploded in 1974. We didn't believe in ghosts but we knew that what lingered in those places was very real. Sometimes we went to a basement bar to see a band called The Boomtown Rats and we listened with delight to the singer, Bob Geldof, as he railed against the police, the priests and politicians. Outside on the street afterwards, still dazed and made giddy by the music and the mood that Geldof created, we knew we were standing at a corner where a car bomb had been ignited and people had been blown to pieces. The walls still bore the marks of the blast.

We haunted the city centre bars we thought were our literary homes, McDaid's, Grogan's, Bowes and Mulligan's. If the bar had been mentioned somewhere in James Joyce's work, all the better. These bars were grotty, cold and damp, but we didn't care. We lived on cheese sandwiches and chips. We sat in Grogan's in an intoxicated condition because there was a chapter in a book that began, "We sat in Grogan's in an intoxicated condition." We took no interest in sports. We didn't watch television except for *The Muppets*. It was a secret dream to have a woman interested in us in the way that Miss Piggy was smitten with Kermit. Once, in Bowes, I caught a glimpse of the Ireland I was living in. Three of us were in the snug, drinking pints. The snug door opened and four large, wary men entered. The first studied us carefully and waved the others in. They sat, hunched over a small table, and talked in deliberately low voices. Joe Gormely was among us and he said,

"Guards." He told us he could tell from the shoes and the attitude. He had a brother in the guards. The men at the table began to relax, and I watched as one reached up to the bar for his pint. As he did, his anorak fell away from his side and I saw the gun in a holster there. The police in Ireland hadn't had guns. There had been no need until the IRA had started making trouble.

Mam and Dad would come to visit on occasional weekends, and one Saturday Dad drove up with a television set in the back seat. It was an old one that a neighbour in Carlow was throwing out. I remembered the first TV arriving in Nenagh, and this time I carried it in myself, hauling it up endless flights of stairs. It was an old black-and-white set, on its last legs, and it only received RTÉ. But some nights, when we had little money for drinking, the lads would gather with me to watch TV. Among us, a cult grew around *Hawaii Five-O*. We adored Jack Lord as Steve McGarrett, the steely cop who talked in staccato and gave orders that nobody dared disobey. He wasn't a man to mess with. "Book 'em, Dano," became one of our catch-phrases as we delighted in the dilemmas of the baby-faced detective Danny, suffering under Steve McGarrett's orders. Mostly, we loved it because it was American and about a sun-drenched paradise that looked like heaven.

We could not escape the seriousness of our studies and the guidance of our teachers, but what we really craved was escape from the dullness of Dublin and the weight of all the political, moral and religious issues that we were expected to dwell upon. I dutifully watched serious drama on the BBC and ITV. I watched and admired Tom Stoppard's play "Professional Foul," and was heartened that a literary man was writing drama for TV. The play highlighted how basic moral issues of right and wrong are perversely twisted in a dictatorship, but to me it felt abstract, unreal. I sympathized with the university professor in the play—the bad guy—who would rather watch a soccer game than talk about ethics at an academic conference. Stoppard didn't need to set his TV play in Czechoslovakia. He could have set up his ethical dilemmas next door to him, in Ireland. We at UCD had our fill of moral issues daily, because the government acted like the secular arm of the Church. On *Starsky & Hutch*, which we took to with abandon, the lack of seriousness was a saving grace. The show was violent and preposterous, but the main characters used a wry humour to deal with every situation. In Dublin, there wasn't enough wry humour in supply to deal with the intensity around us.

In the summer of 1977 we all went to London to work. Some of us had been before, on brief trips, but living and working among the English was a vastly different experience. We worked in bars, factories and shops, living together but relocating constantly to cheaper rooms and flats. We bought books all the time, mainly the books that were still banned in Ireland. Some were even by Irish writers. We bought J. P. Donleavy's *The Ginger Man* and all the Henry Miller books we could find, and we mailed them back to Dublin. We stuck together because getting along with the English was difficult. You could be cornered anywhere if people thought you were Irish and given a lecture about the horrors the IRA were committing. Once, at a hostel, the woman in charge refused to let two of us stay there, on the grounds that we were Irish and the police and the army would be coming by to check up on us. Couldn't have that sort of disturbance. The Irish should stay in Ireland. The Australians and even the Jamaicans were all right, but the Irish were trouble.

We spent nights in Soho, going to see the punk bands that everybody was talking about. We'd wander down streets where prostitutes lined the pavement and called out to us as we searched for the makeshift club or underground pub where The Clash, The Strangers or The Sex Pistols would be playing. We decided that punk had actually been inspired by the house band on *The Muppets*. The English lads we met thought we were insane for saying that. One night in a bar on the Fulham Road, a few of us gathered for drinks. Fiona, a girl who had been at Sandymount school with me, lived nearby and she joined us. Tall, pale, with long, red hair, she was a striking figure. We were in a corner and a short, stout, tipsy Englishman came over to chat up Fiona. She ignored him, but he kept talking to her, getting more aggressive all the time. She told him to leave her alone, and then one of us, Joe, told him to go back to his friends, that Fiona wasn't interested. The Englishman heard Joe speak and gazed at the group of us. "Irish kids," he said with a sneer. "Fuckin' Irish!" Then he tried to put his arm around Fiona and she pushed him away. We decided to leave. As we hurried out the door, I was the last to leave. A hand grabbed my arm and swung me around. I heard the angry little Englishman say "Irish bastard" before he smashed his beer glass into my face.

I went back to Dublin with a scar. I'd met the English, felt their derision and been bloodied by it. I had at last experienced what I'd been reading about since I was a child in Nenagh.

CHAPTER TWENTY-ONE

GET OUT

Back at UCD, we took over the English Lit Society. The lad who had been running it was ill, and supported by my cronies, I was put in charge. At UCD, apart from lectures and drinking, student societies were the main social activity. There were many of them, the most famous and long-standing one being the Literary and Historical Society, always called the L&H, which was, by the 1970s, neither literary nor devoted to the study of history. It was a debating society and a social club. James Joyce had addressed it decades earlier and laid out his artistic vision, but he wouldn't have dared in my time at UCD.

The L&H met every Friday evening. Meetings were held in a large lecture hall and important guests were invited to address a topic. Politicians, entertainers and journalists were the favoured guests. Before they spoke, students debated the topic in front of a raucous audience. Anyone could interrupt from the audience, and did. Everybody involved, from the official speakers to the wits in the seats, had to have a sharp mind and a quick tongue. Almost every president and prime minister of Ireland had been involved with the L&H and had honed his debating skills there. In the 1970s the society had become a grooming ground for barristers.

The L&H set were notorious for being pompous windbags. The society was controlled by a coterie of south Dublin middle-class students on the make. They all wanted to be lawyers or politicians with the big political parties, and they perfected their sneering skills. Still, with so little going on, the L&H debate was often the highlight of the week on campus, a theatre of arguments and insults. Once, the Member of Parliament Oliver J. Flanagan, who had uttered the phrase "There was no sex in Ireland before television," was invited to speak. He was greeted with a standing ovation from the audience of hundreds. They jeered him, ironically saluting his status as an icon. He misinterpreted the ovation and acknowledged the greeting as if he was being hailed as a hero. I saw him lapping up the applause from the smirking students and knew he still didn't grasp the ridiculousness of what he'd famously said.

The English Lit Society was tiny and irrelevant in comparison. But it had a small budget to invite speakers and entertain them with dinner before the talk. A distinguished poet was among the first we invited. He accepted the dinner invitation, but turned up at the dining room of the hotel, across the road from UCD, in an agitated state. He declared that he didn't want dinner, he wanted drink. After one drink in the hotel bar he announced that he didn't like the place and he wanted to go to the student bar on campus. He refused to walk, so a taxi was ordered for the three-minute drive. In the bar, he drank three pints in half an hour and announced he was ready to read from his work. The reading went well, all things considered, and the small audience hardly noticed that he was shellacked. As soon as he ended the reading, he wanted more drink, so we took him back to the student bar. There, he searched for academics he said were his enemies and would fight on the spot if he could find them. None were on the premises. We were exhausted from the tension of dealing with him and relieved when some students who had attended the reading turned up, seeming anxious to meet the great man. A young woman offered to buy him a drink, which he gladly accepted. He drank it in a gulp and then began drinking the pint of beer she had bought for herself. When she protested, he swore at her. Then she asked sweetly if she could buy him another pint. When she returned with it, he was beaming. But I sensed what was coming and moved aside just in time. The young woman threw the pint of beer at him and walked away. The poet didn't seem at all surprised by this turn of events and, soaked, only asked that we get some paper napkins and call him a taxi. When he left, he grinned and waved at us from the back of the taxi. We knew that as far as he was concerned, he'd had a fine evening out.

The encounter dismayed us. There wasn't much fun in the drink-sodden literary life. It was grim and squalid. We invited other poets and writers, hoping that they would be less trouble and that perhaps some of their glamour and success would rub off on us. Seamus Heaney accepted our invitation but then he didn't show up. He had gotten his appointments all mixed up. He apologized profusely and promised to make an appearance the following week, when the novelist John McGahern was reading. He duly did and apologized some more. In the bar afterwards, we sat around with Heaney and McGahern, who didn't drink much and had little to say to us. They talked about teaching jobs they'd had in the United States and how there was a huge appetite in America for Irish studies. We were awed by them and too shy to say anything. We certainly said nothing about the poet who had ended up with beer all over him. All those literary gents were probably close friends. They were polite, but seemed puzzled by our interest in sitting in literary pubs, several of which they had never heard of. Heaney gave two of us a ride home in his white Volkswagen Beetle and on the way cheerfully suggested that we might be having more fun at university in another country.

We ran a campus club but were pipsqueaks on campus. Around us, student politics was intense and brutal. A variety of left-wing groups battled for control of the student organizations, and rarely succeeded. They argued for the availability and sale of contraceptives to everyone and wanted the laws changed to allow divorce. Exactly how mere students could help realize such dramatic change was never made clear. These were attractive policies for many students, but what bedevilled the left-wing groups was the North. Taking a stand on Northern Ireland was the kiss of death. At big meetings when elections for the student union were under way, anyone who proposed action to support the Catholics in the North was booed. Sometimes it only took a Northern accent to start the jeering. Joke candidates started winning the elections and set to work on issues that would never be controversial. Students were more interested in lower food prices in the cafeteria and cheaper drink prices in the bar. There was outright hostility toward the far left and a deep suspicion that the IRA or Sinn Fein had infiltrated every left-wing movement. Nobody wanted that kind of trouble. The left-wing groups grew ever more angry at the apathy and fought among themselves.

Rebellion against the establishment was low key and often childish. Because I ran the English Lit Society, I was asked to contribute to a new magazine that would circulate on campus. It was a secret project because it would be filled with mockery of the university, the professors and anyone who was thought to be pompous. It would also have rude jokes, copied from *Playboy* magazine, which was banned in Ireland. The magazine, when it appeared, was called *The Catholic University News & Times*. The initials caused immediate outrage, and it was banned. My contribution was a guide to dirty books in the library. It felt good to be banned.

It was the handful of foreign students that gave the campus some little sophistication and brought news from other places. There was always a group of students who came to study Irish literature. Many came from America, and the rest from all over Europe. An occasional bewildered student from England turned up and complained at length that university life in Dublin wasn't half as stimulating as it had been in England. They moaned that everybody was obsessed with the politics of the North and the petty issues of contraception, divorce and abortion. Students in England had gotten over those issues years ago. There were too many priests, the students from England said, and pointed out that the priests undoubtedly belonged to secret conservative organizations such as Opus Dei. We knew that.

It was among the foreign students that I found a girl-friend. Rayna was a Polish-American from New Jersey and came to Dublin because she'd become enamoured with Ireland through reading W. B. Yeats, John M. Synge and Sean O'Casey. She was an oddity among the foreign students because she wasn't an Irish-American, whose roots were in Ireland. She had left an American university and transferred to UCD because the country intrigued her. She had a clear, bemused outsider's perspective on it. In many ways the country appalled her. Tall and striking, with long, dark hair, she stood out because she wore clothes she'd brought from home. Men followed her everywhere, knowing she was from somewhere else and therefore exotic.

Their fascination at first amused her and then the crudeness made her angry. When she was looking for a flat near UCD, the landlord at the first place she saw put his hand up her skirt and told her he could make "an arrangement" about paying the rent. At the post office a young man behind the counter had slipped her a note and offered her money to meet him in a nearby park after dark. The first man she'd dated in Dublin had announced on the first date that he expected to lose his virginity to her because she was a Yank and therefore used to sleeping with the men she dated.

When she told me these things, I felt ashamed of Ireland. But Rayna said it wasn't worth worrying about. She said Ireland was still growing up, still stuck in adolescent conflicts with authority, and it would be years before the country matured. The rigmarole of acquiring contraception in Dublin was a lark the first time she'd been obliged to do it, but then the joke faded. She hated having to go through the charade of pretending she was married. She said Ireland was built on lies that everybody agreed to ignore.

Her outsider's eyes gave me a new view on Ireland. Rayna was a serious student of literature but wanted her fun too. She hated the scarcity of pop music on the radio in Dublin and thought that rationing it to a few hours a week on RTÉ Radio was backward. She discovered the pirate radio stations that had begun cropping up all over Dublin, inspired by the punk spirit and the gap in the market for pop radio. At one point there were twenty of them on the air. Occasionally the authorities closed one down, but the owners simply moved their equipment to another location and started up again a few hours later. On the pirate stations we could hear music by U2 and other young bands who were playing in bars around Dublin. There was a faint glimmer of hope in the existence of the pirates and the music they promoted. But most of the talk on the pirate stations was angry. They were angry that they'd been forced to operate outside the law. When the young musicians were interviewed they all talked about leaving Dublin for London.

Ranya had a taste for melodramatic American TV shows, and we spent hours in bed watching the mini-series *Rich Man, Poor Man*. It was a rags-to-riches and happiness-to-heartbreak saga. Two brothers dominated it, and one was evil while the other was pure of spirit. It spanned decades from the 1940s to the late 1960s. Rayna told me that it showed how the United States had changed in those years but Ireland hadn't. She enjoyed *Monty Python* too, and I explained how it had mattered in the madness of my first years in Dublin and after Bloody Sunday. I'd been looking forward to seeing the new Monty Python film, *Life of Brian*, but it was banned in Ireland.

One night we sought out Mick Mulcahy in a city centre bar. I wanted to show her that Dublin wasn't as depressing and rigid as she'd come to believe. Mick fussed over her, paid her elaborate attention and asked many questions about New York City. He was wearing a white suit, trying to look like John Travolta in *Saturday Night Fever*, but wearing the suit made him more angry than it gave him pleasure. Schoolboys on the street had called out, "Howya, sailor!" and made limp-wristed gestures at him. He said he wanted to go and live in a place were he could actually wear a white suit all the time and not stand out like a sore thumb. He asked many questions about what men were wearing in America. He was going to leave soon, I knew, and so was Rayna.

Finding jobs in other countries or simply leaving Ireland, even without job prospects, was preoccupying students at UCD as graduation approached. Only those who were heading directly into the professions looked forward to a career in Ireland. They were the smug ones, the middle-class Dublin boys and girls whose fathers were lawyers, judges, doctors or powerful businessmen. They had already had success and made connections running the L&H society. They belonged to a private club, like the gentry had years ago. They had nothing to fear.

Part of the mystique that surrounded the L&H was the parties. It seemed everybody on the organizing committee hosted a party every Friday after the debate. If you couldn't afford to host a party, you didn't belong in that set. Because I ran the teeny English Lit Society for a while, I was occasionally invited. And one Friday night I went to an L&H party at a large, ancient house near the campus. I took Joe and Eddie with me for protection and fun. The house smelled of damp and camphor, but it reeked of wealth. We drifted through it, staring at the stars of the L&H set as they talked only to each other about their law degrees, their parents' connections and their plans for the future. We drank copiously from the free bar and left. As we made our way out, we spotted the owner of the house, the man who was obviously the father of the young man who had hosted the party. Eddie, being a countryman who believed in old-fashioned courtesy, stopped and said we had enjoyed the evening and he wanted to thank the gentleman on behalf of all of us. The man looked us over, each of us, head to toe. He could tell we weren't part of his son's crowd. "Get out!" he shouted. "Get the hell out of my house." Eddie smiled back at him. "We're leaving," he said. "We're leaving your house, leaving Dublin and leaving Ireland. You're welcome to it." I was reluctant to be so certain. I still wasn't sure where I could go.

CHAPTER TWENTY-TWO

YOUNG PEOPLE OF IRELAND,
I LOVE YOU

THE POPE AND J. R. EWING arrived in Ireland within a few months of each other. I don't remember the day J.R. arrived, but the Saturday morning in 1979 that the Pope came to Ireland was sunny and breezy. People had been praying for good weather, because no Pope had ever been to Ireland and they wanted him to see an Ireland bathed in sunshine. The day the Pope came, one of the papers carried the giant headline, "Ireland's Greatest Day."

The Pope's visit lasted three days, and there was round-the-clock coverage on RTÉ. I watched his arrival sitting at home alone. The streets of south Dublin were eerily quiet outside. Hardly a car passed on the road. I felt like I was the only person in Dublin, possibly the entire east coast of Ireland, who was watching on TV. Apart from shut-ins and those confined in hospitals, I probably was. Mam and Dad were back living in Dublin, in a pleasant house where south Dublin stretched toward county Wicklow. They had left hours earlier for the Pope's appearance in Phoenix Park. They were part of a crowd of more than a million, the size of the entire population of Dublin. They'd left at dawn, with their folding lawn chairs for sitting in the park. For weeks, every street corner in Dublin seemed to have a fella selling the fold-up chairs for the Pope's visit. On the Thursday evening, drunk to hell in town, as much intoxicated by intense conversation about Joyce as by Guinness porter, I'd emerged from a pub and watched a chair-seller loudly telling anyone who passed that he had only a few chairs left and if people didn't want to be sitting in the wet grass catching their death on Saturday morning, they'd better buy a chair now. Somewhere in the back of my mind, I was reminded of Uncle Paddy and his once-thriving business selling Sacred Heart pictures and miraculous medals at the missions. Little had changed, now that the biggest mission of all was coming to Ireland.

After four years at university, there was no way on earth that I was going to Phoenix Park. So what if the Pope was coming to Ireland for the first time? A person with years of book reading and a taste for watching the adventures of libertines on TV wouldn't want to get caught up in that kind of mass hysteria. For weeks, every member of the Catholic clergy had been on TV, from the old codgers who'd be basking in the glory of hanging around with the Pope to the young, trendy ones whose vocation was persuading teenagers that they were better off without contraception and that divorce and abortion were evils that should not be allowed into Ireland. There wasn't a word from anybody who thought that the Pope's visit was dangerous religious hysteria, that the country couldn't afford it and that the money involved would be better spent on supplying condoms to young fellas and young women so that the nightly boat to Liverpool wasn't filled with Irish women going there alone for an abortion. According to one newspaper report, written in the time before the Pope's imminent arrival and therefore before all bad news about Catholic Ireland was banished, about six thousand Irish women went to England for abortions every year.

During most of 1979, the year the Pope came, the country was rapidly declining into an economic and social malaise. Dublin bus drivers and conductors went on strike for months. The army was called in to run a skeleton service. The postal workers went on strike, and that too lasted for months. Visitors from other countries were astounded that the place could function without mail or public transportation, but somehow it did. Inflation and unemployment rose. The trade unions and employers were locked in a bitter battle over wage increases. Even my dad's trade union, which represented men who were managers and worked in offices telling other people what to do, talked about industrial action. Income tax was forever rising. There were marches in the streets by an endless stream of workers complaining that they were carrying the country on their backs because of high taxes.

The burden of heavy taxation was electrifying those who still had jobs. Nothing seemed to result from the enormous taxes they paid. The government did nothing except make bland statements. In my parents' new house in Dublin, there was no telephone. Mam and Dad were told that there was a three-year waiting list for new phones to be installed in Dublin. A government department was in charge of the telephone and postal systems, and exactly what the department's workers accomplished was a mystery to everybody. Using the literary skills acquired at UCD, I'd written an angry, impassioned letter to the Department of Posts and Telegraphs, demanding that a phone be installed. The response, when it eventually came while postal delivery was operating, suggested that I cease using intemperate language if I expected the application to be successful, and said that the only motivation for the department to install a new telephone line in the area would be the arrival of a priest or doctor in the neighbourhood, such persons obviously being entitled to priority service.

Ireland was a banana republic, with people living by their wits and using ingenuity. The students at UCD had been hit hard by the lengthy postal strike because many were trying to arrange jobs in other countries, especially America. With no way to communicate, they feared being stuck in Ireland without jobs for the summer or after graduating. Some students secretly devised a solution. A few clever lads tampered with several public phones on campus and managed to override the charging system. A couple of pay phones became free phones, and students lined up to make calls all over the world, in search of jobs. This secret system lasted for ages.

The issue of the availability of contraception was still simmering, years after the courts had decided that the total ban on contraception had to be erased. Anyone of my age had watched closely as Charles Haughey, back in government as minister for health, made a tortured attempt to have contraception available in Ireland without raising the hackles of the Church. His plan was to make contraception solely available to married couples, by prescription from a doctor, for "bona-fide family planning purposes only." He'd called it "an Irish solution to an Irish problem." The phrase was repeated over and over as a joke, to describe every crackpot element of the crumbling Irish economic and social system.

In the North, the killings continued, as steady as the rain. The IRA had grown cocky, out of control, and appeared to be more powerful than the British army or the governments in Britain or Ireland. A month before the Pope came, the IRA assassinated Lord Mountbatten, a British war hero and cousin of the Queen, while he was on a fishing boat near Sligo, in the Republic. Later that same day, the IRA killed eighteen British soldiers with a bomb in the North. The public reaction wasn't shock. Even the assassination of Mountbatten failed to startle them. Jokes that captured the weary cynicism did the rounds. "They found out that Mountbatten had terrible dandruff. Yeah, they found his head and shoulders on the beach."

Somehow, the Pope's visit was expected to erase all the

cynicism and help solve the country's problems. Just before he came, an air of ecstatic joy enveloped Ireland. On the day of his arrival, RTÉ's coverage started early, with images of the Pope's plane visible in the sky above Dublin. The multitudes cheered at the news that the dot in the sky might actually be the Holy Father arriving. At Dublin airport the Pope got down and kissed the ground. Sitting in my empty house, feet up and watching avidly, I wondered if that piece of ground would be for sale before the Pope left Ireland. The TV commentators were bursting with pride and grew more excited by the minute. The president, Patrick Hillery, greeted the Pope, and there followed a long session of grinning, nodding, ring kissing and more grinning. I watched as rows of bishops and priests, their large arses covered in stately silk outfits for the occasion, beamed at the Pope and at each other. There wasn't one of them under the age of fifty and I wondered if among them was one of the stuck-up, self-important priests who had bluntly ignored me when I'd said hello on the street in Nenagh, when I was small and knew no better.

I had little interest in the Pope himself. The previous year there had been three popes, and if you weren't paying close attention, you got confused about who was in charge at the Vatican. The newest one, the stocky bruiser with the shrewd eyes, was Polish and cunning. I could see the self-possession and egotism in his every gesture as he accepted the fawning welcome in Ireland. He looked around with a deliberately vague sense of where he was but a certainty about his own charisma and power over the crowd. His were actor's gestures, offhand but emphatic. He had the manner of a politician you'd see glad-handing during an election, always looking at the next person while shaking hands with somebody else.

All of Dublin was there in Phoenix Park, row upon row of people in chairs, stretching for miles, united and quiet, listening to the Chieftains play "Carolan's Welcome" for the Pope. His arrival was greeted with a sound that started as a low buzz of anticipation and grew to a deafening roar as the Popemobile finally entered the park. The parade of small children who went to the altar to greet him walked in a dreamlike state. The mug of tea went cold as I watched and watched, noting the adoration and excitement that arose from the crowd at the Pope's every little gesture and movement, and the smile of satisfaction on his face as he looked out and saw people as far as the horizon stretched. The commentators on TV were awed, hushed, and said that everyone there would remember the moment the Pope arrived and that they'd seen him. Watching the event on TV, I knew instantly, was better than being there. On TV I could see the Pope intimately, his words and movements isolated by the camera, ready for the plucking by a skeptic like me.

Later that Saturday the Pope went to Drogheda, and in his speech he pleaded with the warring communities in Northern Ireland to stop the violence. "On my knees I beg you to turn away from the paths of violence and to return to the ways of peace . . . Let history record that at a difficult moment in the experience of the people of Ireland, the bishop of Rome set foot in your land, that he was with you and prayed with you for peace and reconciliation, for the victory of justice and love over hatred and violence."

It was galvanizing television, his voice rising in that slightly slurred, accented English, to address the North. He meant the IRA, of course. I knew that. There was no use in the Pope aiming his remarks at people who spent a lot of the summer marching around Ulster with signs that read "No Pope Here." He was talking through his little silk hat, as far as I was concerned. I knew that if you were there in Drogheda or up in Phoenix Park, the grandiosity of the occasion and the charisma of the man gave it all some weight. But on television, even in RTÉ's fawning, excited coverage, the stocky little man over from Rome looked like a strutting little parish priest, drunk on his own power. It was the way he inserted himself into the plea to the IRA that was most irritating, and that stood out on television. He wasn't only asking them to quit shooting, bombing and maiming people. He was asking that history might show that they had listened to him. It was all about him.

While he was in Ireland, of course, the Pope wanted to remind the country of its glorious past as the cradle of Roman Catholicism in northern Europe. He made a point of stopping briefly at Clonmacnois, the site of the ancient monastery. We were told that he wanted to personally give thanks for the Irish monks who had kept the faith in Christianity alive in Europe in the Dark Ages. He was telling Ireland that the Irish had saved northern Europe from paganism. He was saying that Ireland could still be a model to the rest of world by keeping its faith in Roman Catholicism, the sort of Catholicism that was old and unyielding.

On the Monday, the Pope was in Galway for what was promoted as a meeting with the youth of Ireland. This was going to be good. Almost every junior holy roller in Ireland had got the bus to a field in Galway. Some of them had walked, according to the papers. I could picture them, the legions of farmers' sons and daughters who devoted their time at university to handing out leaflets about the dangers of letting contraception into Ireland, how abortion was sure to follow and we'd all be going to hell in short order if the student union clinic, which was telling students how to get condoms, wasn't shut down immediately. They were the ones who went to the student union concerts and danced around with each other in what Mam called the Legion of Mary Stance. They were stiff dancers, adhering to the Legion of Mary's code, avoiding all holding, groping and kissing during the slow numbers. One night, at the students' fancy dress ball, I'd seen a girl from Mayo dressed as a cat, trying to do the Legion stance with her boyfriend. She was in a skin-tight outfit, with bits of fake leopard skin on it and a little furry tail hanging off her arse. Her bosom looked enormous in the tight outfit. She'd had a few drinks, I knew, because she had that sleepy, shiny-eyed country-girl look, the one they all got in the student bar on a Friday night after their ration of two drinks. Her boyfriend, a loud Dubliner who studied commerce, looked like he was going to burst, staring at her in the cat outfit. As they danced, he moved in and she moved out again. He'd pull her close but as soon as his hand rested on her arse, she'd push him back. On and on it went, as he hummed along to the music, buzzing like a bee around a sweet cask. I could picture her walking to Galway to meet the Pope, with half a dozen strapping lads traipsing after her, their tongues hanging out when they weren't saying their prayers.

The day was cold, the rain sweeping in from the Atlantic turning the field in Galway into a sea of mud. It was filled with hundreds of thousands of teenagers. A bishop and a priest warmed up the crowd, reminding them how special it was to be in the presence of the Pope. They were both famous from their TV appearances. Bishop Eamonn Casey, a grinning, roly-poly man, had a reputation as a people's bishop. He'd been on *The Late Late Show* several times, singing songs, telling jokes and being a lovable country-man, steeped in the down-to-earth wit of the west of Ireland. He was an expert performer, a man with a genius for understanding the power of the camera and shrewdly able to reach through it to people's living rooms. He took a hard line on moral issues, but told the Irish that they should be happy with their lot. He'd seen people who were truly poor in South America, where he did a lot of work. Father Michael Cleary, a bearded Dubliner with a rough working-class accent, was known as the Singing Priest. He carried a guitar and belted out old ballads or hymns at the drop of a hat. Also a regular on *The Late Late Show* and other pro-grams, he was the Dublin version of Casey. He claimed to be familiar with the problems of the working class in Dublin and was devoting his life to helping the poor. He wrote a column for a newspaper and gave speeches all over the place. Even more hard line than Casey on banning contraception, divorce and abortion, he was full of energy and wisecracks. He had a good showbiz act.

In Galway, Bishop Casey and his co-cheerleader Father Cleary whipped the crowd into a frenzy. The sound from the multitudes of youngsters was deafening. The Pope then made his usual statements about Ireland keeping the faith, but the noise from the crowd seemed to invigorate him. He was feeding off it. He said, "Young people of Ireland, I love you! Young People of Ireland, I bless you!" The response was otherworldly, a noise beyond mere cheering people. It was at once guttural and low, but some of the youths were screaming in a high-pitched wail. It sounded like the entire crowd had lost their minds in ecstasy. My heart sank. I knew what the echoes from it would mean—no contraception, no divorce and no abortion. Soon we'd all be expected to be on our knees every night saying the rosary, like they did back in Cranna when I was small. Holy Ireland was revived. Plump priests, high on the Pope's popularity and the tonic he'd given the clergy, would appear on television and dismiss any need to liberalize the laws, to accommodate a changing world. The insufferable arrogance of the lot of them was enraging, and I knew the power of the priests and conservative politicians would expand and expand until it suffocated all efforts at change.

The Pope left, but J. R. Ewing stayed on. He was on RTÉ week after week. *Dallas* was an instant hit in Ireland. J.R. was the man everybody knew and secretly admired.

Holy mother of God, but that J. R. Ewing was a rogue. You couldn't keep up with him and his mad antics. And the things that came out of this mouth were rich beyond compare. There was the time that his poor wife, Sue Ellen, sat across from him and asked, "Which slut are you going to stay with tonight, J.R.?" Well, J.R. looked at her, that brazen smile spreading like an oil slick over his face. "Whoever it is has got to be more interesting than the slut I'm looking at right now," he said to her, cool as you like. An awful man, that J.R., but full of strokes and schemes, the way an Irishman would be if he had all that money and he was involved in a feud with another family. J.R.'s strategy for dealing with trouble was the three B's: booze, broads and booty. Wasn't it the same three B's that ran things in Ireland? It was a wink and a nod, money under the table, the few pints or a bottle of whiskey as a gift and, if it could be arranged at all, a session with some fine hoor of an agricultural girl who wouldn't say no to a few pounds for letting some ould fella get his hands on her in the nip.

From the first episode that aired, Ireland was besotted with the Ewings and the Barneses on *Dallas*. Even at university, students watched it closely and with relish. Among my crowd, the literary set, the trick was to pretend that you got suckered into it, by joking that you'd thought you were going to watch a good documentary about the oil business and then you found yourself absorbed in a soap opera about that malicious J.R., the goody-two-shoes Bobby, their pair of gorgeous-looking wives and that little slut Lucy. Now there was a girl you didn't see in Ireland. The round face, the blond hair and the smirk on her. Man-mad she was. Not a brain in her head, but the bubs on her! There were a lot of fellas who'd sell their souls to the devil himself for a quick courting session in the hay barn with a girl like that.

I'd watched the first episode of *Dallas* because there had been a big fuss about it. It was taking America by storm, according to RTÉ. From the beginning, I watched it with greedy attention, and it was wonderfully broad television, its luxurious quality delectable in pinched and gloomy Ireland. At the start, it was obviously a Romeo and Juliet story. Bobby Ewing brought home his new wife, Pamela, to the Ewing family home at the Southfork ranch. Then it was revealed that she was the daughter of the Barnes family, the arch-enemy of the Ewings. You couldn't take your eyes off Pamela. Tall, leggy, ripe and big-eyed, she was an apparition, a fine example of American munificence, tanned by the sun and gorgeous in that casual American way. While she was a figure from beyond Irish experience, the story going on in *Dallas* wasn't so far from Ireland at all. The Ewings and the Barnes family had been feuding for years over land and oil. J.R.'s wife was an alcoholic, but they wouldn't separate. J.R. would just keep manipulating her and go tomcatting around when he had the urge. There wasn't a parish in Ireland that didn't have a similar story about families who hated each other because of some age-old fight about the land. Half the plays staged at the Abbey Theatre were about such bitter feuds.

But while the feuds over land and the bitterness between brothers could have taken place in any county in Ireland, there was a big difference. On *Dallas* there were marital affairs galore, infidelities and betrayals, divorces and an abortion. They happened so casually in the *Dallas* plots that in Ireland people could only marvel at the vast difference in social restrictions. These characters couldn't be bothered to cock an eye or express remorse. All that sex, infidelity and cavorting amounted to a way of life like any other.

I could see J. R. Ewing in Ireland, just as I'd imagined Bat Masterson in Nenagh years before. Always the rogue, he would understand Irish ways. The country lived on vendettas. It was all about power, showing off your status and never forgetting an insult. I could see him behind a desk at an Irish company, using his cunning to massage the system and keeping a cold eye on his enemies. He operated under the guise of respectability but ignored the rules in private. Rural Ireland was full of fellas like that, smooth-talking fellas who had chanced their arm at something, like running a dance hall, and ended up millionaires, and then acted like they owned the town and everyone in it. They bribed politicians and ignored laws. J.R. would be one of the boys. He proclaimed loyalty to family and to Texas, as Irish gombeen men did to family and Ireland, but really the only allegiance they had was to money.

All the family in-fighting and political jiggery-pokery on *Dallas* was lapped up in Ireland. Ireland needed a J.R. too. For all the ecstatic reaction to the Pope's visit, there was a gnawing feeling that some things needed changing. The country was poor, exhausted and decrepit. But fortunes were being made. It was an open secret that rules were bent to accommodate the rich and the well connected. Charlie Haughey had manoeuvred his way to prime minister despite the taint of corruption and scandal that still hung over him. He went on television and addressed the nation. He said, "We are living beyond our means," and most of the population laughed. If ever there was a rogue living beyond his means, it was Charlie.

The Pope could do nothing to fix any of those problems. The IRA had dismissed his plea for peace with utter scorn. The attitudes of everyone were hardened by the election of Margaret Thatcher and a Conservative government in Britain. The Conservatives weren't going to talk to the IRA about concessions and ceasefires. People were leaving Ireland in droves. Most of my friends from university were now in London, Lisbon, Hamburg or Rome. They were teaching English, working in factories or digging ditches. They were glad to be gone.

At university, my professors told me to leave too. They encouraged me to do postgraduate work in America or Canada. I was ready to leave Ireland and allow the Pope and J. R. Ewing to fight it out for the country's soul. The professors provided names and references and I duly wrote away to Boston, New York, Chicago, Montreal and

Toronto. The replies came back, some encouraging and others, like the one from a man in Canada, blatantly coaxing me with a vivid picture of life at a university there—the many cultures, the acceptance of newcomers, the hard winters followed by soft summers. In Boston and New York, I knew what I'd find. The bars called The Blarney Stone, the cops called Murphy and O'Brien, the devotion to an old Ireland shrouded in mist and peopled with holy saints.

One night that winter on the *RTÉ News* there was a special report about Canada. An election was under way and, according to the RTÉ reporter, it could mean big changes in Canada. It was the second election in a matter of months. Pierre Trudeau, who'd lost the last election and resigned, might be back in power. The strange issue of Quebec separating from Canada was going to boil over again, and Trudeau wanted to fight to keep Quebec in Canada. Trudeau's name meant something, but not much, to me. He seemed to have been around for ages and was a sort of Beatles-era figure who'd set out to modernize Canada and bring the French-Canadians closer to the rest of the country. He was charismatic, suave, brave and witty and enjoyed needling Richard Nixon. These impressions had registered with me. His wife, Margaret, had left him the year before, in a lurid affair that involved the Rolling Stones. The British and Irish papers had played up that story, suggesting she was mad, a woman gone insane after being trapped in a marriage. Now, according to the RTÉ, Pierre Trudeau was arising like a phoenix from the flames.

The reporter was besotted with him, I could tell from the way she talked, in a rushed, reverent voice, as if she'd discovered somebody special and significant to her. Trudeau's career in Canadian politics was presented in a collage of images and sound bites. The voice cut through the sounds around me—the traditional music on RTÉ Radio in the kitchen, Mam and Dad talking at the kitchen table about Charlie Haughey—and it had a fine, clear ring to it. Trudeau was seen in old clips and recent ones. In each, the assuredness was obvious. Trudeau let fly at people—reporters and voters—without hindrance, as if he was daring anyone to challenge the logic of his words and intent. "Well, let them bleed," he said with scorn to a reporter who had asked him about the opinions of people who were worried during the crisis when he called the army into Quebec. When the reporter asked him how far he'd go, he said, glaring at him, "Just watch me." Now this was gripping television. The flavour of it was fully there. I thought of old Jack Lynch and his speech to Ireland when the North was exploding all around us in Carrick. "We cannot stand idly by," he'd said, and it meant nothing. In another clip Trudeau said, "Canada must be a just society." And then he was saying, "The state has no place in the bedrooms of the nation." That remark struck me hard on that night. Rain lashed against the windows and the coal fire sagged.

Canada had been a blur to me, but now it came into focus. That man in Toronto had written a sweet-natured, coaxing letter. This man Trudeau was elegant, smart, vigorous and direct. In his three-piece suit and gunslinger pose he reminded me of Bat Masterson, swinging through the doors of a saloon, looking for trouble and afraid of nothing. He was unfettered, roguish, and yet he had integrity. He couldn't care less about the Pope, the bishops and the priests. The program on RTÉ was continuing, going this way and that to explain the complex layers of Canada, but always coming back to Trudeau. I sat transfixed by the candour and charm. I looked at the screen and said to myself, "I'll go there." And I did.

AFTERWORD

Dallas RAN ON RTÉ FROM 1979 to 1991. The two cheerleaders for the Pope's Galway meeting with Irish youth became significant figures in Irish history. Bishop Eamonn Casey resigned as bishop of Galway in 1992 when it was revealed that he had had a long relationship with a divorced American woman and had fathered a child with her. The people of Ireland met Bishop Casey's mistress on *The Late Late Show* and, hearing her story, began to change their minds about the Catholic Church. Father Michael Cleary died in 1993. Shortly after his death, it emerged that he had fathered two children with his housekeeper. You can buy condoms anywhere in Ireland now. *The Late Late Show* is still running on RTÉ. Between 1993 and 2003, Ireland had the strongest economy in Europe. J. R. Ewing won.

And I became a Television Critic.

ACKNOWLEDGEMENTS AND SOURCES

MANY PEOPLE HELPED IN many ways. My agent, Denise Bukowski, steered me carefully into the publishing world. I am very grateful to my editor at Doubleday Canada, Martha Kanya-Forstner, who handled the gnarly manuscript with great patience and skill, and to all the staff at Random House of Canada for their flair and precision.

My parents, Sean and Mary Doyle, brought the past to life and encouraged me. My sister, Máire, with Stephen McBride, provided invaluable help. In Nenagh, Brendan Treacy, a great town historian, provided a ton of material about the town. My first teacher, Joe Daly, has written numerous columns, "Down Memory Lane," for the *Nenagh Guardian*, and those were a joy to read. At RTÉ in Dublin, Brian Lynch of the archives department gave me excellent help. Hilary Read, who runs the BBC office in

Toronto, was exceptionally kind, gracious and helpful.

At *The Globe and Mail*, my friend, collaborator and sometimes editor Henrietta Walmark was endlessly encouraging and shrewd, as usual. Among my colleagues, special thanks are due to Alexandra Gill, Rebecca Caldwell and Simon Beck for their friendship, support and wit. Dianne De Fenoyl allowed me time off and for that I am very thankful. Outside the *Globe*, outstanding advice and help came from Heather White, an exceptional editor, who gamely read an early draft of the book's beginning. Dave Bidini offered sound counsel. The brother, thankfully, stayed out of it. I must also thank Kevin Quain, who, by doing what he does, as a writer and singer, provided inspiration and a model of integrity. At home, the mott, Suki and Mick deserve extra-special thanks for cheering me throughout, sometimes with a dry sherry.

The story of the awful events in and around Carrick-on-Shannon during the famine is told best in David Thomson's classic memoir *Woodbrook* (Barrie & Jenkins, 1974). Thomson's book has informed everyone who has written about the famine, including me. There are numerous histories of Ireland in print and many books of opinion about Ireland and the Irish. All can spur fierce argument. I have taken inspiration from the work of Fintan O'Toole, a classmate at UCD and now a columnist for the *Irish Times*. Two of his provocative books are *The Ex-Isle of Erin: Images of a Global Ireland* (New Island Books, 1998) and *The Lie of the Land: Irish Identities* (Verso, 1998).

INDEX

ABOUT THE AUTHOR

JOHN DOYLE, one of Canada's most popular newspaper columnists, was born in Nenagh, County Tipperary. He attended University College, Dublin, and escaped to Canada in 1980. He has been a critic for *The Globe and Mail* since 1997 and has written the *Globe*'s daily television column since 2000. His writing has appeared in *Report on Business* magazine, *Elle Canada, Books in Canada, The Irish Times,* and the *Toronto Star,* among others. John Doyle lives happily in Toronto.

A NOTE ABOUT THE TYPE

A Great Feast of Light is set in Monotype Dante, a modern font family designed by Giovanni Mardersteig in the late 1950s. Based on the classic book faces of Bembo and Centaur, Dante features an italic which harmonizes extremely well with its roman partner. The digital version of Dante was issued in 1993, in three weights and including a set of titling capitals.